"*Strays* is a window into another world, and gives a compassionate and honest account of what it feels like not to have a place to call 'home,' and to seek comfort in unexpected places. And any cat lover will fall head over heels for little Tabor!"
—Ruby Warrington, author of *Material Girl, Mystical World*

"No doubt *Strays* will be seen as a cat book, but make no mistake, this is a book about humans, and how animals, especially cats, can reach a paw into our hearts and pull out the best of us. Part love story, part adventure epic, part travelogue, part social commentary, *Strays* will give you insight into the kindnesses of strangers, the healing capacity of our furry friends, and the resilience of both man and cat in the face of blizzards, long nights on sidewalks, wild beasts, and dark memories."
—Caroline Paul, author of *Lost Cat: A True Story of Love, Desperation, and GPS Technology*

"A powerful tale of a drifter saving, and being saved by, a stray feline. This book is a reminder that the animals that shadow us in our lives help to make us more human."
—Scott Carney, *New York Times* bestselling author of *What Doesn't Kill Us*

STRAYS

THE TRUE STORY OF
A LOST CAT, A HOMELESS MAN
AND THEIR JOURNEY ACROSS AMERICA

BRITT COLLINS

With a foreword by Jeffrey Moussaieff Masson

SIMON &
SCHUSTER

London · New York · Sydney · Toronto · New Delhi

A CBS COMPANY

First published in the United States by Atria, an imprint of
Simon & Schuster, Inc., 2017
First published in Great Britain by Simon & Schuster UK Ltd, 2018
A CBS COMPANY

1 3 5 7 9 10 8 6 4 2

Simon & Schuster UK Ltd
1st Floor
222 Gray's Inn Road
London WC1X 8HB

www.simonandschuster.co.uk
www.simonandschuster.com.au
www.simonandschuster.co.in

Simon & Schuster Australia, Sydney
Simon & Schuster India, New Delhi

A CIP catalogue record for this book is available from the British Library.

Paperback ISBN: 978-1-4711-5465-2
eBook ISBN: 978-1-4711-5466-9

Interior design by Kyoko Watanabe
Printed and bound by CPI Group (UK) Ltd, Croydon, CR0 4YY

Simon & Schuster UK Ltd are committed to sourcing paper that is made from wood
grown in sustainable forests and support the Forest Stewardship Council, the leading
international forest certification organisation. Our books displaying the FSC logo are
printed on FSC certified paper.

CONTENTS

*For Bobby Seale, my gorgeous ginger
girl, always in my heart. And for anyone
who has loved and lost a cat.*

FOREWORD

When I think back to some of the happiest moments of my life, I think of the midnight walks I would take on our beach in Auckland, New Zealand. Our house, surrounded by sea and subtropical rain forest, was only fifteen minutes from downtown, but it could have been hundreds of miles. There was no road down to our community of ten houses, and therefore no cars: you had to walk through a forest to get there. When we found this patch of land, my first thought was: *This is an ideal place for cats.* We lived with five cats and our dog, Benjy (about whom I wrote *The Dog Who Couldn't Stop Loving*), and the greatest thrill for the cats was to wait until there was nobody out, when I would take Benjy for his last walk along the beach. It was especially wonderful on full-moon nights, the waves gently lapping the shores and bioluminescent fish creatures lighting up the sea. The five cats—Yossie, Minna, Miki, Moko, and Megala—thought it was enormous fun to race ahead, hide behind a sand dune, and then jump out and ambush Benjy, who always played along by pretending to be totally surprised and freaked out: he would race along the beach into the warm ocean, the five cats chasing behind him. They loved it. He loved it. I loved it. We would walk to a stand of pohutukawa trees, giant flame-red trees hundreds of years old that thrived near seawater, and the cats would race up the branches, high into the trees, far above the water, and then start meowing piteously, as if they could not possibly get down. I would come to investigate, pretending to begin climbing the trees, and then they would race down the trunk and leap onto the sand. They were ecstatic. Then all seven of us would stand quietly by the shore, gazing out at the small offshore island, and I knew that the peace that I felt was felt by the six animals as well. Such a sense of all being right with the world, even when, as right now, all is not all well with the world. At those moments of intense happiness for me I could see what people meant by the cliché of animals living in the moment, not preoccupied with what had come, or what would come, but just enjoying that moment of glorious peace.

But at the same time I knew there was another reason that gave me intense happiness: the knowledge that the cats, the dog, and I were all enjoying something together and in a similar way. It was interspecies understanding: we all were enjoying the moment more because we were enjoying it together. I realized then something about cats that I knew made them different from their sometime bad reputation for being aloof and stand-offish. I felt this so strongly that I knew I had to write about the complicated and deep emotional lives of cats, and eventually I did. I called the book, a little bit cornily (most of my titles were corny!): *The Nine Emotional Lives of Cats*. You had to enter their world instead of forcing them into ours. This was something I first learned when I read Elizabeth Marshall Thomas's book *The Hidden Life of Dogs*. Every animal has a hidden life, and to discover it you must be willing to live life on their terms instead of the other way around.

Reading Britt Collins's wonderful account of Michael King and Tabor, the injured stray he rescued on the streets of Portland, made me realize that this is exactly what happened: both cat and human decided to live the life of the other. This makes for a peculiar bond, one that perhaps cannot be had in any other way. As Michael learns the ways of the cat, he feels a sense of purpose caring for someone else and opens his heart in ways he hadn't before. Moreover, the intimacy and intensity of their life on the road is something else that allows you to know an animal in a way that simply sharing your house with them does not. (Perhaps unfairly, I feel that confining a cat to an indoor life is depriving them of the ability to truly be a cat, even though I recognize that statistics show they will live much longer inside than outside.) Michael and Tabor rarely spent time apart and slept together every night for almost a year while traveling across the American West. Bliss for cat and for man. And by the way, I recommend anybody who lives with a cat in their house to share their bed with them. Sleeping with cats is surely one of life's great joys. It can be tricky: I slept for years with my cat Megala (not to mention Leila, my wife, who was such a good sport that she allowed herself to lose her allergy to cats by extreme exposure), and on cold nights he would slip under the covers, stretch out his little body next to mine, and purr loudly until he fell asleep (I have claimed this discovery for myself: cats only purr when there is a living being near them, not on their own, but my discovery may be false, as many of my readers have written to me explaining they have seen examples of cats purring when nobody was present). The great writer Doris Lessing, surely more knowledgeable about cats than I, told me so, and then nonetheless graciously reviewed my book for the *Guardian*, omitting to mention that and other possible errors, because she so admired my passion for cats. But I digress: the reason it was tricky was that every once in a while I would do something to annoy Megala (no idea what it was—perhaps I moved in the wrong way), and Megala would punish me with a swift bite of my leg. It hurt. My feelings were hurt, too, and I would banish him from our bed. He would leave in a huff. But an hour later he would return, and how could I not relent, knowing the pleasure that awaited me. This happened at least two or three times every night, and Leila marveled that I did not decide against allowing him to sleep with us altogether. But who could resist the soft fur (Megala was a Bengal and looked and behaved like a small leopard), the stretched-out body, the purr of pure pleasure?

Can you love a cat and not be changed? I would think not. I adore dogs, too, and have written much about them (including *Dogs Never Lie About Love*—another corny but true title), but there is this important difference: dogs don't need to let you enter their world. We already live with dogs in the same world. Not so with cats. I maintain that cats were never truly domesticated. They just deigned, for reasons of their own, to move in with us. But when they allow you to enter their world, you are suddenly in a different realm. The reason we think of cats as mysterious is that in fact they are mysterious, and once they permit you a glance into their mysterious world, you are forever changed. You might not be able to say how, you might not even realize it has happened, but it has. Michael felt the full force of this, in continuously sacrificing for the needs and wants of the other person (yes, a cat is a person, for sure—a being with a full personality, and the subject of a life, as the great animal-rights writer Tom Regan reminded us so well in his many seminal books) he had perhaps loved most deeply and unconditionally, and found a fuller purpose to his life as well. Michael learned to care about the street kids, the helpless, the vulnerable, those less fortunate than ourselves, while he was down-and-out, and to help them just as this little lost cat he named Tabor helped him. By entering Tabor's world, he was able to see what before he could not take in.

What I especially loved about *Strays*, or rather, about the real-life adventures of Michael and Tabor on the road, was seeing how cats and humans alike crave adventure and how they come alive when faced with dangers most of us never have to face. As the pair hitchhiked for thousands of miles, there were times when I wondered how they could be so trusting of anyone who offered them a ride, even hitching a lift with a guy covered in tattoos and guns in a red state after spending a week stranded in the stifling summer heat. More surprising were the unexpected acts of kindness that awaited them seemingly at every turn, helping them to survive raging snowstorms, fanatical evangelists, hungry bears and coyotes, and stampeding cattle.

Perhaps this self-possessed, lovable cat with a drifter's spirit was exactly what Michael needed as much as she needed his care and protection. Tabor has utterly stolen his heart and before their road trip ends, Michael is transformed. To read how Ron Buss, the cat's original guardian, grew and remained for nearly a year desperate at her disappearance and how her littermate Creto waited for her on the porch every night made the true story all that much more compelling. Speaking of compelling, the story itself is written in such a way and in detail so lush that you feel you are there as it all takes place. Everything is vividly observed: the grass, the trees, the smell of the sea, the quality of the light, the shifting moods and emotions of Michael and Tabor of roughing it and being on the road. And yet Britt Collins, the author, is delightfully self-effacing. No small achievement. Returning Tabor back to her original home in Portland was perhaps the hardest thing Michael had ever done, but letting go of what you love was the deepest lesson he had learned from Tabor and now he put it in practice. While Michael's struggles and sorrows are not magically fixed by adopting a stray, I am sure that Tabor turned out to be his salvation, literally: he was on a path of destruction—drinking himself to death until she brought calm and purpose to his day-to-day existence.

I am deeply impressed with how hard Britt has worked to capture this warm, witty, absorbing story in all its color and complexity, giving an insightful glimpse of the vulnerability and hardships of life on the streets for both man and feline. How much passion and love of truth she has brought to this task, for its own sake. Or should I say, for the sake of Tabor and other cats. For every page makes it clear that Britt understands and loves cats in the best possible way: she allows them to be cats. Almost everybody who lives with a cat loves cats. How can we not feel strangely blessed that these wild creatures are willing to live with us, however briefly (alas, too briefly)? But only now, it would seem, are we more inclined to allow them to be what nature designed them to be.

It would seem the world is just beginning to show a deep love of cats: how else to explain the sudden explosion of interest in all things cat? Books like this one, movies, TV shows, Internet memes, cat-obsessed social media, feline superstars (Grumpy Cat, Bob, and all), and the endless videos of cats and kittens of every size, color, and circumstance doing crazy things. My wife, Leila, insists that if I could, I would happily spend all day simply watching them. (There are worse ways to spend a life.) This is no fad, I am sure; it is the world catching up with the reality of cats: They accept us. They love us. Lucky us. For those of us who love them, the reward is immense, for with no other animal is it easier and more enchanting to cross the species barrier than with cats.

JEFFREY MOUSSAIEFF MASSON

BERLIN, GERMANY

DECEMBER 28, 2016

I was born lost and take no pleasure in being found.

—JOHN STEINBECK

Chapter 1

Portland, Oregon: Round Midnight

It was after midnight, the streets were deserted, and Michael King was drunk again. A heavy rain was falling, cold for mid-September. Water streamed down Michael's long gray-streaked hair and scraggly beard, and his ragged clothes were sopping wet. The sidewalk was so waterlogged that he and his companion felt as if they were wading through a swamp. Michael didn't mind too much. It had been fifty-one days since the last rain, a record dry spell, and the cool rain felt good. And, living on the streets, he was used to feeling grimy.

Almost ten years earlier, Michael had been a chef in St. Louis making good money and living in a nice house. Then he lost someone precious to him, and he hit the road. Now at forty-seven, Michael looked old and worn, with a missing front tooth and a collection of scars. His vivid blue eyes were shadowed by dark bags, his sharp cheeks sunken and heavily lined after years of hard drinking and sleeping on roadsides and under freeway overpasses in cardboard boxes. He had less than three dollars in loose change rattling around in his pockets.

Stopping under a store awning, Michael popped open a can of Four Loko and dumped it into a half-empty bottle of cheap malt liquor he'd already started on. He added a bottle of apple cider he'd scavenged from the trash earlier and called it a Sidewalk Slam. After a few swigs, he felt numb.

Michael passed the bottle to his friend Josh Stinson, a slight, unshaven twenty-seven-year-old, clad in a fraying red-and-black flannel shirt and grubby, ripped black jeans held up by a safety pin at the waist.

Stinson took a big slug of Michael's concoction.

"Good, right?" Michael said.

Stinson swallowed hard and cringed. "That's lethal," he said, handing it back. "Did you siphon it from someone's car?"

Michael downed the rest as they walked along Hawthorne. At night, every few blocks of the boulevard were lined with homeless encampments.

Michael stumbled over the corner of a soggy mattress wedged in a doorway.

"Damn it," he muttered. He preferred to sleep in the bushes and in out-of-the way areas, where there were fewer people to deal with, rather than bedding down on the sidewalk.

Slogging through the downpour, Michael and Stinson headed toward their usual squat beside a UPS loading bay on a forlorn corner of Hawthorne and SE 41st Avenue. They slowed in front of the Tabor Hill Cafe, a dingy old-time diner that was closed for the night. A stab of hunger broke through Michael's intoxicated haze. The pictures of eggs and waffles, burgers and fries plastered on the windows made his mouth water.

A flash of white under one of the café's outdoor picnic tables caught Michael's eye. Stooping down, he looked into the shadows, thinking maybe the white flash came from a takeout container with some leftover food. He started fantasizing about macaroni and cheese, and mashed potatoes with mushroom gravy. Michael had a knack for finding unlikely treasures: coins, broken jewelry, and half-eaten sandwiches all had value on the street. He was so good at it that the other drifters called him Groundscore.

"What're you looking at?" Stinson asked, kneeling beside him.

Two glowing eyes stared back at them. A soaked, shivering cat was cowering from the rain. Michael was disappointed— food would have been better—but something about the way the animal looked disturbed him. Her stripy white fur was covered with dirt and motor oil. One of her eyes was swollen, and she had a raw gash on her face. She looked even more beat-up than he was, and she was scared.

"Grab the cat," he said to Stinson, who was closer to the animal. "And try not to spook it." Cars still rumbled down Hawthorne even at that late hour. If the cat darted out, she'd likely get run over.

Stinson reached out for the cat, but she sprang back, her eyes fixed on him. When he tried again, she jumped sideways and gathered herself to shoot past them.

Michael turned and saw a lone car heading down the street, its headlights glowing in the rain. "Damn it," he said.

Stinson lunged and grabbed the cat before she could launch herself onto the sidewalk. As he pulled the little animal to his chest, she was panting, but she didn't fight to get away. He looked down at her, the muddy fur stuck to her face, and gently ran his dirty hand over her head. The cat burrowed her face into his hand.

Stinson looked up at Michael through the fogged lenses of his wire-rim glasses. "I think we should bring her back with us."

"Lemme see," Michael said, taking the cat into his arms. She was so thin she was almost weightless. Michael had been on the streets longer than Stinson and believed that when you had nothing to offer, it was best not to try to help. But he loved cats and wanted to get this poor, raggedy little one out of the rain and off the busy road.

"Maybe we'll keep it for a night," Stinson said. A homeless young veteran who came from a small town in the Midwest, Stinson had a natural sense of rightness about things, especially when it came to vulnerable animals.

The cat looked at Michael with big, luminous eyes, shivering pitifully as she lay in his arms.

"Hey there, kitty cat," he said in a soft, reassuring voice. "What's happened to you?"

Michael tucked her inside his jacket, and he and Stinson took her back with them to the small alcove behind the UPS store that they called home. It was a good place to bunk down without worrying about being mugged and assaulted or rousted by the police. During the day, it was a busy loading dock, with delivery vans driving in and out. They had to get up before the business opened, stash their sleeping bags in the nearby bushes, and stay away till the shop closed. But after hours, it was quiet and isolated, shaded by a sprawling red maple tree. The lot was also just across the street from the New Seasons supermarket, where Michael and his friends sometimes panhandled.

"Here we are, puss," Michael said, setting her down on the dry patch under the doorway while he pulled his backpack and sleeping bag out of the shrubbery. He expected her to bolt, but she stayed close and sniffed around as Michael set up camp.

Stinson grabbed his pack from the bushes, too, and unrolled his sleeping bag onto a folded cardboard box he'd stashed beneath the sheltering boughs of the maple. He sat down, cross-legged, and riffled through his things, taking out a hooded sweatshirt and slipping it over his head. The rain had invaded his tangle of strawberry blond dreadlocks beneath his dark-blue seaman's cap. They smelled dank.

The cat wandered over to Stinson's sleeping bag. She looked like she'd been out on the streets for a while, just like they had. She didn't have a collar and scratched occasionally at fleas on her belly. Stinson reached down to stroke the damp, matted fur on her back. The open, weeping wound on her face made him wince with pity. "You've had a tough time, haven't you?"

The little tabby gazed up at Stinson with her good eye and meowed, pressing the back of her head into his hand again. Then she climbed into his lap and drifted off to sleep.

Stinson stroked her. "She's all bones," he said, looking over at Michael.

Michael didn't say anything, but, after a moment, he stood up.

"Whaddaya doing?"

"Going to the store for some cat food."

Stinson watched him walk off. It was the first time in a long while that Michael had spent his last few dollars on something other than booze.

Michael and Stinson had first run into each other in a doorway in Santa Barbara in the spring of that year and were drawn together by their rambling spirit, dry sense of humor, and love of animals. Stinson had done four years in the navy before getting kicked out for smoking pot. Just prior to moving to Portland, he had been a mailman in Japan—he still had his Japanese driver's license.

Fifteen minutes later, Michael came back with a pint of milk and a can of Meow Mix. The little cat woke up and, when she saw the food, opened her mouth and let out a faint, hungry squeak. Michael lifted her off Stinson's lap and set her on the sidewalk. He opened the can, spilled the mushy contents into an empty burger container, and put it in front of her. She meowed weakly and nibbled at the food, but within seconds, she was gulping it down in giant bites. Michael poured the milk into a plastic lid he found on the ground and she lapped that up quickly, too.

Both men sat quietly, watching the cat. After she ate, she nuzzled each of them and kneaded their chests to show how grateful she was. She snuggled back into Stinson's lap, purring loudly. Then she shifted to Michael's lap, purred some more, and fell back asleep.

"That cut on her cheek looks pretty nasty," Michael said, looking closely at her war wound.

He dug into his backpack without waking the cat and took out a stack of napkins from Taco Bell and a mini first-aid kit. One of his friends had bought the kit for him because Michael was always scraping himself up from stumbling over after drinking. He carefully cleaned the red cut across the cat's face and then cleaned mites out of her ears with a little iodine. The cat didn't even flinch, barely stirring from her sleep. She seemed to know what he was doing.

He rummaged through his bag again and dug out some evening primrose oil, which another friend had given him to heal the eczema on his arms. He never used it himself but thought it could help the cat's injury.

"It's not too deep," he said, dabbing a bit of the oil on her torn cheek. "She was probably attacked by another cat. Or at least I hope it was a cat."

Handing her over to Stinson, Michael unrolled his ratty sleeping bag on a pad of cardboard and slid wearily inside. He'd been sleeping on the hard ground for years—the only way to make it comfortable was to get wasted, but he had drunk all the Sidewalk Slam and just spent his bedtime booze money on cat food.

The cat had woken up as the men prepared to sleep. After Michael was settled, she crept to the edge of the bag and sniffed around him. Then she came closer and sat to the side of the bag, in front of his face, her tail twitching slightly.

"What do you want? I don't have any more food."

"I think she wants in your bag," Stinson said.

Got to be desperate if she wants to bed down with me, Michael thought. His buzz was wearing off and he just wanted to crash. He closed his eyes for a while but sleep didn't come. When he opened his eyes, the cat was still there, staring down at him.

"Okay, kitty," he said, lifting the flap. "You can sleep with me tonight."

She crawled inside and snuggled up against his chest, purring softly, like a hypnotizing personal heater.

Michael looked over at Stinson, who shrugged. "She likes you," he said.

Whatever, Michael thought, *she'll be gone by sunrise.*

But in the morning something rough wiped across his cheek, and Michael awakened to find the cat standing on the pavement, licking his face. Not yet alert, he pulled an arm out of his sleeping bag and rubbed behind her ear. She looked at him, one eye still swollen, and meowed, clearly hungry.

"You should find someone else to take care of you," he said, getting up for the day. He didn't have anything else to give her. He stashed his gear and picked up and held the cat for a minute, stroking her. Then he set her down near the bushes and walked off to do some panhandling. He didn't expect to see her again.

But later that afternoon, he came back to squat, and the cat was waiting for him. He had half hoped she'd be there and had bought a couple of cans of cat food from the supermarket, as well as flea treatment and a compress to put on her swollen eye.

After they'd both eaten, they settled contentedly into the sleeping bag, to make it through another night, at home with each other.

Chapter 2

Stray Cat Blues

"Maaa-ta," Ron Buss called out, peering into the gloom of the crawl space beneath a neighbor's porch. His cat liked to hide there and disturb the nests of mice. He got down on his hands and knees so that he could shine a flashlight into every shadowy corner, but all he saw were spiderwebs, dried leaves, and crickets.

He got up and shook a bag of crunchies to tempt her out of hiding. Usually Mata could hear treats rattling from a block away. He'd been searching for her for hours, but there was no sign of her anywhere. Ron was beginning to suspect the worst.

He rubbed his shaved head and straightened his black Ministry rock T-shirt. A short, stocky man in his early fifties, Ron still had an earnest, boyish look, to which a gap between his front teeth contributed. As a kid, he had dreamed of becoming a successful musician and traveling the world, and that wide-eyed sense of possibility had never left him, even after he joined the family business, a storage locker company.

After twenty-five years, he sold his share of the company to his sister and brother-in-law and used his earnings to begin a career as a collector, eventually opening a guitar store, Boojumusic

Guitar & Crazy Crap Inc., in a disused office of the family storage company. He wallpapered the insides with tattered posters of Bowie and Bolan and '70s concert memorabilia. A Beatles fanatic, he specialized in collectible Beatles records, vintage mikes and amps, and rare '60s Fender Stratocasters worth as much as $10,000 each. It wasn't much of a business, but it reignited his passion. He collaborated with other musician friends, putting out small-scale indie R & B albums, and kept his dream alive.

The only things Ron loved more than rock 'n' roll were his two cats, Mata Hairi and Creto. He raised them almost like children, giving them enriching experiences. He took them to the beach (waves scared them, but Ron thought the exposure was "character building"); he threw them fancy birthday parties ("cats are thrill seekers, too"); and he wrote songs for them on his acoustic guitar ("cats are rockers at heart"). He also cooked for them, buying organic chicken and wild-caught salmon from Whole Foods.

His father, a retired lawyer, was mystified by his obsession. He thought it was pathetic and often told him: "You can go anywhere, do anything, but you just want to be around your cats."

Ron never had pets growing up, despite constantly begging his parents for a cat or dog. Once, when he found a stray dog as a kid, his mother said it had to stay out in the garage. When Ron came home from school the following afternoon, the dog was gone. His mother had taken it to the pound. It broke his heart. He didn't get his own cat until after he graduated from college and moved in with his first boyfriend. That cat, a black charmer, got him hooked. Now his cats meant the world to him.

Ron had spent the morning at the auto-repair garage collecting his 1967 Chevelle and running an errand for his father, Donald, who lived less than half an hour away across town. Not long before, Ron and his sister Teresa had promised their dying mother that they'd look out for their dad, even though she had divorced him decades earlier. After the divorce, Donald had married a woman named Judy, his former secretary, who was a good decade and a half younger than Ron's father. For a long while, Ron had thought of Judy as a home wrecker and hated her for causing his mother so much pain, but his mother had let go of her animosity by the time she died. Eventually Ron had as well.

Ron had rushed to get home from his errands in anticipation of the long weekend ahead. It was a bright, balmy Indian summer afternoon, the Saturday before Labor Day. He had plans to meet up with friends at the annual Last Chance Summer Dance along the Willamette River—and to take along his cats. Most of the summertime tourists had left, so Portland felt like a ghost town. The only sounds in his neighborhood were the crows cawing, the scuffle of falling pinecones, and the distant whistle of trains.

But when Ron pulled up to his white-and-gold Craftsman bungalow on the corner of SE 37th Avenue, in the lush, leafy Richmond neighborhood near Berkeley Park, he knew something was wrong. The picnic table on his front lawn where Mata usually waited for him was empty.

Thinking that Mata might have been chased off by a dog or was taking shelter from the heat somewhere nearby in a shed or under a shrub, Ron started searching his neighbors' front yards, calling her name. Her littermate, Creto, a black-and-white tom, shadowed him, sniffling and calling out plaintively for his sister.

On hearing Ron, Ann, his next-door neighbor, came out to say that Mata had been following her around earlier that morning while she was trimming her roses, but she hadn't seen her since then. Ann had a big black, yellow-eyed pirate cat named Gordon that Ron had rescued. Ron was constantly finding and rescuing strays.

"Maaa-ta," Ron called again, gingerly sifting through the

prickly holly hedges that fringed Ann's front yard, where Mata sometimes liked to nap.

"Come on, Mata," Ron said. "Don't do this to me."

Mata had always been a bit of rambler, spending her days roaming a three-block patch in the peaceful neighborhood of neatly pruned roses and shady sycamores, but she never went too far. And she always came when Ron called her. Both she and Creto stayed close to the house, and if they didn't come in before dark, he grounded them for a day or two. So they tended to listen to him.

Mata and Creto were part of a litter of five that had been dumped under a neighbor's porch. When Ron had peered down into the box in his neighbor Stefanie's kitchen at the five trembling kittens—tiny weakly mewing bundles of fluff and bones with gummy eyes—he knew he had to help them. She was in the middle of packing up and moving out, and Ron's last two cats had recently died, so he took over caring for the kittens. He fed the malnourished two-week-old orphans with an eyedropper several times a day and saved their lives. Two months later, he found homes for two of them and Stefanie took one. Ron kept the remaining two and named them after characters from his favorite children's TV show from the '70s, *Lancelot Link, Secret Chimp*, starring chimpanzees dressed in clothes who ran a detective agency: Mata Hairi was the glamorous sidekick of Lancelot, the star, and Creto, their mustached chauffeur, was a double agent and archvillain.

Now Ron fished out his cell phone from his shorts pocket and anxiously called Evan, a thirty-five-year-old photographer and Irish transplant with whom he'd become fast friends. Evan and Ron had met the previous spring at a sunset picnic on Rooster Rock beach on the Columbia River Gorge. They clicked instantly and became each other's wingman.

"I think Mata's gone again," Ron said, tremulous and close

to tears. "I'm worried that psycho across the street has done something to her."

Evan did his best to calm him, but Ron had reason to fear for Mata. Ron had lived in the area quite happily for more than twenty years, even when it was grittier and less gentrified, way before the shinier hipster Portland emerged. Back then, a Mexican gang leader had ruled the area, and there had been a halfway house for mentally ill people, both long since gone. Ron knew most of his neighbors, and no one ever gave him any trouble until a big guy named Jack had moved in a couple of years before and quickly developed a reputation around the neighborhood as a sketchy character with a hair-trigger temper.

A hulking, muscular ex-wrestler in his midtwenties, Jack was an out-of-work welder and construction worker who lived off his girlfriend. He took perverse pleasure in tormenting Ron, whom he hated for being gay, overweight, and a cat fancier—and everything that's gone wrong with America. Tall and tattooed, with a scraped-back fascist haircut and long hipster beard, with face piercings, Jack towered over Ron, and he made it obvious that he didn't like animals. Ron had not thought that he would actually try to hurt the cats, but whenever Jack walked by his house, Mata hissed and Creto ran to hide. And when friends with their dogs visited Ron, the dogs growled at the sight of Jack.

Mata had disappeared almost a year earlier, on December 21, 2011, one of the coldest, snowiest days of the year, and Ron suspected that Jack had something to do with it. That morning, when he left for work, he had locked both cats inside the house. But when he got home early that evening, the back door was ajar, and when he crept cautiously inside, he saw his bedroom door, which he had closed, was also open. The bedroom was a mess, his things overturned, and a water bottle that wasn't his was on his nightstand. What was particularly disturbing was that

a blanket had been stuffed into the space under his dresser—
something someone might do in order to try to trap a small animal. Creto was hiding in the closet, freaked out. Mata was gone.

Someone had clearly broken into the house and taken Mata.
Nothing else was missing. But Ron didn't call the police because
he didn't think they would believe that someone would break in
just to steal a cat or let her out of the house.

Ron searched frantically in the neighborhood from morning
till evening for three days. On the third day, Jack drove onto the
street and got out of the car. Seeing Ron searching and calling
for Mata, he told him that if Mata was still alive, she was probably in a forest in nearby Washington State. Jack claimed that
Mata had stowed away in his trunk, and he had driven her to
his girlfriend Suzy's place in Vancouver. Jack insisted it had been
an accident and he had no idea she was in there until he popped
the trunk to get his things and Mata shot out and into the woods
behind Suzy's house.

Ron immediately called Suzy, who he knew and liked from
seeing her in the neighborhood whenever she stayed at Jack's.
She always apologized for her boyfriend's moodiness and barbed
comments. Suzy told Ron that she suspected that Jack had something to do with Mata's disappearance because he'd been acting
strange, as if he were hiding something. As soon as he got off
the phone, Ron drove the forty-five minutes to Vancouver, and
he and Suzy, and Suzy's neighbor, a former cop turned detective,
walked through the woods until dark, searching for Mata.

When the three of them turned back toward Suzy's, the ex-
cop said that Jack's story sounded ridiculously improbable. "I
know from experience that things like he said just don't happen,"
he told them. "It doesn't make sense. Cats don't jump into trunks
of idling cars, especially cars owned by people they hiss at."

For weeks afterward, Ron went back to those snowy woods

again and again, looking for Mata and leaving food out for her. After several months with no sign of her, Ron became convinced that Jack had killed her.

But six months later, on June 21, 2012, Ron got a call from the microchip company letting him know that Mata had been found and handed over to the Humane Society for Southwest Washington in Vancouver, which he'd already visited several times during those first fraught, desperate weeks. He immediately drove there to pick her up and took her home. For a while, she seemed almost feral, skittish and shell-shocked, but she had slowly settled back into her home life with Ron and Creto.

Now she was gone again.

Ron stayed up all night searching for her. The next day, he saw Jack's car parked in his driveway and crossed the road to knock on his front door. Since Mata's return, they had maintained an uneasy peace after Ron apologized for accusing Jack of kidnapping his cat and gave him a case of beer. But Ron was still scared of him. Sensing that even asking if he'd seen his cat might spark another war, he wanted to gauge his reaction, so when Jack answered the door, he simply told him that Mata had strayed and asked him to keep an eye out for her.

Jack was annoyed by Ron's neutral request. "I'm not a cat snatcher. Now get the fuck off my porch," he snarled and slammed the door in his face.

His hostility made Ron more suspicious.

For weeks, Ron walked up and down the streets, looking for Mata. He called her name until his voice was hoarse. He sat in the nearby park at night with open cans of cat food. Whenever he saw similar-looking or tabby cats lounging on porches, he'd check to see if they were Mata, then knock at the house. He'd show a picture of her to whoever came to the door, asking if they had seen her. He jumped at every mewing he heard outside and at the screeches of cat fights. Sometimes, in the middle of the night, he would suddenly wake up, worried that Mata was locked in a basement or trapped in a shed. Then he would crawl out of bed and walk from one of his neighbors' backyards to another, even venturing onto their porches to peer inside windows, hoping to spot Mata inside.

Ron left dried kibble and water for Mata on his back porch every night, contacted all the local vets and shelters, and printed up "Lost Cat" posters, plastering them around his neighborhood. Beneath a photo of Mata, he'd typed: MISSING, MISSING $$$ REWARD $$$, *Have you seen me in SE Portland? Mata's very sweet and intuitive and will come up to anyone she senses won't mean her any harm. She also has a chip, so any vet or humane society can scan her. I miss her sorely.* He included his phone number and Facebook link, since he had heard stories of lost pets being reunited with their owners via social media.

As Ron posted his flyers, he surveyed the other signs. There was a flyer for a missing teenager, a strawberry blonde fourteen-year-old girl. Among this patchwork of little mysteries was another runaway, an intelligent-looking brown alpaca with huge liquid-black eyes and a crazy fuzzy cloud of fur that looked like an Afro. Along with the promise of a $1,000 reward was a warning: *Check your backyards and sheds. If you see him, don't surprise him, he'll spit on you. But lure him with dandelions and wheatgrass.*

Only in Portland, Ron thought. Over the next couple of weeks, a few people phoned to say they'd seen a white tabby with gray patches. One man had seen her rummaging through his trash cans. "She'd looked bone thin, like those strays in Mexico," he'd said. "You could see her ribs."

As the weeks went by with no further sightings, though, Ron was devastated. He became more and more despondent, a drifter in his own life.

Chapter 3

Gimme Shelter

While Ron was searching for Mata Hairi those first several weeks after her disappearance, she was a few blocks away on the scuzzier edge of Hawthorne Boulevard, settling into her new digs in the UPS parking bay.

Her rescuer, Michael King, had not wanted a cat. Depressed, alcoholic, and homeless, living outside and begging for scraps, he had a hard enough time feeding himself. Yet now he found himself wanting to take care of this little, injured creature. Every morning Michael would wake up with the cat lying beside him, stretching and letting out a sweet, breathy little yawn. And every day he thought, *She'll probably run off on her own.* Part of him wished she would, but part of him looked forward to seeing her.

Michael and Stinson developed a little routine with the cat. Michael would stash his sleeping bag in the bushes and head out with Stinson on their daily rounds, leaving the cat alone in the shrubs to do her own thing. First they would find an outlet at a diner or café to charge up their phones. Like many of their homeless friends, they used pay-as-you-go cell phones and social media for day-to-day practicalities like finding meals, beds when the weather turned bad, bits of work, and vital social services. Some shelters in Oregon even gave free secondhand phones to rough sleepers, which helped them to stay in touch with friends and family.

Michael, Stinson, and many of their friends used Facebook. For them, like everyone else, it was a virtual home. There, they felt visible; they kept up with their buddies and built support networks. It was free and easy. All they needed was a phone and access to Wi-Fi, and Portland was full of Wi-Fi hotspots.

Usually Michael and Stinson went to El Cubo de Cuba, a bright-orange stucco café-canteen on the corner of Hawthorne and SE 31st Avenue. In the morning before the café opened, they sat at picnic tables tucked along the side to charge their phones and brew their own coffee. In the early autumn, they would pilfer apples, plums, strawberries, and tomatoes from community gardens, collect half-smoked cigarette butts, and forage for discarded, partly eaten breakfast burritos, pastries, and grilled-cheese sandwiches behind the food trucks on Division Street.

And every morning for that first week the cat watched them go and, when they returned at sunset, was waiting for them there. "Damn it," he'd grumble to Stinson, in spite of his happiness at seeing her, "this cat's sticking around."

After a few days, Michael took to calling her Tabor, the name of the café where they'd found her.

"Tabor," he'd say each evening, "we're home." She would shoot out of the bush where she'd been hiding, tail up in the air, and run over to welcome them, meowing all the way. Always hungry, Tabor would slink around Michael's legs, sniffing for treats. Stinson would feed her a piece of egg sandwich or other morsel he'd dug out of the trash behind the food trucks, and the cat would devour it in twitchy, panicked bites. When it was gone, she'd lick the pavement for any crumbs she may have missed. Then Michael would feed her a can of cat food. At first

Michael thought it was just the food that made her stay. Even though he grumbled about her, it comforted him to be able to help someone in the same position as he was in.

By the end of the first week, he found himself worrying about Tabor and thinking of ways to make her comfortable. He lined an empty produce box with one of his sweatshirts, converting it into a sort of crèche where she could sleep undisturbed. He hid it in the bush and set a bowl of water and dried kibble beside it in case she got hungry while they were away for the day.

Michael noticed that the cat now looked at him differently, purring at the sight of him, and, when he spoke to her, her eyes widened as she listened intently.

"Tabor, look what I got for you," he said one day, showing her a can of tuna. Stinson and he had had a good day panhandling, and he wanted to treat her. Tabor jumped up and meowed with squeaks of hunger, winding herself around his legs impatiently as he tried to open the tin.

Before Michael could even finish scraping the tuna from the can into her dish, she had dived in headfirst and was hungrily snatching mouthfuls of tuna. He bent down to pat her back, which she arched as she kept on eating.

"She's beautiful, isn't she?" Michael said, as if seeing her for the first time.

"Yeah, she is," Stinson said.

She was a beauty, perhaps no more than three or four years old, with tiger-striped gray patches and soulful green eyes the color of eucalyptus leaves. She'd cleaned herself and looked healthier, her coat glossier, and her puffy eye and the wound on her face were healing.

Stinson bent down to feed Tabor one of his cold fries. "It's cool to have a cat around. I love it when they scoop food with their paws. It's so damn cute."

Michael blocked Stinson's hand, saying, "You can't give her junk like McDonald's. It'll mess with her liver."

"Whaddaya know about cats?" Stinson asked.

"I know enough."

The two drifters were easygoing and agreed that Michael would take over Tabor's care, since he knew how to look after a cat properly. In fact, ever since reading the Dr. Seuss books *The Cat in the Hat* and *Green Eggs and Ham* as a little boy, Michael had been a bit obsessed with cats. He wasn't allowed to have a pet as a child, but he had known there was nothing else like the peace of being with animals. Michael had three brothers and a sister, but he was the quiet one who sneaked home broken-winged fledglings that had tumbled from their nest and sneaked out food to alley cats. Before he'd become homeless, Michael had doted on his own pet cats and dogs, bringing home fresh meat and fish from the restaurants where he worked.

Every night after feeding Tabor, Michael and Stinson sat side by side in their makeshift sanctuary at the UPS loading bay, silently puffing on their roll-ups, watching the cat play. They'd split a half-eaten pizza, a bag of cold fries, or whatever food they had scavenged, on plates made out of ripped-up pieces of cardboard. And they drank from a thirty-two-ounce water bottle filled with Sidewalk Slam or what Michael called "a wake-up"—a mix of any available alcohol they'd found or bought.

As they ate, Tabor might play football with a scrunched-up cigarette pack or commandeer an empty box and pretend to ambush invisible prey, plunging into the box with her paws stretched as if she were diving into a swimming pool. She would have ten-minute bouts of feline mania, zooming around the lot, mumbling and meowing to herself. One evening, Michael tossed Tabor a red catnip mouse he'd bought her. She pounced on the toy and batted it around with her paws. Then she tucked it into the bed Michael had made for her. "She's funny," he said. "Last night she dug out a can of sardines from the trash and tucked them into bed, just like she did with that catnip mouse. She's basically more a raccoon than a cat."

Stinson smiled and said, "Maybe you should keep her."

Michael didn't look too enthusiastic. "That's a bad idea."

"Why not? She's cool, cute, and doesn't complain much."

Michael didn't answer.

Even though Michael was his closest friend, Stinson didn't know much about him, aside from what he'd gleaned through bits and pieces of conversation. Michael said little about his past and didn't like to talk about his feelings, the things that made his heart ache. While he seemed pretty grounded and easygoing, he was deeply depressed a lot of the time. It was pretty clear that, at some point, something devastating had happened to him. He'd lived on the street a long time and had good advice on how to get by, and he told some funny stories. Yet Michael was withdrawn and deeply depressed at times. Stinson would've liked to see him happier, so he was glad the cat made Michael laugh and gave them something to focus on.

At night Tabor was like a moth—she'd go back and forth between Michael and Stinson until they went to sleep, and at any little light she would go nuts. She was also easily distracted by sounds of passing cars and scared by police car and ambulance sirens. But she liked to wake early and expected everyone else to get up with her—sometimes she would go off like a broken alarm clock, meowing loudly at 4 a.m. At the first hint of light, she would hop from sleeping bag to sleeping bag, trying to roust the men. If Michael didn't get up when she wanted, she'd pull his beard or swat him across the face with her paw or lick his eyelids.

One late September morning Tabor tailed Michael to the back of the UPS building, where he washed his face and brushed his teeth at the spigot. She meowed and looked at him in a way that seemed to ask, "Are you leaving me again?" That day, as Michael and Stinson walked to the edge of the UPS lot, she followed them. Clearly, she didn't want to be left behind.

Michael stood in front of her and sighed, not sure what to do. In a whoosh, she zipped up his leg and clawed her way up to his shoulder and onto his beat-up beige backpack.

"Guess that's telling you," Stinson said, laughing.

"Okay, Tabor," Michael said, reaching up, and ruffling her head. "You're coming with us today."

But the minute they stepped from the parking lot into the street, she flew off Michael's pack and ran back into the bushes where she usually waited for them. Michael decided he couldn't spend his days worrying that she'd get into the road and get hurt or hit by a car, and so that afternoon he spent all the money that he and Stinson made from panhandling on an elegant red-and-orange checked dog collar and leash. He figured dog collars were more secure than cat collars, which were flimsy and easy to break out of.

The following morning, as he prepared to leave the squat, Michael hoisted on his backpack and put the collar and leash on Tabor. At first, she didn't like it and pulled away from him. "Nope, you're coming with me now," he said, scooping her up again onto his pack, where she immediately balanced herself and calmed down.

As Michael walked down Hawthorne, Tabor alternately perched on the backpack or his shoulder like an oversize parrot. Michael turned to Stinson. "You see this?" he asked, pointing to the cat riding happily. "Isn't that awesome?"

"She's a gypsy cat," Stinson said with a grin. "I wonder if she belonged to travelers."

"Or maybe she's a circus cat."

After that, whenever they were heading out, Michael would strap on his pack, say, "Get up," and stick out his leg. Tabor would scoot up his leg and onto his pack. She didn't quite get the hang of walking on leash like a dog at first, and preferred to hitch a ride on Michael.

With Tabor on his shoulder, Michael and Stinson were stopped every few blocks. People gravitated toward them, handing them money or food. Stinson started calling Hawthorne Boulevard the Green Mile for the money they made just walking around with the cat.

Every time they passed a sidewalk café or restaurant, people smiled. It had been a long time since anyone other than another hobo was happy to see Michael, and most people did their damnedest not to look at him for fear that he might ask them for something. Once he started walking around with Tabor, though, lots of people wanted to talk to them or take their pictures. At first, Michael hated it and got grumpy. But Stinson would tell him, "Relax, Groundscore, and be nice to those people."

The cat, on the other hand, soaked up all the attention.

Tabor lightened their moods. Around the cat they were happier, less on edge. They laughed more. Sometimes, the sight of Tabor brought tears to Michael's eyes. She was so sweet and affectionate. Still, Michael felt that he shouldn't get too attached to her, because sooner or later she might run off or her owner would find her.

· · · ·

October arrived and the leaves turned. The scarlet oaks and Japanese maples were a shimmer of ruby reds, and the Norway maples shades of gold and copper. The shop windows along Hawthorne filled with witches on broomsticks, plastic flying bats, glowing goblins, and ghouls. Posters around town advertised zombie walks, haunted houses, and scary movie nights. Pumpkins were for sale outside the New Seasons supermarket.

Opposite the pumpkin display, as Michael and Stinson left the UPS lot one morning, they saw a friend, a skinny, shaggy-haired teenage drifter named Kyle, who sometimes squatted at the bay with them. Sitting alone on the pavement near the fire hydrant, dressed in denim overalls and a ragged red sweater, Kyle had an upturned cap holding a few dollar bills and coins in front of him. Next to the cap was a cardboard sign with SPARE A LITTLE KINDNESS scribbled on it.

Squinting up at them with tired, bloodshot eyes, Kyle said, "Wow, you got a cat. Didn't know you wanted a cat."

"I didn't," Michael said, hovering over him with Tabor in his arms. "I found her on the street. If I left her, she probably wouldn't have survived. When Stinson and I grabbed her, she didn't meow, hiss . . . nothing. She knew right away that she'd been saved."

"She spends all day hanging out with us. She's kind of like a small-community cat," Stinson said, flopping down beside Kyle.

Michael set Tabor down, flung off his pack, and joined them on the sidewalk. Tabor clambered onto his bag, where she curled up with Buddha-like calmness, and remained for the rest of the afternoon.

"So, you back on the street?" Stinson asked Kyle, who had just returned after spending a couple of weeks looking after his sister's cat while she was on vacation.

"Yeah, pretty much," he said. The tenth child of a woman in prison who gave birth to him while she was behind bars, Kyle never knew his father. He had been adopted as a baby by a Harvard-educated software engineer and his social-worker wife and grown up just a few blocks away, but he had lived on and off the streets of Southeast Portland since he was fourteen. After his parents had eventually separated and moved to opposite sides of the city, he had shuffled back and forth between them but never felt a sense of belonging anywhere and kept running away. On the street, he had taken a liking to Michael and Stinson. Since they were older, worldlier, he saw them as kind of mentors and sometimes tagged along.

"So how have things been in the hood?" Kyle asked.

"Well, no one's been stabbed for a while," Stinson said with a laugh.

"For at least two weeks," Michael added, with his broken-tooth smile.

Petting Tabor, Kyle asked, "So whaddaya gonna do with the cat?"

"Beats me."

"Got a snipe?" Kyle asked.

Michael pulled out a couple of half-smoked cigarette butts from his pocket and lit them. His hands were scarred and callused, his fingernails crusted with dirt. "I was thinking if we carry her around, maybe her owner would spot her more quickly."

"Do you really think she has an owner?"

"Yeah," he said, handing the lit half-cigarette to Kyle. "And I figure since she's recovered from her injuries, she'll go back to where she came from eventually."

"Maybe we should look," Stinson suggested.

"I guess we should," Michael said, a touch reluctantly, petting the cat by his side. Tabor looked up at him, blinking drowsily. Then she clasped his hand between her forepaws and began licking it with her raspy tongue.

After that, whenever they walked around town, Michael and Stinson scanned the lost pet posters on trees and lampposts. A lot of cats and dogs had gone missing in the area. A sign for Freddy, an emotional-support dachshund "snatched from a handbag," read: *Even if you find Freddy and he's dead, send him back home anyway so he can have a proper burial.*

"I think some of these guys must've been stolen," Stinson said, as they surveyed a cluster of faded, weather-beaten posters plastered all over one telephone pole.

"Probably," Michael said, remembering how his own dog, Wylie Coyote, had been taken outside a store in St. Louis and never found. He had left him for only a minute to buy a pack of cigarettes. He'd lived in a rough neighborhood, where criminal gangs stole family pets to serve as bait for fighting dogs and suppliers of medical research labs also routinely paid thieves or dog dealers known as bunchers to steal animals.

Some of the flyers, like a child's drawing of a black kitten, were pleading and heartbreaking. " 'My name is Rosemary and I am twelve years old,' " Michael read out loud from a poster. " 'I lost my kitten outside the Goodwill store.' I mean, how simple is that, she's twelve years old and she put up a flyer?"

He was mystified and a little annoyed that they didn't see a single poster for Tabor. "I just don't get it." They couldn't know that they were eight blocks from Tabor's home near Berkeley Park. Somehow the cat had ended up all the way across the chaos and traffic of Hawthorne before Michael stumbled upon her.

. ˙ . ˳ .

On October 8, about three weeks after they found Tabor, Michael had to go to Montana to attend a court date for unpaid tickets for drunk and disorderly charges, for essentially sitting on the sidewalk and drinking in public. While he was away, Stinson looked after the cat and continued to try to trace her owner. One of their street buddies, Crazy Joe, tried to help them by going on Facebook. He posted, *What to do if you get stuck with a stray cat that won't leave?*

Someone posted back: *Rescue it, you moron.*

Stinson took Tabor over to a girlfriend's house, hoping she'd want to keep her, but Tabor fought with one of her cats, so that didn't work out. Then Stinson snapped a few pictures of Tabor and posted them on Craigslist. But despite his efforts, there was no sign of an owner.

When Michael returned from Montana a week later, Stinson said, "Well, Groundscore, looks like she's yours."

You can't own a cat, Michael thought, *especially when you don't own anything else.* But he smiled.

Chapter 4

Scary Monsters and Super Creeps

On the trendier, leafier fringes of Hawthorne Boulevard, not too far from his house, Ron Buss went to visit a cat lady who was known for taking in strays. His friend Stefanie had told Ron that this lady might have heard if anyone had found Mata. Within the animal-rescue community, she'd become known as the queen of street cats in Southeast Portland and made nightly rounds of bleak alleyways and abandoned buildings feeding ferals. With a small network of other cat ladies, she would capture these forgotten felines, pay to neuter them, find homes for kittens and friendly adult cats, and return the wilder adults to their colonies.

Walking along the overgrown path to the cat lady's old dusty-pink saltbox bungalow, which was buried beneath a canopy of wisteria, Ron saw cats of many colors squashed against the window screens sunning themselves. A slight whiff of urine mingled with citrus-scented incense on the doorstep.

Some twenty years before, Ron had filled his own house

with strays. He'd had four middle-aged cats at that point, and that summer someone had left three Siamese-mix kittens on his doorstep in a cardboard box with cruel cooking instructions scribbled on top. He quickly learned how to hand-feed them with a syringe and otherwise look after them. Some days later, he heard yowling outside his front door and found that their mother had been dropped off with another kitten. Ron named the mother Mama Yoko, and the little feline family moved in permanently, pushing his cat count to nine. Ron became known as the cat man around the neighborhood.

When the cat lady opened the door, she was clasping a chatty brown Burmese in her arms. Both she and the cat had big, bright green eyes and glossy sable-colored hair reddened by the sun. The woman wore eyeliner to accentuate her striking eyes. At least a dozen other cats were behind her—red, yellow, and brown tabbies, tortoiseshells, tuxedos, grays, and blacks—all lounging alluringly across sofas and bookshelves. She didn't look like the typical crazy cat lady with unbrushed hair in a bathrobe. She was very glamorous, and apart from the faint cat-pee smell at her front door, her house looked immaculate.

She listened to Ron's story about his cat who was lost, found, and lost again. "Poor little mite," she said to Ron. "She's not a black cat, is she?"

"No, she's white with tabby markings and kohl-lined eyes," he said, handing her one of the lost-cat flyers with Mata's face.

The cat lady took a good look at the flyer but didn't recognize her. Then she told him a couple of stories of missing cats that were found and gave him a reassuring smile. "You never know— someone might actually be taking care of your kitty."

"I know she's out there somewhere."

"What's worrying is that it's nearly Halloween," she said, her smile fading, "and people do wretched things to animals around this time. It's good of you not to give up on her." She explained that she and her husband were a little overwhelmed with strays at the moment. "The streets just seem to be a dumping ground for animals. People frequently leave cats behind when their lives change or their hearts grow cold. I'm not a cynic, but I've seen the worst of humanity."

"Yeah, I know, I've rescued quite a few myself," Ron said glumly. "Well, if you see her or hear anything about a cat of her description, I'd be grateful if you'd let me know."

"Of course. I'll ask around and keep an eye out for your kitty."

"Thank you," he said, turning away.

Ron walked the five blocks back home, blinded with tears.

* * * * *

After the visit to the cat lady proved to be another dead end, Ron thought he had exhausted his search options. But that afternoon, while pottering around at home and tidying the kitchen, he found a matchbook on which he'd jotted the number for an animal psychic, Rachel. Another friend had recommended he call Rachel, who worked exclusively to find missing pets. A public-service psychic, Rachel didn't ask for any money, so Ron figured she must be legit.

Ron left a rambling message on her voice mail, explaining how Mata had gone missing. When Rachel got back to him, she suggested that she could show Ron how to tune in to his intuition, and they could try to locate the cat telepathically. She explained the nature of spiritual connections and psychic impressions and how to tell if he was having one.

For example, she said, "While you're concentrating on your cat and asking where she is, if you smell freshly cut grass and your cat liked rolling around in the grass, that would be a psychic impression." Ron believed that he had a spiritual connection with his cats, since he got them as tiny orphans, so he was open to trying.

Rachel asked Ron to picture his cat and concentrate and, after a minute, asked, "Are you getting anything?"

Ron didn't see or smell anything.

"Let's try this . . . I'd like you to turn off the lights and light a candle," she said. "It will strengthen the psychic bond with Mata."

Ron put down the phone, found a half-melted red cranberry-scented candle in a small glass on a bookshelf, and lit it.

"Okay, it's lit," he said, switching his phone onto the loud-speaker and waiting for further instructions.

"I want you to clear your mind and concentrate on Mata again, and I will, too."

After a brief pause, Rachel gasped and said, "There's a person, like a rock that was fractured in many places but was glued back together, but the fractures still show," she said. "This person has her."

Ron thought he knew whom she was talking about: his rogue neighbor, Jack. He hung up but was now more worried than ever. He called Suzy, who told him that she didn't think Jack had anything to do with Mata's disappearance this time, as they had been away over Labor Day weekend. But Ron couldn't shake his feeling that Jack was somehow involved.

· · · · ·

Halloween was a big event in Portland. All Ron's neighbors' porches and lawns were ablaze with carved pumpkins and decorated with scarecrows and spiders on giant cobwebs. In the front yard of a house a few doors away, the owner, a film-set designer, had erected a monsters' ball, a theatrical display of life-size vampires and witches in fancy dress draped on deck chairs, with skeletons and zombies springing out of a makeshift graveyard.

The day before Halloween, Ron woke up feeling low. He kept thinking about Mata and tried to distract himself by doing some late-season gardening before the weather turned. In his homey urban garden at the side of the house, a jumble of potatoes, squash, green beans, mustard greens, and a few pumpkins were all hemmed in by a tiny, white picket fence.

Ron picked his biggest pumpkins to make jack-o'-lanterns and bake a pumpkin pie for Ann next door, in thanks for her supportiveness since Mata's disappearance. Ann was a bit of a curtain twitcher who reminded him of Gladys Kravitz from the '60s sitcom *Bewitched*, but she was well-intentioned and kind. Brushing the dirt off the pumpkins, Ron thought back to when Mata and Creto were kittens and they always wanted to be involved in everything: if he was tearing up carpet and pulling nails from the floorboards, they tried to pull the nails out with their tiny teeth; if he was gardening, they'd come out and help dig holes, their little white paws getting smudged with dirt.

Now Creto sat on the edge of the little vegetable patch, nervously watching him work.

Creto had been shy and skittish since Mata's first disappearance. In fact, shortly before Mata went missing the first time, Creto himself had disappeared for two days. When he had come back home, he'd had a swollen eye and bloodied mouth. Someone had obviously kicked him in the head. One of his fangs was broken, a few bottom teeth were knocked out, and the skin on his chin was torn. For two months, the cat couldn't see straight and kept bumping into things. The vet said Creto was lucky to be alive.

Since Mata had vanished again, Creto had become much more fearful. He hid from everyone but Ron and hissed at them, even if he knew them. A lovely leggy tuxedo tomcat with silvery-green eyes and a crooked mustache, he had become positively clingy ever since his sister had disappeared, staying constantly at Ron's heels when he was working around the house or in the garden.

Ron stopped gardening to finish his coffee. Suddenly he heard Creto hiss and saw a swish of black and white fur flick past. He glanced over his shoulder to see Creto frantically scrambling up the back-porch steps. When he turned back around to see what had scared the cat, he spotted Jack walking by his house. Ron flushed with adrenaline and launched himself up and out of the garden, running toward Jack on the sidewalk, his fingers muddy from digging and still holding his mug of coffee.

"I know you killed her," Ron shouted, stepping in front of Jack and blocking his path.

Jack hesitated, momentarily confused, and Ron couldn't stop himself—he shoved Jack. Ron didn't believe in violence, but in his hurt and rage, he lost his head. Jack pushed him back, easily knocking him to the ground. The coffee mug bounced on the grass and rolled away.

Jack loomed over Ron, furious. "I didn't touch your fucking cat, you fat faggot," he shouted, his face flaming and the blue-green tattoos on his herculean neck pulsating with rage. "I'm not an animal abuser. I might stomp at them to scare them away, but I'd never light them on fire."

Ron staggered to his feet and started screaming, "You're a terrorist. I'm sure it was you who kicked Creto in the face and knocked out his tooth. Why else is he so terrified of you? And everyone knows you kidnapped Mata and dumped her in the woods last year. What'd you do with her this time . . . did you kill her?"

"What the hell are you talking about?"

Red faced and seething, Ron grabbed the coffee mug off the

lawn and flung it at Jack, hitting him in the head and cutting his temple. This time the mug shattered.

Jack touched his face and, seeing blood on his fingers, turned feral and hysterical. He charged and head-butted Ron like a crazed rhino, and then punched him in the ribs. "If you run around telling people I killed your cat, you will disappear," he said, jabbing a finger at him. "I'll take you out, and no one will ever find you."

"Fuck you, loser," Ron spat back. He straightened up and went for Jack's throat, but Jack quickly grabbed both of his arms and put him in a guillotine choke.

"You live and breathe because I say so," Jack said, menacingly, before releasing Ron, leaving him gasping and sputtering. "I'm telling you now, watch your back." Then he stormed off, spun around, and shouted from across the road with a taunting grin, "That was a pretty good shot, faggot. I was actually rooting for you."

"Junkie scumbag," Ron fumed under his breath, turning away.

Ron limped back to his house to get a broom and swept the broken coffee mug pieces off the sidewalk. He picked up the basket of pumpkins and hobbled inside.

The moment he opened the back door, Creto popped out from behind the fridge where he'd taken refuge, his glittery gem-green eyes wide and questioning. Ron washed the dirt off his hands and, picking up his frightened cat, slumped into a chair and cuddled and comforted him.

They were both shaking.

· · · ·

That same afternoon before Halloween, Michael, Tabor, and Kyle wandered over to the New Seasons. It was windy, so they huddled together in their usual spot by the graffitied fire hydrant. A few years earlier, the street kids had spray-painted the hydrant with a likeness of Michael, with his street-name "Groundscore" above it. It had proved surprisingly durable. Now they held out their flimsy SPARE A LITTLE KINDNESS sign next to their totem.

Stretched out on Michael's pack between him and Kyle, Tabor was wearing a shiny new red heart-shaped metal ID tag Michael had got her, with his phone number and "LC Tabor" inscribed on the front. The LC stood for "Love Cat."

Just a few days earlier, Michael had asked Stinson and a buddy of theirs, Whip Kid, another young drifter who also sometimes crashed at their squat, to look after Tabor for five minutes while he popped across the UPS parking lot and into the New Seasons. When he came out of the supermarket, he saw them chasing Tabor across the sidewalk toward him, her leash trailing behind her. The street kids couldn't handle her—she was willful and feisty and had come after him. She didn't want to let Michael out of her sight. The new tag was more protection for her.

Tabor had become something of a star along that stretch of Hawthorne. Moments after the men and cat arrived in their spot every day, passing locals and shoppers stopped to greet the cat. Many came out of the supermarket and handed Michael bags stuffed with cat food, treats, and accessories. Others gave him coffee and sandwiches, even a bag of candy corn. Many of these same people had been walking past the panhandlers all summer long, but the sparky little cat suddenly made them visible that fall.

Tabor lapped up all the attention, swishing, prancing, and doing little belly rolls. She was a born showgirl, a fool for ad-oration.

A young couple in their twenties stopped to put some change

in the guys' cup and to pet Tabor. She popped on her hind legs to reach the girl's hand like a tiny show pony.

"Awww, soooo cute, she does little jumps!" the girl said as she took out her phone and tried to snap a photo of the cat in action.

"She does tricks for treats," Michael said, laughing.

A little while later, Michael and Kyle were sitting quietly, smoking and staring at a swirl of leaves on the sidewalk. Tabor had been curled on Michael's backpack between them when suddenly she rolled over on her back and started yowling and screeching in a way she had never done before. Michael and Kyle looked at each other, stunned.

"Tabor, what's wrong with you?" Michael asked, scooping her into his arms and hugging her tightly. "Kyle, know what she's saying?"

Kyle put on a high-pitched voice and said, "They're killing me . . . heeeeelp."

Michael broke into an amused smile, but he guessed something bad had happened to the cat before he'd stumbled across her. "When I found her she was like, 'Don't fucking touch me. I've been traumatized.'"

"Come to think of it," said Kyle, "the other day someone was trying to open a bag of weed beside me, and Tabor shot onto his lap. I think this cat's a stoner."

"I wouldn't be surprised. She's mental. She chases lights all night. It must be kitty stress. I've seen it in dogs that belong to potheads."

Even though she was unpredictable and sometimes incredibly stubborn, Michael, Stinson, and Kyle had fallen hard for the sweet, plucky little cat.

* * * *

As the days got colder, Michael grew more anxious about being able to care for Tabor. He had had other street cats: Sunshine, a tiny tiger-striped orange kitten he'd found in an alley, and a brown tabby kitten, who had first belonged to a friend who went to jail. But neither of those cats had taken to living outside or accompanying him on the road when he was drifting south for the winter, so he had found them proper homes.

The homeless had a code of ethics—they always took care of their animals first. Living on the street without anyone or anything else, they were usually devoted to their furry companions. One of Michael's buddies suggested that he take Tabor to a no-kill shelter, but Michael had visions of Tabor looking sad, sitting beside a tiny pink suitcase with all her bowls and toy mice, waiting in line with a bunch of other cats and dogs at the shelter. He couldn't bear the thought of abandoning her.

Tabor had now been with him for two months, but he still had moments of doubt about the wisdom and practicality of keeping her. Somehow, Tabor always sensed these moods and would look into his eyes or lick his fingers until he melted. Michael realized he had become attached to her—he loved the way she burrowed into his chest, pulled at his beard to wake him, and chirruped to her toy mice. She was super needy at times, but he was grateful to be needed by anybody for anything. He hadn't cared for anyone for a long time, and part of him longed for it.

Before Tabor had appeared, Michael would start every morning with beer, progress to Steel Reserve, then to whatever slop was left. But, quite unexpectedly, Tabor had affected Michael's drinking habits. He'd got off the malt liquor and now only drank at night. He felt that he needed to keep it together so that no one would call the police on him and take the cat away.

Now, as Michael reflected on how much Tabor meant to

him, he resolved to make whatever sacrifices necessary to take her with him wherever he was going. It was time to make plans to head south to warmer weather.

Nevertheless, the thought that she might have an owner out there somewhere was always on his mind.

Chapter 5

Born to Run

Michael William Arthur King grew up in an ordinary clapboard house in Webster Groves on the outskirts of St. Louis, Missouri. A leafy suburb, lined with pretty shuttered bungalows, Webster Groves had a sleepy small-town feel. It was a safe, decent, and peaceful kind of place, with long, winding streets surrounded by woods and creeks where kids and dogs played outside and ran wild. But for Michael it was mostly a quiet little corner of hell. His family lived on the poorer end of town and his parents, whom he thought of as bad-tempered strangers, were overwhelmed with trying to raise him and his four siblings. His father worked around the clock at two jobs, but money was still tight, and his mother remained home alone looking after five kids. A teenage bride when she moved to the United States from England, she struggled to assimilate into a new culture without any help from family or anyone.

Michael's parents had met in England in 1955. Clarence, or Clancy as everyone called him, was an American soldier stationed at a U.S. Army base in Cambridge. Kathleen was a nineteen-year-old British orphan for whom marrying a dashing

American soldier opened the door to a new life. Clancy brought Kathleen back to the States with him and became a police officer in St. Louis. Kathleen had their first child at twenty.

The five King children were expected to be quiet and do as they were told. They weren't allowed to have friends over, couldn't use the telephone, couldn't play music. But Michael was willful and talked back, and his mother used to hit him with his dad's police belt, among other punishments. One of his most disturbing memories was being locked in the upstairs closet while the rest of the family ate dinner. To Michael, Kathleen seemed angry all the time, which got worse as he got older.

An anxious, worried child, Michael attended Mary Queen of Peace Catholic School with his twin brother and their three older siblings. All the nuns there were fiercely protective of Michael. They saw the welts on the back of his legs and knew he got hit at home, so they made sure he was never touched at school. His second-grade teacher, Sister Maureen Teresa, took him under her wing. Michael adored her, and for a while school was a refuge from his troubled home. As he got older, however, he became more willful and withdrawn, skipping school and hanging out by the railroad tracks near his house, nurturing dreams of escape.

After all the kids were in school, Kathleen took a job working night shifts as a nurse's assistant at the local hospital. Left alone and unattended, Michael and his brothers prowled the railway and parks at night—although Michael spent most of his time by himself, kicking around the back alleys, reading books about animals and plants, daydreaming, and learning how not to be lonely.

When he was thirteen years old, in June 1978, Michael ran away for the first time. School was out for the summer, and he told his friends he "was getting the hell out of that house." He packed a little duffel bag and sneaked out in the middle of the night along with his twin brother, John Patrick, who went by the nickname JP. They walked down the railway tracks and out of St. Louis. Without any money or place to stay, they raided vegetable gardens and apple trees, ate wild blackberries, and slept in derelict garages or dense thickets. They got as far as New Mexico before being arrested for truancy and hauled back home in handcuffs.

By fourteen, Michael would often sleep in bushes along the train tracks and survive by dining in local restaurants and skipping out on the bill. For a while he lived with neighbors, a family called the Bekemeyers who took pity on him, but he always got dragged back home.

When Michael was fifteen, his father caught him and JP smoking weed in the backyard. They were just experimenting, but he flew into a rage. Thinking the boys had a drug problem, he checked them both into a month-long, lockdown treatment program.

A few days later, Michael, along with another fifteen-year-old kid, Mike, escaped and hitchhiked out of town.

The boys headed to Seattle, where Mike said they could live with his mother, but they got arrested in Wheatland, Wyoming. Since they were minors, the boys were placed in a holding cell. The sheriff called Mike's parents first, who said he was a runaway and they wanted him back.

Then the sheriff got on the phone with Michael's parents. His parents had put out police reports initially but then had stopped searching. At the end of the call, the sheriff hung up and uncuffed Michael: Clancy didn't want him back and Kathleen was resigned to the fact that Michael was unhappy at home and liked to roam and sleep under the stars. For her, it was probably a relief to have one fewer child to deal with. The sheriff took Michael back to the car, drove him out of town, gave him twenty dollars, and said, "Good luck, kid."

* * * * *

Sometime in the summer of 1981, Michael wound up in Montana. Its sawtooth mountains and sun-scorched plains were the wild, uncultivated place he was looking for. "All you could see is a little landscape and a lot of sky, and not a soul for miles," he wrote on a postcard to JP back home. He got a job delivering milk for a local dairy farm in Helena, found a cheap apartment, and forged his dad's signature on the enrollment form at the local high school.

Michael thought of himself as an old soul, and, in some ways, he was mature beyond his years. He could easily pass for eighteen or nineteen, but after a few months he was found out by the authorities and told he couldn't stay in Montana without a legal guardian.

He returned to St. Louis but hated being home and, after a couple of months, hitchhiked back to Montana, determined to find a legal guardian. The dangers of riding with strangers never occurred to Michael. He was convinced that multiple angels followed him and nothing bad would happen to him—besides, he'd already been through the worst. Once he got to Helena, he jumped in the first battered pickup that stopped for him. The driver turned out to be a beer-swilling hippie on his way to his AA meeting. Having nowhere else to go, Michael joined him, figuring that Alcoholics Anonymous was as good a place as any to find a legal guardian. During his own short stint in the rehab program the year before, he had appreciated the honesty of the adults he'd observed.

That Tuesday afternoon in October at the AA meeting, Michael met Walter Ebert, a Vietnam veteran and divorced recovering alcoholic who worked as a recruiter for the army.

Michael sensed Walter was a good guy. He had an earthy

wholesomeness about him. Michael asked if Walter would pretend to be his dad so he could stay in school, explaining that he'd
run away from a bad home but had a job and could take care of
himself. He just needed a signature. "Sure, I'll help you," Walter
had said, but insisted on talking to Michael's mother first. Over
the phone, Kathleen told Walter that if Michael wanted to live
in Montana, that was fine by her. His parents signed him away.

Walter would become Michael's foster parent and a caring
presence for the next three decades. Having had a Jesuit edu-
cation and spent some time in a Franciscan seminary, Walter
often told Michael that "in nourishing others, we sometimes
find ourselves."

Shortly after moving in with Walter, Michael got his GED
while continuing to work as a gardener during the day and occasionally as a dealer for an illegal underground casino in Helena
at night. Those first few years that they lived together they split
the rent, food, and bills. Michael went on to the state university
in Bozeman, Montana, studied business and horticulture, but
dropped out when he realized he didn't need a degree to start
his own landscaping company, which he did. He would live and
work in Montana for nearly a decade.

Over those years, Michael had minimal contact with his
family, aside from JP, who'd also moved to Montana, but he
went back to St. Louis for his dad's funeral in August 1990. He
intended to stay in town for only a couple of days, but on the
night of the funeral, after skipping the service, Michael and his
brother Robert went out to a bar in St. Louis to get wasted.

As Michael knocked back his drink, he spotted an old high
school friend, Michael Mercer. His hair was shorter, his face a
little thinner and older, but Mercer was just as good-looking as
ever. They had first met when Michael was sixteen, in the lino-
leum-lined hallways of Mehlville High School in St. Louis. Their

connection was electric. Mercer was a couple of years older than Michael, and they looked very similar, both six-two, with dark, messy hair, sharp cheekbones, and sparkling blue eyes. After Mercer finished high school and joined the military, they kept in touch briefly through letters.

It seemed like those nine years apart passed in a blink. In a matter of minutes, they were doing shots together, smoking, talking, and laughing like nothing had changed since high school. The next day, Michael and Mercer met up again, and Michael decided to delay his return to Montana. His friend was laid-back, generous, funny and fun to be around. He felt more at ease with Mercer than anyone else. With Mercer, Michael finally felt at home.

He returned briefly to Montana to pack up his stuff and shut down his landscaping business, then moved into Mercer's place in St. Louis in a ramshackle row house apartment building in a rough black neighborhood. The owner, who was a friend of Mercer's, offered Michael a job as building manager, so Michael collected the rent, did routine maintenance, and tended the grounds in exchange for a very low monthly rent for several years.

Eventually Michael got a job as a chef at a fancy bistro, and Mercer worked as a cable guy installing cable TV into people's homes. They settled into a quiet, domestic routine, punctuated by poker games and occasional drug binges. They took camping trips and enjoyed being outdoors. They even talked about eventually retiring to Montana. On television after work, they watched as the Soviet Union fell apart and South Africa abandoned apartheid. A host of countries signed nuclear nonproliferation treaties. It seemed like the whole world was actually improving; things could change.

In this new comfortable existence, Michael was able to admit something he would have hidden before: he was in love with a man. Michael was raised to think of it as a sin, but this new, unexpected love felt like a blessing.

For five years, they enjoyed a fairly peaceful and contented life until Mercer confessed that he was HIV positive. He'd gotten it a couple of years before they had reconnected and now was struggling to cope. Almost overnight, Michael went from having the beginnings of a life and a future with Mercer to preparing for his partner's death.

Michael held out hope that they could contain the disease and, for almost thirteen years, they did. They got on with their lives. Then, in the summer of 2003, Mercer got very sick and was hospitalized. Michael felt a rising panic, then a numbing sadness as he waited for the inevitable.

Michael was working sixty-hour weeks, but every morning before work, he would go to the hospital and have breakfast with Mercer, making sure that he had everything he needed. One day he found out that the nurses were forgetting to give Mercer his pain medication. Michael flipped out. He didn't like the way Mercer was being treated, so he pretty much kidnapped him and took him home. The doctors warned, "You can't do that—he'll die in two weeks." But with Michael's care and a hospice nurse to look after him while he was at work, Mercer lived four more months.

Almost every day, when Michael got home from the restaurant, Mercer looked worse: skinnier, paler, and weaker. When Mercer started having trouble breathing, Michael got him an oxygen tank. All throughout this time, he kept contacting Mercer's family to let them know that he was dying and hoping they would help look after him or at least visit him. But they were in complete denial and refused to accept that his death was even possible. They didn't come to see him once during his illness.

Mercer died on October 20, 2003, at the age of forty. Michael held him as he passed, gazing at his one great love through tears, memorizing the details of his face and the way his dark, silver-flecked hair fell across his cavernous cheekbones.

Five days later, Michael managed to stay calm through the ordeal of the funeral and burial. He had been grieving for Mercer months before he died, as well as during those last days when he had felt his fragile body crumbling in his arms. But after the burial that Saturday afternoon, he went home shell-shocked and sank into the sofa on which they had talked so many nights together. He turned on the television and muted it. And for the next few days, little by little, he fell apart—his eczema flared out of control, his hair came out in big silver-dollar clumps when he ran his fingers through it. He barely moved off the couch.

When he finally did get up, he faced the many little losses in the wake of the enormous vacuum that Mercer had left in his life. In the bathroom, he spotted Mercer's toothbrush. As he tried to throw it away, it hit him that Mercer would never use it again.

Everything he looked at—the chairs, the ceramics, the art they had started collecting not long before Mercer passed away—had meant something while they were together, but now it was all oppressive clutter.

Michael thought, *There's too much stuff in the world and most of it's pointless.*

He started pulling things off shelves, making a pile in the bedroom and a pile in the kitchen. He made a mental inventory of all the things in their driveway: the brand-new Subaru, the Ford F-150, the trailer, the boat. They had accumulated about $250,000 worth of stuff. He thought about having a garage sale, but then immediately felt guilty about making money from Mercer's death.

Still, Michael had the heartbreaking task of emptying their house. Only a week before Mercer died, he had given away their cat, Mau Mau, a big-boned tabby girl, and dog, Aggie Jr. to Mercer's brother. He'd already known he would be leaving St. Louis.

Now, a week after the burial, Michael went upstairs one last time to sift through their photos, snippets of their life together. His eyes lingered over a picture of Mercer, smiling with Mau Mau in his arms. Mau Mau, named after the African rebels, took up half the sofa and fetched like a dog. Mercer had adored her. Aggie Jr. was one of the puppies of a brown stray mutt Michael had found beneath a restaurant dumpster in southwest Missouri. Flicking through all the happy memories, he came apart again.

He went back downstairs and grabbed a bottle of whiskey. He collapsed on the couch, staring into space, and swigged straight from the bottle, lying there until the whiskey ran dry. He looked up at the muted TV and caught a glimpse of himself reflected in the screen, his face wet and swollen from crying.

Not long after, in the middle of the night, Michael packed a backpack with a few clothes and precious photos. He emptied the contents of the fridge and wandered around the backyard, leaving the food in heaps for the squirrels and raccoons to eat. He filled all the bird feeders with seeds and then sat by the pond he had built under the willow he had planted, next to the lovely brick courtyard he had constructed with its honeysuckle, mimosa, and rose garden. Michael and Mercer used to sit there in lawn chairs in the summertime, talking and smoking, with Neil Young songs floating from the house.

He went back into the house to grab his backpack. He wanted to be light on his feet again, and unsure of how to escape this sadness, he did the only thing he knew and ran away.

Leaving the front door unlocked, Michael left the house for the last time and put his thumb out on the nearest highway. It felt strangely liberating to be walking away with nothing.

Chapter 6

On the Road Again

In Portland, by late November, winter had blown in, turning the landscape gray and ghostly. The wind coming down the Columbia River Gorge brought the type of chill that cut to the bone and made eyes water. Michael struggled to keep dry as the frequent rains seeped into his tatty, moth-eaten sleeping bag.

Sometimes five of them were sleeping out in that UPS bay or banding together in the doorways on busy streets: Michael, Stinson, their friends Kyle and Whip Kid, and Tabor. Rough sleepers on their own were vulnerable to attacks, particularly in city parks and secluded areas, which was one of the reasons some kept dogs—to have some sense of protection as they slept.

Almost ten years before, when Michael had walked away from his home and life—everything—he had thought that a few months on the road would help him escape his grief. He hadn't planned to walk into homelessness. But he'd become a heavy drinker and, after lightning strikes of bad luck, had nothing to fall back on. He found himself broke and alone on the streets and eventually fell in with the community of other drifters and adapted to their way of life.

Living outside also meant drifting with the seasons. Ordinarily, Michael rolled out of Portland by mid-November to find somewhere where the elements weren't so fierce, but he had hung on a little longer this year, hoping someone might reclaim Tabor as their missing cat.

One morning during a brutal cold snap, Michael woke up to find frost covering his bag. Tabor had climbed inside his sweatshirt, shivering, to press against him and absorb as much warmth as possible. She couldn't live out in the cold for much longer. They had already endured too many wild and windy nights. Michael knew it was time to head south for the winter.

After the hard freeze, on December 3, his forty-eighth birthday, Michael started the day bright and breezy with a can of Steel Reserve. He wanted to have a birthday party and a farewell party. Before he got on the road with Tabor, Michael went with Stinson, Kyle, and Tabor to several drinking spots around Hawthorne, but they were kicked out or moved along after owners called the police. They wound up at the Lone Fir Cemetery on Morrison Street, where they would be left alone to celebrate.

Crazy Joe and the other pals had collected enough money to buy Michael a bottle of Wild Turkey, as well as a few six-packs of beer and store-bought sandwiches. Deep in the heart of the old pioneer cemetery, beneath the three tall ponderosa pines, they huddled in a circle, listening to classic old country music and passing around the bottle, each taking a swig. That way, if the police showed up, they would only have to pour out one bottle.

Near a large crypt, Michael stood swaying under the wintry, moonless sky, and Tabor wandered around in the shadows. When they were among friends in calm, empty places like the cemetery, Michael let her off her kitty leash to roam a little. She batted around acorns and pinecones that littered the muddy, threadbare grass, swished her tail, and slunk in and out of the choke of weeds at the base of the mossy graves.

From behind the crypt, two figures suddenly materialized out of the inky darkness, like vampires, sending everyone scattering. Crazy Joe, a small, whippet-thin guy in his late forties, with short, peppery dirty-blond hair, leaped up, spilling beer all over his trousers.

The vampires were actually Whip Kid and Jane. A slouchy indie kid, Whip Kid wore green army pants and a flannel shirt beneath a sweater and a denim jacket. His girlfriend Jane, cute, pale and freckled, with short chestnut hair and skinny as a colt, stood beside him, shy and watchful.

"Y'all scared the bejesus outta me," Crazy Joe said in a thick southern accent. "Thought you'd both risen from the dead."

"Sorry, didn't mean to scare you," said Whip Kid as he joined the group.

"Are you from the South?" Jane asked Crazy Joe.

"Sure am, mama," he said as he ripped open another can of beer. "Georgia . . . from the sticks . . . from a town you ain't never heard of." Crazy Joe looked like a tough guy, tightly wound and highly strung, and he traveled with a big black mellow female rottweiler, who was curled up against a weeping stone angel nearby. "My mama was a redneck, my daddy was a scumbag, and I ain't no good." He had come to Portland to find work painting, picking fruit, anything. When he couldn't find work, he scratched out a living growing and selling pot and magic mushrooms in the community gardens.

While everyone was drinking and talking, Tabor had come to sit inside the circle, grooming herself. Whenever she heard her name, she paused, with tufts of damp fur sticking out of her side. The rottweiler, a sweet-natured dog, kept looking at Tabor with her soft, cow-like eyes and wagging her tail. Then, the rottie rolled over across a carpet of pine needles and dried leaves, trying to persuade the cat to play. Tabor ignored her and just kept grooming.

"We found twenty dollars outside of Rite Aid," Whip Kid said, taking out two beer bottles from his bag and handing one to Michael. "And you know what that means—"

"The sound of angels," Michael said with a laugh, and clinked his bottle against Whip Kid's.

Jane had slumped against a pine tree to sit beside Michael and was now crouched over her phone. "Why are you having your birthday in the cemetery?" she asked with a giggle, without taking her eyes away from her phone.

Michael grinned and said, "Guess cemeteries are the natural ground for strays."

"It's the right place to be diggin' yer own grave," Crazy Joe broke in.

"And the cops kept kicking us out of all our usual spots," Michael added.

Crazy Joe took another swig of beer and cast his mournful gray eyes around the circle. Then he looked at Michael and said, "I got some produce here if you'd be in-ner-rested," he said, opening a crinkled brown paper bag of magic mushrooms.

"Don't need 'em. I got the cat and plenty of brew," Michael said, turning back to his beer and to Tabor, beside his bag, playing with an acorn like it were prey. "Just glad you're here." He never had birthday parties as a kid, so he was touched that all his regular street buddies had showed up. He took a slug of Wild Turkey and checked his phone. He had birthday texts from other friends around the country and tapped out a quick message on his Facebook page in response: *Wet in Portland . . . cat is sooo good.*

It was a bone-chilling night, a little above freezing with a light rain falling. The whiskey could only do so much. Michael realized he needed to get away from the bitter chill as much as from himself. He imagined Tabor wearing tiny red sunglasses and a cardboard sign around her neck that said CALIFORNIA BOUND.

As he passed the bottle, he announced, "Tabor and I are going to Cali."

"We'll go with you," Whip Kid said. "Me and Jane are heading south, too, for some sunshine."

"Yah, I can see that," Crazy Joe said, nodding. "In my heart, I'm on a tropical island in a hut. I think it's better for y'all's sake and the cat's. But how d'you plan on travelin' with a cat? First class or coach?"

Everyone except Kyle and Stinson laughed.

Traveling with the cat wasn't as far-fetched as it seemed, sure she was going to make Michael's trip harder to do, but he couldn't leave her behind. "I want to show her the sights," he said.

Tabor had stopped her ramble and returned to Michael. He zipped her into his jacket, and he and Stinson and Kyle started back to their squat. They left Crazy Joe passed out with his dog inside the grandest crypt, a redbrick pile with spires and stained glass windows.

"Taking Tabor on the road south," Michael said to his friends as they walked out of the cemetery, "is a compulsion of the heart."

Chapter 7

Oregon to California:
Riders on the Storm

A couple of weeks after his birthday party in the Lone Fir Cemetery, Michael and Tabor were hitchhiking with Whip Kid and Jane on the side of Interstate 5 in Oregon in the middle of a snowstorm. Michael had strapped a durable zip-up nylon pet carrier firmly to the top of his backpack, inside of which Tabor huddled under a fluffy fleece donated by one of the sympathetic shop owners along Hawthorne.

Earlier that morning, Michael had filled his battered backpack with scavenged winter clothes from the discarded boxes outside the Buffalo Exchange thrift store. He packed a small camping stove, a pan, a can opener, some spices, beans, and saltine crackers, a jar of Nescafé, a blanket, a rain tarp, a portable radio, a handful of paperbacks, his notebooks, pens and markers, a tin cup for panhandling, and cat food and accessories.

He had left a cardboard box of fifty-odd cans of cat food under a note pinned to the maple tree on the street side of the UPS lot: FREE CAT FOOD. *Please take this to the local humane soci-*

ety. People were very kind to me and the cat, but I cannot carry all this. Over those three months since he'd rescued Tabor, Michael joked he carried around enough food to feed a whole herd of cats. His buddies had helped him carry some of the surplus at the bottom of their packs, and they also hid some in bushes along Hawthorne, in case they ever ran low. But since her first outing on the top of his backpack, he hadn't had to worry about providing food for her.

Michael had said good-bye to Kyle, who was being taken in by friends, and Stinson, who had bought a used car and was heading to New Orleans to spend the winter with his girlfriend. Then he strode over to Hawthorne Cutlery, to see the owner, a former Miami cop he'd become friendly with, who had asked him to drop by before leaving town. The shopkeeper gave Michael fifty dollars for helping to prevent a robbery.

Just before finding Tabor, Michael had passed out beneath a food truck across from the cutlery store and woke up when two guys tried to break into the food truck. Michael shouted, "Hey, whaddaya doing?" and they took off. He reported them to the police and told the officers to be on the lookout for those guys. He had a feeling they'd be coming back, and, sure enough, they had returned the following evening. Shortly afterward the cutlery-store owner saw Michael sitting in a doorway and told him, "I heard what you did. You've been looking out for us, and I'm going to look out for you." He gave Michael fifty dollars and, later, when he found out Michael was going to California for the winter, wanted to give him something more as a send-off.

After collecting the money, Michael and Tabor met up with Whip Kid and Jane. It started snowing lightly, so they got some 7-Eleven coffee to warm up and struck out south. Oregon is the only western state where it isn't illegal to walk on highways.

Between them, they had enough money for train tickets,

but they couldn't sneak a chatty, overly friendly cat on the train without drugging her, which Michael wasn't about to do. So they had to hitchhike.

Whip Kid was great with maps, directions, and bumming rides, but the highway was mostly deserted, except for an occasional truck. Truckers rarely picked up hitchhikers, trucking companies didn't allow it since their insurance wouldn't cover riders in an accident. They walked for miles on the side of the highway, and theirs were the only footprints in the snow. Every now and then, Michael stopped to check on Tabor by shoving his hand through the zipped opening and into her nest of blankets.

By the afternoon, the snow was swirling in all directions. It had covered the highway and piled up on their clothes and packs. Big rigs blasted past them, splattering them with more snow and slush. Whip Kid waved his sign, SOUTH OR CALIFORNIA, to try to attract their attention, but no one was even slowing down, let alone stopping.

By mid-afternoon, they saw a strip of dilapidated outlet stores and fast-food restaurants surrounded by straggling fir trees. But they decided to keep walking to the next exit, off of which they knew there was a bare-bones convenience store and gas station. When they got there, though, the businesses were closed. Racing against the fading light, they got back on the highway, hoping they would get to a cheap "hodey"—what drifters call a motel—where they could bed down for the night.

"We need to find somewhere to crash soon," Michael said every couple of miles. "I don't want to keep hitchhiking with a cat in a snowstorm. Someone might call the cops on us. And Tabor is not liking this."

"Don't worry, Groundscore, we'll find something," Whip Kid kept telling him. "I'll get us a ride soon."

But it had gotten dark, and they still had no ride. Hours

before, the patchwork of suburban neighborhoods south of Portland had turned into rolling, forested hills. They were beat, so they found shelter beneath a thick border of shaggy fir trees on a grassy median strip. It was dry and cushy with pine needles underneath the trees, so they spread out their bedrolls. Jane, Michael, and the cat instantly fell asleep from exhaustion. But Whip Kid wrapped his sleeping bag around his shoulders and sat on the side of the road, leaning on his pack with his cardboard sign and phone flashlight, waiting for passing cars.

Around 4 a.m., the snow still falling hard, Whip Kid woke Jane and Michael. He had not slept at all, and somehow he'd gotten them a ride to the next rest stop, in Wilsonville. They scrambled to collect their things and walked toward the small pickup waiting for them on the road. Jane, Michael, and Tabor could cram into the front seat with the driver, but there was no room in the cab for Whip Kid. They had to roll him up in a piece of carpet in the bed of the truck, and hope that would protect him from the cold.

The guy was a terrible driver, and the truck kept slipping and sliding through the slushy snow. Michael kept Tabor in her carrier on his lap, trying to keep it as still as possible. But she rode in the car peacefully, without complaint—most cats would've meowed from Oregon all the way to California. Michael and Jane were more worried about Whip Kid the whole time, thinking he might be jolted out onto the freeway and then run over by a car. Luckily, the rest stop was only about forty miles down the road.

"That was sketchy," Whip Kid said to Michael when they unrolled him from the carpet at the end of the ride. He'd been tossed back and forth in the cold truck bed for almost an hour.

The Wilsonville rest stop—where Michael had hitchhiked many times—was freezing, but it had free coffee, a service to drivers provided by nonprofit organizations. Because Christmas was just days away, Oregon rest stops were also handing out cookies and doughnuts.

Michael took Tabor out of her carrier and put her on his lap. He warmed his hands on a cup of coffee and pressed them against Tabor to warm her up. She purred and rubbed her cheek against his face.

It was still so early in the morning that they couldn't get a ride, so Michael led them through the snow to a nearby squat just off the highway at the edge of some woods where they could crash. A long-deserted shell of a house with a screened-in back porch, the moss-covered ruin smelled of dust, mold, and cedar. Trees grew through its broken windows, and weeds pushed through warped cracks. The woods were slowly reclaiming it.

When Whip Kid and Jane stepped inside, carefully skirting the broken floorboards, they brushed against a doorway. Paint chips fell from the ceiling like autumn leaves.

Clinging to the cat carrier, Michael followed behind. "I think the Zodiac Killer lived here," he said with a laugh.

It did look like a fugitive's hideout, but its back porch held a couple of collapsed sofas, which they pushed together, and then they laid their sleeping bags close together for warmth. Tabor curled up with Michael inside his bedroll, and they hunkered down for the rest of the night, getting a couple of hours of deep sleep.

As soon as the sun came up, they continued their march south to another rest stop. After a few coffees and doughnuts, they hitched a series of rides in quick succession. They were south of Salem heading east to Prineville, a former logging town with alpine valleys and glacial-green lakes, when their luck ran out. Still, they were able to make it to a friend's house in Prineville and crash in her living room. The next day Michael posted a Facebook message: *In Prineville with Whip and*

Jane . . . raging it in the snow. After three days, their friend got sick of them and the four companions went back to the highway, hitching and ending up in Redmond, a high desert city once famous for slaughtering wild and unwanted horses. Horse blood overflowed the local sewage system, and locals constantly complained about the stench and the screams of horses before eco-saboteurs burned down the slaughterhouse.

From Redmond, they caught another ride all the way to Sisters, a picturesque ski town in central Oregon backcountry, cocooned by swaths of evergreen forests and bustling with people. The three of them spent that night, half-frozen and wearing virtually everything they owned, sleeping outside on the cold concrete, with Tabor buried in blankets inside her carrier alongside them. Whenever Michael stuck his hand in her carrier, she'd place her paws on his hand to warm him. She was toasty, even though it was about eighteen degrees outside.

The next frosty morning, they rolled up their gear and settled outside a local grocery store scraping up some money. After collecting about eighty dollars, they bought food and coffee and waited along the roadside trying to hitch. After a long wait, Whip Kid and Jane, desperate to get out of the deep freeze, got into a car that Michael didn't like the look of. The driver held a beer in one hand and appeared half-drunk. Michael said goodbye to his friends. He and Tabor would take their chances with another ride.

Now it was just Michael and Tabor—alone together for the first time in the months since they had met. Few cars were on the road. After a couple of hours of walking with no ride in sight, Michael felt like he was about to collapse. Aside from several coffees, he had eaten only a sandwich early that morning. His stomach was grumbling. He could barely feel his fingers and feet. Mostly, he was seriously worried about Tabor. Every now and then, she mewed as though she wanted to let him know she was still there. Whenever he set the carrier down to check on her, she blinked at him through its mesh window.

A sudden gust of wind nearly swept Michael off his feet. They needed shelter or they wouldn't make it through the night. When he checked on Tabor again, she looked anxious, her eyes wide and searching as she peered from beneath her blankets.

"I'll find us someplace warm," he promised the cat, sticking his hand through the zipper to rub her ears and chin affectionately. "Soon we'll be in the sunshine by the sea, and you're gonna love it." Tabor gazed up at Michael and slowly closed and opened her eyes, giving him the feline equivalent of a kiss.

He gave her an eye kiss back and then bundled her up in her blankets and zipped up her carrier. He glanced around, raising his hand to shield his eyes from the blowing snow. On either side of the freeway, there was only a blinding sweep of snow and trees—spruce, yews, and hemlock everywhere. Below him, just off road, Michael saw a ramshackle barn through the jumble of snow-dusted pines.

He hoisted the cat carrier and hurried down the incline from the highway to the barn. It looked deserted, but it would give them some protection from the wind and snow for the night. Rotting pasture fences surrounded it, like the ruins of an old horse farm. An upside-down horseshoe hung over the nearest stable door, which was blocked by an immense drift of snow. Michael dug through it frantically and cleared enough so that he could wrench open the door, which was rusting off its hinges. He scanned the dark interior to make sure nothing was lurking inside, then shrugged off his pack and set it down along with the carrier with Tabor inside. He pulled the door shut as tightly as he could, shutting out some of the fierce wind.

The stables smelled of manure and mildew, although they

looked as if they had been abandoned long ago. The barn was dusty with straw and seed husks, but it was dry. In the farthest corner, he found a thick pile of dirty, decomposing old horse blankets and empty burlap grain sacks. He slumped down against the wall on the blankets and checked on Tabor, taking her out of the carrier and rubbing her back to warm her up. He held her as he fumbled with his bedroll and small bag of belongings. His fingers felt like icicles beneath his gloves.

Even inside the shelter of the stables, it was so cold that Michael could see his breath. The wind blew puffs of snow through the broken wooden slats and the cracks between them. He wrapped Tabor up again and set her in her carrier as he tried to block the blasts of cold air by propping some of the horse blankets against the corner walls to cover the openings. Then he pulled out his orange-and-black North Face sleeping bag and foam sleeping pad and spread them on the ground.

He had acquired that sleeping bag on his birthday the previous year. He had been on the sidewalk, midway through writing a sign saying *It's my 47th birthday, December 3rd 1964. Help a brother out*, when a man in a Mercedes stopped and asked, "What do you need?" Michael had said, "A new sleeping bag," and the man replied, "Hop in," and drove him to a sports store across town. Even though the bag was one of the nicer ones, after so much wear and tear from living on the streets, it was already giving way at the seams.

Michael set Tabor on the bag and gave her a snack of dried kibble. While she was busy eating, he sneaked out into the pitch-blackness to gather some firewood. From living in the city, he had almost forgotten how dark it got in the country. He crossed a small clearing to the nearby woods, where he quickly gathered all the fallen branches and twigs he could carry. Something about being alone in the woods at night had always scared him. It brought back the fear he felt as a kid walking out of the woods near his house after dark by himself.

Just as he turned to go back to the barn, he saw a flash of shadowy movement from the corner of his eye. It was Tabor, flitting between the trees and sprinting toward him.

"Tabor," Michael shouted out as she ran over. "And where do you think you're going? Don't you worry your little head, I'd never leave you." She was too scared to stay on her own in that spooky old barn.

Michael walked back as quickly as he could, Tabor following close behind. He paused inside the doorway cautiously. When he stepped farther inside, he had an unsettling sense that they weren't alone. He heard straw rustling, and Tabor's eyes were wide, her ears flicking and whiskers twitching. The noise seemed to be coming from the hayloft above: either it was rats, bats, or some other mystery guest. Michael suddenly thought: *What if it was a serial killer?*

Panicked, he glanced around for a heavy object. He put down his armful of wood and pulled out his battered old phone. But he'd run out of credit, the battery was almost dead, and there was no reception anyway out there in the sticks. Who could he call?

Suddenly a flock of roosting crows erupted from the hayloft above their heads and flew outside through a hole in the roof. Michael nearly jumped out of his skin, and Tabor scurried off in a flash, bumping her head into the wall, then burrowing into the deepest pocket of the sleeping bag.

He drew a deep breath, thinking he could really do with a smoke to calm down, but first he needed to build a fire. He picked up the wood he'd gathered and went over to the protected corner he'd created with the blankets and cleared an area of straw on the ground near them. He set down the wood and stoked a small fire that would keep them warm through the night. Then, firing up the camping stove, he warmed his numb fingers and prepared two dishes: a can of beans and crackers lightly seasoned with sea salt and cracked pepper for himself, and a metal bowl of Meow Mix salmon pâté mixed with warmed-up cat milk for Tabor.

Once he'd been a chef at fancy restaurants, and now he was cooking for a cat in a falling-down barn in a blizzard. In some ways, it was an improvement—and it was nice to have someone special to cook for again.

At first, Tabor refused to come out of the sleeping bag for dinner, but Michael coaxed her with some small treats. She scarfed down her salmon and warm milk, all the while looking around furtively. Then, still licking her lips and burping like a trucker because she'd eaten so fast, she retreated back inside the sleeping bag.

"Coward," Michael said, teasing her.

Normally he would fix himself a nightcap to deal with the cold and discomfort, but tonight he was grateful to have hot instant coffee. The beans and crackers barely filled the emptiness in his stomach. Despite his exhaustion, he knew he couldn't sleep, so he sat up and rolled one cigarette after another to stave off his hunger. To get through the night, he remembered the dishes he used to make as a chef at Obie's restaurant back in St. Louis: his Texas French toast with cream cheese and strawberry jam and his Italian omelets with provolone, pepperoni, green peppers, and onions.

The sound of the snowstorm outside grew wilder, rattling the rickety old barn door. The wind howled shrilly, and tree branches scraped against the roof. Michael kept looking apprehensively at the dark, shadowy stalls at the other end of the barn, wondering if something else was going to leap out. He waited tensely, listening out for every sound, getting a little paranoid in his anxiety. At one point, he even thought he heard muted footsteps crunching through the snow, and his mind looped to horror movies about isolated houses in the woods and psychotic killers.

In the firelight, cobwebs glistened with drops of condensation. The flickering flames illuminated the walls, which he now could see were covered by decades' worth of graffiti, as well as scrawls of skulls, crosses, and band names. He could just about make out the crude hearts with initials and dates carved into the decaying woodworm-eaten planks, which got him thinking about Mercer when they were teenagers, smoking weed and laughing about everything. After they'd first met in the school hallway, they'd seen each other every day in between Michael's runaway trips, cutting classes and sharing cigarettes, beer, or dope in the park.

The thought of Mercer made him smile and calmed his fears. As the fire burned down, Michael slid into the sleeping bag and eventually dozed off into a disturbing dream about Mercer and the day he'd almost blown up their house. A week before Mercer died, Michael had come home from work to find him so zonked out by the morphine that his chest was covered in a trail of cigarette ash, which had burned slowly all the way up his T-shirt. An oxygen tank was two feet away from his bed. Shaken, Michael told him, "You can't have cigarettes anymore. Somebody has to be here if you're going to smoke." Mercer was shocked to realize that he could've blown up the house and killed their cat and dog.

When shards of light filtered through the broken slats and the fogged, half-moon window in the hayloft above, Michael's eyes snapped open. It took him a moment to figure out where he was. Then he felt a warm, gentle pressure on his chest and face. It was Tabor standing on him and looking down at him, kneading his beard and drooling into his eye. He smiled, scratching her fluffy head, and she purred loudly and rubbed her face against his.

They'd survived the blizzard through the night, and by morning their love for each other only deepened.

Chapter 8

Backwoods Oregon: Memory Motel

Michael and Tabor were back on the road before the cold blue light of dawn had fully broken. Michael shivered in his four layers and worn hoodie, over which he wore a well-worn old UPS driver's work jacket. He'd wound a wool scarf tightly around his neck. The cat was swaddled in her tiny fleece blankets in her carrier with only the tips of her ears sticking out.

Trudging along the highway, he got a short ride back to Sisters, where he and Whip Kid and Jane had parted ways the day before. He needed to get some coffee and supplies.

In the center of town, the main street looked like it hadn't changed much since the 1800s, with covered walkways and bars with names like Bronco Billy's and Three Creeks Brewing. Outside a grocery store, Michael sat on the pavement as tourists and shoppers hurried past. He took out a handful of colored markers and a piece of cardboard and drew a Christmas tree, snowman, snowflakes, and the words *happy holidays. thank you for caring* on it. He set out the festive sign beside the dented tin cup that he'd had since 2005 when an older homeless black guy named Mystery had first shown him how to panhandle. Then he made a little stack of homemade Christmas cards from bits of cardboard to hand out to people.

It was Christmas Eve. Tabor lay in Michael's lap under her pile of blankets, half-asleep. Only her head and one paw she'd extended on his arm were visible, but this drew people to them. Upon spotting the cat, they gave Michael food for himself and for her, as well as blankets, hot drinks, spare socks, and sweaters. As Michael sat there, he remembered when he used to buy Christmas presents back in St. Louis at Grandpa Pidgeon's, a quirky retro discount store long gone out of business. Until he'd gotten together with Mercer, Christmas had had little meaning for him. As a chef, Michael had usually worked over the holidays anyway.

On that Christmas Eve, people were especially generous, handing out ten- and twenty-dollar bills, and, by the time the daylight was fading, he had gathered well over a hundred dollars. He was thinking about packing up when a big, burly woman, who looked like a bricklayer, came out of the store, and her young daughter sprinted ahead of her, excited to see the cat. As the little girl bent down excitedly to pet Tabor, the woman yanked the child back and hissed, "Don't touch that cat."

Michael glanced over at Tabor, who looked hurt and confused, and said, "Oh, Tabor, I'm sorry!"

The woman gave him a hate-filled look and started screaming at him for showing her up in front of her child. Tabor got scared and tried to run away, but she had her collar and leash on, so Michael was able to grab her in the nick of time.

That nastiness threw him a bit. Having been homeless for so long, Michael had learned not to take personally the snickers and taunts some people directed at him. Most people avoided him, but he had his share of abuse, mostly from carloads of kids flipping him off or clean-shaven but drunk young men who'd had a bad day, yelling, "Get a job, hippie."

Sometimes Michael reminded himself what Sister Maureen Teresa had told him: "When people say mean things, it's usually how they feel about themselves. Don't take it to heart."

But now that he had Tabor, it had become harder to let that stuff roll off his back. He felt a rush of anger at this woman who took her aggression out on an innocent little cat. He wanted to scream insults right back at her, but instead he stood up, swept his bag and belongings off the ground, put Tabor back in her carrier, and called it a day.

Normally whenever he gathered a fair bit of money, he blew it all on booze, but tonight, restraining himself, he bought just a half pint of Wild Turkey. He was responsible for someone else now, and he had to consider Tabor's needs first: her hunger, her fears, and her discomforts. He was going to treat Tabor to a proper bed for once.

He walked to the edge of town, where, through the snow flurries that had started up again, he spotted an old-style motel, which looked faded and run-down, and was likely the cheapest place around. Eager to get out of the cold, he rushed toward it, but slipped on the icy concrete of the motel parking lot and fell headfirst. As he hit the ground, Tabor shot out of her carrier and vanished into three feet of snow.

"Shit, shit!" He flung off his pack and staggered back to his feet. "Taaa-bor, I'm sorry . . . I'm sorry," he said as he pawed through the snow on his hands and knees. He didn't see anything. "Tabor, where are you?"

Then he heard a low, anguished cry from deep within the snowdrift. He dived into the drift with his whole body, waved his arms around until his fingers brushed against something warm. He grabbed her and scrambled out, pulling Tabor free. She looked bewildered and had a pile of snow on her head like a little cap.

"I've got you. I'm here," he said, brushing her off and cradling her in his arms. He headed for the front door of the motel.

Inside, Michael was greeted by an old lady with blue-rinse hair and '50s-style cat-eye glasses on a chain around her neck sitting behind the counter. She looked at Michael a little disbelievingly when he walked through the door dusted with snow, Tabor stuffed inside his jacket, her little wet cat head peeping out.

Michael had enough cash to stay for three nights. He lay the money for the room on the counter and, as the woman counted it out, said to the cat, "Look, Tabor, we're outside." It was a silly little in-joke among his pals. Since he lived outside, and everyone from Walter to Portland social services tried to get Michael off the street, whenever he took the cat indoors he would refer to it as the outdoors.

Moments later, he slammed his motel room door shut against the blustery wind. Tabor was ecstatic and immediately hopped onto the bed. When Michael went into the bathroom and turned on the tap to fill up his water bottle, she came rushing in and leaped onto the sink to sip from the tap. He gave Tabor her dinner and then spent a long time in a hot bath trying to thaw out and soothe the blisters on his feet.

The floral bedspread was frayed, the orange carpet was stained, and the bathroom had patches of mildew, but to Michael it was as good as the Ritz. Tabor seemed at home, too. She knew exactly what to do and where to go, and she'd meow by the door to be let out whenever she wanted to relieve herself, which made Michael think again that she was housebroken and definitely belonged to somebody. The motel room had a sliding patio door that opened onto a small patch of grass that was buried in snow deeper than the cat. Seeing it was a struggle for her trying to pee in a foot of snow, Michael borrowed a shovel from the front desk to create a pathway for Tabor so she could do her business and then get back inside out of the cold. But it was so chilly and windy outside that every time Michael slid open the patio door, a small blizzard blew in.

That first night in the motel room, Michael turned on the TV, settled into the bed, and flipped through channels. He had rarely watched TV, even when he had owned one, as he thought most Hollywood actors were unbelievable and terrible. But *Babe* was on, and Tabor was glued to the screen, mesmerized by the talking barnyard animals. Every so often, she'd leap toward the TV and look behind the screen to investigate how to get to the talking pig and her pals. She made Michael laugh.

On Christmas Day, they ate dinner in bed: a cheese and tomato pizza from the vending machine for Michael and a can of pink salmon for Tabor. He checked his Facebook and read all his Christmas messages from Walter and his friends around the country. This was one of the nicest Christmases he'd ever had, shacked up with a cat in a musty motel.

After his father died, Michael had tried to make amends with his mother. For many years he hated her, and their relationship seemed beyond repair. She had moved to a gated retirement trailer park in a small, dusty Arizona desert town, where she lived alone with two dogs for a while before meeting a retired truck driver named Burt, who moved in with her. She never married Burt because she didn't want to lose her husband's police pension, and after Burt passed away, her life revolved around the dogs and the Cowboy Church, a simple white steeple in the desert that had live blue-grass bands and social events, where you could even take your horses.

Michael felt sorry for her and thought she might be lonely, particularly since his brothers had stopped speaking to her. A few years back, Michael had drifted through Arizona twice and called her. Once, he had met up with her in the middle of the desert while she was out walking her dogs, but she didn't invite him to visit. She later told him that she didn't think the guards would let him in her trailer park looking the way he did— grubby and unshaven. Ever since then, Michael just kept in touch by calling her on Sundays after her church service. Often, she didn't answer, and when she did pick up, their conversations were usually short and stilted.

Now, sitting against the plump pillows with Tabor cradled in his arms, he switched the channel to *The Wizard of Oz*. Tabor couldn't take her eyes off the army of monkeys with red jackets and the green-faced witch.

"And that's how I learned that you can melt mean people with water," he said to Tabor as she watched, wide-eyed, as the wicked witch shrank till nothing was left of her but her hat, robe, and a puddle of steam.

As the credits rolled, Tabor made a nest under the covers and nodded off. Michael watched her as she chattered to herself in her sleep. She was a really heavy dreamer. Sometimes her ears, whiskers, and paws twitched at the same time as her teeth clicked, making a crunching *ack ack* sound that cats make when they see a bird out the window, out of reach.

It all reminded him of a past life, a time when he slept in a normal bed with his boyfriend and the warm furry bodies of their cat, Mau Mau, and dog, Aggie Jr. At moments like this, he thought he and Tabor must have sought out each other.

As they lay together in the blankets, snow filled the street outside and the red neon sign cast a warm glow across the frosted windowpanes. Michael stared at the red reflection, thinking that things were getting better. That night, he had a dream. He saw a house with a wood-burning stove, a cozy bed, cupboards, and a fridge full of fresh food. Tabor was lying on a basket full of clean laundry.

When he awoke, he felt the memory of someplace half-known sink out of reach.

Chapter 9

Baby Please Come Home

Ron's father, Donald, and his wife, Judy, lived in a big, rambling, two-story house surrounded by rolling lawns. In a gated community in the upscale West Hills of Portland, their lavish but cozy home was stuffed to the rafters with art and antiques. The living room, a wash of dazzling whiteness with cathedral ceilings, had big picture windows that overlooked the garden and a koi pond and let the evening light stream in. Vases spilling over with white flowers were arranged on every table. A white baby grand piano took up one corner of the living room, and a giant beautifully decorated Christmas tree, glittering with silver and gold ornaments, took up another.

From early December until Christmas Eve, Ron was usually caught up in a whirl of shopping and parties. But this year, he didn't have the heart for it and simply went with Creto to his father's house for the family's Christmas gathering. Ron was hoping that visiting for a couple of days would be a welcome distraction for both of them, and he was afraid that if he left Creto alone in the house, even for an evening, he would be abducted, too. His father was allergic to cats but felt so bad for his son that he allowed him to bring Creto. They put the cat in the guest room, which had a bathroom en suite, where Creto found comfort in curling up in the bathtub.

Donald, Ron's father, was mourning the death of one of his closest friends, who had died a few days earlier. At eighty-two, Donald was of an age when he was losing old friends, one after another, like falling leaves. Ron had known this family friend since he was a kid and had gone with his father to the funeral. As they had sat in the Catholic church during the somber service the day before, Ron broke down and wept uncontrollably—not for his dad or his dad's dear friend John—but for Mata and what she had suffered, and for what he thought she might still be suffering. He couldn't shake off the sadness that he might never see her again or know what happened to her.

The Christmas party the next day only made Ron more anxious and lonely. He couldn't switch off his sorrow to make small talk. His two adult nieces, whom he barely knew, and Judy's son, who was close in age to Ron, tried to cheer him up. He could see that everyone thought he was losing it.

While they were all chatting happily, Ron sneaked away to check on Creto, up the graceful sweep of staircase covered with holly and garlands like overgrown ivy. During the course of the evening, everyone at the party had visited the bathroom to say hello to Creto and make a fuss over him. Someone had given him a stocking with a stash of wrapped-up toys—a windup mouse, balls that lit up, and a catnip cigar, which he had sniffed sullenly and batted once or twice before losing interest.

Judy had followed Ron upstairs, carrying a huge carpeted scratching post wrapped with a big red bow. "Look, Creto," she said, placing it in front of the cat and stooping to stroke his head. "Look what I got for you, pussycat."

But Creto turned away. Ron sat down on the floor beside

him twirling the feathers attached to the scratching post to catch his interest, but the cat jumped out of the bathtub into his lap and buried his head like an ostrich in the crook of Ron's arm.

"I'm sorry," Ron said, looking up at Judy, knowing she had made a special effort, particularly as she wasn't an animal lover. "This is what he does when he's sad and depressed." Creto missed his sister and it showed. Judy persuaded Ron to go back downstairs for dinner.

After a long dinner feast, everyone exchanged gifts and then settled in the living room for homemade eggnog and sugar cookies shaped like angels, stars, and snowmen. A vintage Christmas song played in the background, a wistful Motown number, "Baby Please Come Home," and the yellow tree lights twinkled.

Mata had loved having a Christmas tree in the house. She would climb it, paw the ornaments, sharpen her claws on the tree trunk, and drink the water from the stand.

As the night wore on, Ron's sorrow turned to anger. He fantasized about running over Jack with his car and making it look like an accident. At one point, he even thought about making a voodoo doll and sticking pins into it. Then he felt guilty for having such dark thoughts. Ron used to be a sunny, optimistic person who always made the best of things and was rarely down or depressed for long. Now he was living beneath a tidal wave of grief and negativity that was drowning every aspect of his life.

Seeing Ron sitting alone on the couch, Judy walked toward him with a bottle of cabernet and two glasses and sat beside him. They had had a complicated and frosty relationship but, after years of friction, had warmed to each other.

"Howya doing?" she asked, pouring him a glass. "I don't know what to say except that I feel terrible for you."

"It's so freakish," Ron said, staring blindly at the fairy lights strung up over the mantel. "How could this happen twice? It's like being struck by lightning twice. I'm sure it was the Neanderthal across the street . . . he's unhinged. He probably killed her."

"You don't have any proof, and you can't make an accusation like that go away," Judy said, with a look of concern.

"I don't understand why I have to share this city with vile savages like him."

"You have to remain hopeful."

"What do I have to be hopeful for?" he said irritably. "It's been a terrible year. . . . I lose my cat once, barely have her three months after getting her back, only to have her snatched away again. And now I'm at war with a crazy person. I'm so done with 2012." He felt guilty about complaining, knowing that Judy had spent days shopping and preparing for this gathering, and he didn't want to seem self-indulgent or ungrateful. "It's just like I have this raging storm inside my head that no one can see."

"You don't have to justify yourself," she said, reaching for his hand and patting it. "Stuff happens. You just have to deal with it and not allow yourself to be crushed by it." She put an arm around him and said, "Miracles do happen. Remember you got Mata back once."

Chapter 10

Anyway, Anyhow, Anywhere

On December 27 the snowstorm finally broke, and Sisters, Oregon, was a postcard of whiteness, the sky clear and blue. Michael and Tabor left the motel and went to a bus stop. He did not want to get back on the highway.

A bus heading south toward Eugene pulled in and Michael hopped on with the cat in his arms. The driver shook his head and looked at him as though he were carrying an assault rifle. "No way," he grunted. "Can't let you on my bus."

Michael stepped off. He didn't know whether the driver wouldn't let him on because of the cat or because he didn't want a homeless guy riding his bus. Having slept in his rumpled clothes for days, Michael did look the worse for wear, with his messy hair and dark circles beneath his eyes, but he was clean after holing up in the motel for three days.

The owner of a café beside the bus stop saw the interaction from the window and rushed out. "What happened?" she asked. "Why didn't he let you on?"

"Dunno," Michael answered. He was used to being shunned and didn't want to cause any trouble.

But the lady was genuinely concerned and upset. "It's disgusting," she said, shaking her head. "I should've gotten his number and reported him. I can't believe anybody could treat a pair of living souls this way."

"It's no big deal," Michael said, forcing a smile. "I'm used to it."

"It's cold out," she said. She was a lady of a past era, with frosted-pink lipstick and white hair twisted into a bun. "You come inside and warm up."

Even though she smiled when she said it, her tone made it clear that she wasn't interested in a debate, so Michael followed her inside the small old-fashioned diner. Stuck in the '50s, the well-worn interior was a little dusty and in disrepair, but Christmas trinkets and potted poinsettias were arranged sweetly around the white Formica counter. The lady pointed Michael to a corner booth by the window.

Michael set Tabor onto the red vinyl seat and slid down beside her as the café owner poured him some coffee. Then she disappeared behind the counter, and Michael could hear the cappuccino machine steamer. After a minute, she brought out a teacup saucer of milk that she had warmed. Tabor watched her, purring.

"Aren't you a sweet pussycat?" the lady said cheerily. Tabor's eyes were fixed on the saucer as the woman leaned over to set it down in front of her. "She's such a pretty kitty."

"Yeah, she could easily make the cover of one of those magazines, *Modern Cat* or something," Michael said, looking over at Tabor with a twinkle in his eyes.

"I don't know that magazine. Is it a new one?"

"No, I made it up. . . . I was just saying."

She watched Tabor scarfing up the frothy milk and said, "Cats are good for the soul."

"Yeah," Michael said, smiling and looking down at Tabor. She definitely got him out of himself. He worried about her so much that it stopped him from worrying about his own dark moods and small things like wet socks. She was teaching him to shut out the world and just chill out.

Michael told the café owner the story about rescuing Tabor, and the lady's cornflower-blue eyes became misty. "Oh, bless your heart, darlin'," she said. "So where do you live?"

"Out in the street. We're heading to California to get away from the cold."

"The way some people live on the street just isn't right."

He laughed. "At least I can say I live exactly where I want."

"It must be hard. How d'you do it?"

"Well, every morning I feel my pulse, and if I still have one, I get up and carry on," he said, trying to make light of things.

The lady smiled and went off back behind the counter. Michael overheard her talking to someone on the phone complaining about the bus driver.

When the next bus came, she walked out with Michael, ready to take up their cause. "Wait here a sec," she said, and went to talk to the driver. She pointed at Michael and Tabor, and the driver nodded. She waved Michael over.

He flung on his pack, picked up the cat, and hurried over.

"You won't have any trouble now," she said to him.

With Tabor cradled in his arms, he stepped onto the bus heading to Eugene and glanced back at the lady and said, "Thank you for looking after me and Tabor. We're very grateful."

He thought back to something his foster father, Walter, had told him: "Never be inhospitable to strangers, because a little kindness can take you a long way and sometimes last a lifetime."

The café owner clearly lived by these words. And Michael felt the continuing blessing of having stopped for this little lost cat. The kindness he had shown Tabor was now taking care of them both.

Chapter 11

California:
Ride into the Sun

When Michael and Tabor got off the bus in Eugene a couple of hours later, it was noticeably warmer. Michael shed some layers. Then, with dusk setting in, he staked out camp under a canopy of dense, shaggy fir trees along the roadside, and they crashed for the night.

The next morning, by foot, bus, and car, Michael and Tabor continued south across ribbons of lonely highways on their one-man, one-cat expedition. After catching a short ride and then walking the rest of the morning, they reached Ashland, an arty liberal enclave also known as the People's Republic of Ashland, sixteen miles from the California border. Michael was worn ragged and stopped by a roadside general store and gas station for some water and to rest his feet. Michael had passed through and squatted in fields around there on past trips, so after stopping in the store, he headed to a small sloping hill that customers would have to pass right outside. He had Tabor on her lead and a cardboard sign scrawled with black marker—NEED RIDE TO VENTURA

WITH CAT—pinned to his backpack. He didn't want people to stop for him and then refuse to take him after they saw Tabor. But as it turned out, motorists stopped because of Tabor.

A young woman with a wavy pixie cut and wide smile in a little red Mazda swung in for some gas. "I'd like to offer you and your cat a ride, but I'm alone and probably shouldn't be picking up hitchhikers. But I want you to have something," she said, handing him a crisp twenty-dollar bill out the window.

"How about that, Tabor," he said to the cat sprawled out across his bag. "Everybody loves you."

Before he even had a chance to give Tabor a snack and roll a cigarette, a shiny RV with Texas plates rumbled up. "Hey, buddy," a man in mirrored aviator sunglasses called out. "I saw you walk in. You and the cat need a lift?"

"Yeah, we do," Michael said, picking up Tabor and collecting their things. As soon as he clipped on her leash and set her back down, Tabor sprinted toward the RV, like she'd been hitching all her life and understood what a ride was and was afraid of losing it. He wondered again about how she had wound up alone on the dark, dangerous streets of Southeast Portland.

"Hop in," the guy said, swinging open the passenger door. He was about the same age as Michael, with cropped peppery gray hair. He wore black Levi's and a faded gray, long-sleeve T-shirt with LOTTO, GUNS, AMMO, BEER in big letters across the front. "Name's Ray," he said, taking off his sunglasses to reveal steely gray-green eyes.

"I'm Groundscore."

Ray extended his hand to take Michael's bag. "Where you heading? I'm going just south of Santa Cruz."

"That's good for us, too," Michael replied, pleased to get a good long hitch. He settled into the passenger seat with Tabor on his lap. Because he carefully maintained Tabor's feeding-time routine while on the road, he never had to worry about having to stop for toilet breaks for her on the longer rides.

Tabor gazed up at Ray, blinking slowly, and raised a paw to touch his arm. "Tabor needs to win everyone over," Michael said. "And she likes everyone as long as they touch her."

"Cute cat," Ray said, glancing down at her and ruffling her scruff.

"She's my good-luck charm."

Hitchhiking was always a gamble. Michael had no way of telling where any ride would take him, but most people had been pretty decent and kind to him. Michael had been picked up by all sorts: families with kids; stoned college students; a drunken sheriff who threatened to shoot him like a muskrat if he grabbed the wheel but then gave him a bed for the night at his house, since he had nowhere to go. On the other hand, one of his homeless friends had once hitched a ride with a guy who deliberately drove him fifty miles in the wrong direction and dropped him off in the desert outside a tiny town called Truth or Consequences, New Mexico, out of pure meanness.

Ray had driven down from Seattle, more than 450 miles. As they rolled out along the snowy, twisting mountain roads past dense pine forests, Ray headed west on Oregon Route 66 and crossed over to I-5. The snow-capped mountains faded away as the Californian towns rolled by: Weed, Redding, Willows.

"So how'd you get the name Groundscore?" Ray asked with a sidelong glance.

"A bunch of hippies gave it to me," Michael replied. "About ten years ago I was in Trinidad, California, hitchhiking up the 101, and this pickup truck with a bunch of hippie girls stopped. I told them I was heading to Arkansas for the Rainbow Gathering. And they were going there, too.

"On the way, we stop at a convenience store around three

a.m. I see a grocery cart with a box in it. I take off toward it. And just before I reach the shopping cart, I look down and see a twenty-dollar bill, and I stop and pick it up. But it's actually two hundred dollars, ten twenty-dollar bills, and at the bottom of the cart is a cold six-pack of Henry Weinhard's. My name at the time was Montana Mike, but the hippie girls in the truck started calling me Groundscore. All my homeless friends in Portland loved it, so it stuck."

All the folks who picked Michael up had their own stories—and some shared a little too much, pouring out all their midnight confessions like sinners to a priest, knowing they were unlikely to see him again.

Ray turned out to be a good traveling companion, mostly because he did much of the talking. He was an army dog and spoke with the gravelly voice of someone who smoked a hundred Marlboro Reds a day. "I left my wife. Made a mess of my life. It was good for a long while, then it all went to hell."

Michael didn't reply, since he was tired and concentrating on Tabor, who buried her little chin in her paws, half-asleep, and with a purring sigh, drifted off.

"What you running away from?" Ray asked him.

Startled by the question, Michael stumbled over his words. "I'm, ah . . . not running away from anything. Just trying to get away from the cold and the rain of Portland. There was a time when I'd hitch all over America, but now I'm just trying to survive another winter. That's all."

Ray looked at him and smiled. "Well, you look like some kinda outlaw."

People had told Michael that before. The guy at the DMV who took his picture for his driver's license had told him that he looked like Billy the Kid. Michael liked the thought of it.

"I'm just a drifter."

"We're all drifters," Ray said, laughing, "fugitives from some-thing or other. My grandparents escaped from the famine in Ireland, my parents from the poverty and dead ends of a small town. I ran away from the suffocation of my life and the brutal-ities of war."

Five hours into their journey, in Sacramento, the smell of California farmland rose up around them. They passed rice pad-dies, walnut orchards, and cow pastures. With the sun shining and in the homey comfort of the RV, it was an easy ride.

Passing through San Francisco, they cut over to the scenic coastal Route 1 in Daly City. Rolling down the window as they headed south to Big Sur, Michael felt the chilly sea breeze on his face and thought about all the places Mercer told him he had visited during his time in the air force. The gusty draft woke Tabor, who suddenly sprung up, the hairs around her head fluffed out from sleeping.

"I always wanted to see the world," he said to Ray, "to cross the ocean out of curiosity as much as anything else."

"That's what I thought when I went into the army. But I gotta tell you, curiosity sometimes kills."

The Pacific came into view. "Look, Tabor . . . look, it's the ocean," Michael said, holding the cat up to the window. "That's where we're going."

Sprawled across Michael's lap, Tabor watched everything, owl-like, purring at the excitement of it all: the low-flying clouds scud-ding past, the shoots of puff plants waving in the wintry breeze, and the cars whooshing by. She was even unfazed by the big mon-ster trucks and never flinched when she saw one approaching.

Beneath a hazy purple sky, Ray swerved along the twists and turns of Highway 1, frighteningly close to the cliff, the fierce, foamy water of the Pacific swirling below.

By the time they reached Half Moon Bay, a lovely coastal

hamlet of misty bluffs and beaches, everyone was tired and quiet. A little further south, Michael smelled the kelp forests and listened to the elephant seals barking along the shore—Tabor slept, snoring away on his lap, her fluffy little head nestled on her paws.

They drove all the way down to Watsonville, listening to the Dead Kennedys, the Violent Femmes, and a mix of 1980s Californian punk bands, sharing a bag of Cheetos and a steady stream of Cokes.

* * * * *

It was dark by the time Ray let Michael and Tabor off in Watsonville, an agricultural town a short skip away from Santa Cruz. Michael found an out-of-the-way sleeping nook under a bushy black walnut tree on a patch of green off the main road. He gave Tabor her dinner, made a fire, and heated up some canned spaghetti hoops. Then they both fell sleep, exhausted after nearly ten hours in the RV.

Waking up in the sunshine the next morning with Tabor at his side, Michael felt a lightness and sense of relief at being outside, even in the cold and gloom of dawn. Soon after Tabor guzzled her breakfast, he clipped on her leash and stuck her in his jacket and they explored the quaint little shops along Third Street before taking a short bus ride to Santa Cruz. The mellow beach town overlooking Monterey Bay—once a stopover for Jack Kerouac—prided itself as being the last holdout of '60s counterculture, and it buzzed with old hippies, surfers, stoners, and college kids. University of California, Santa Cruz, even had its own on-campus trailer park for students.

Getting off in the heart of the city just off Pacific Avenue, Michael cruised over to a little mom-and-pop taco bar on the edge of the waterfront that he knew fed the homeless for free most mornings. The owner, a recovering alcoholic, ran the restaurant with his wife and two adult sons. He'd started his charity work about twenty-five years earlier, when he had seen an old man digging in the trash for food. He gave him something to eat and, ever since, had been handing out food to anyone destitute and hungry, in the spirit of Jesus Christ, he said. Every morning, the area's homeless quietly lined up at the side window for a plate of freshly cooked food, in exchange for the pass code: "Beans and rice for Jesus Christ."

After getting his bowl, Michael found a bench close by. He and the cat sat next to each other, and he gave Tabor her meal. She dug into her lunch as Michael ate his rice and beans. It amazed him how much he'd grown to love her. Calm and trusting, she was turning out to be the perfect road cat, adapting to everything and living life to the fullest.

With the whole day stretching ahead, Michael walked the length of Pacific Avenue with Tabor riding on his backpack, her eucalyptus-green eyes big and wide, absorbing everything, the colorful street musicians, the arty vintage storefronts shaded by tall trees soaring toward the sky.

They wove around the side streets named after trees—Willow, Maple, Laurel—and just when Michael thought he was beat from walking and carrying his pack with a shifting cat, he saw a little roadhouse-style bar tucked on a backstreet. It was a friendly, seedy neighborhood dive, the type of authentic crumbly bar found in small towns, with local color, heavy pours, and dark, snug corners where he could disappear with a cat. He had lunch at the farthest end of the bar and hung on for happy hour since it was New Year's Eve. The dimly lit room had a musty elegance, with ripped wallpaper, a jukebox, and vintage surfing snaps on the walls behind the long wooden bar.

By three o'clock, the lunchtime crowd of locals and out-of-towners had dispersed. Five people remained at the bar, the same old spooks and toughs who came regularly, putting in a hard day's drinking, with golden oldies on the jukebox providing the soundtrack.

The bartender, a slim, brown-eyed boy with a soft dusting of freckles and trendy haircut and a goatee, recognized Michael and Tabor from sweeping past the bar earlier. He set out a shot of whiskey in front of Michael and said, "This one's on me. Celebrating a bit early, aren't you?"

Michael smiled and said, "I don't need an excuse. I drink every day."

Tabor enjoyed the fuss as the barflies reached across and stroked her and scratched her chin. But when she wasn't getting any attention, she'd wander off and plop down in the doorway, greeting people passing by with a friendly chirrup. Michael worried that someone would step on her or she'd wander into the street, so he dragged her back inside. But whenever he looked away from her, she would scamper off to her self-appointed post by the door. When he brought her back for the third time and placed her onto the velvet bar stool and clipped on her leash, she protested with a series of loud, whiny meows.

"This is our first disagreement," Michael said to the bartender. "I don't force her to do anything. I think of her as a human being, but unfortunately I have to carry the little bastard around."

"She's a queen."

"She's the queen of frickin' everything . . . thinks the world turns around her."

The bartender spoke to Tabor in a high-pitched voice, "Are you all right there, kitty?"

Snippy and impatient with his customers, the bartender waited hand and foot on Tabor. He gave her fresh cream in a scotch glass. Tabor cupped it and drank it with her paw. The bartender screeched with excitement. "My God, that is the cutest thing ever." He'd had cats back home in the Black Hills of South Dakota, where he grew up facing Mount Rushmore, a town that he'd found to be too small and too sleepy, so he'd moved to California.

Tabor finished her cream and looked up at Michael with drops on her chin. Still annoyed, she stared at him accusingly, as though he'd smuggled her into the bar and was holding her hostage.

"I haven't chained you to the radiator," he said to Tabor, smiling, and picked her up to prevent her from running off again. "She makes me look terrible sometimes, like I neglect her. She has everything she needs, but still meows for strangers."

The bartender brought her a handful of maraschino cherries to play with. She hopped onto the bar to bat them around. Whenever she pushed them onto the floor, she'd wait for Michael to pick them up. After a few minutes, she lost interest and sat on his lap again.

"Look at your paws . . . they're all sticky," Michael chided her, but she just blinked at him.

"Cats aren't wired for submission," he said to the bartender. "They're used to having servants. I have to say no to Tabor about twenty-five times before seven a.m. every day. Always has to have her way."

He dug into his pocket and pulled out a bag of Purina Party Mix to appease her. He scooped out a handful, and she arranged herself on his lap, gobbling them up from his hand with an appreciative deep-throated purr. Then she moved onto the empty stool next to him, with one of her back legs dangling over the side, and promptly fell asleep.

The bartender placed another shot glass of whiskey in front of Michael and poured himself a shot.

"I'm on the clock and have to look after this one," Michael said, gesturing to the sleeping cat curled up on the stool beside him. "I can't overdo it, but thanks."

They raised their tiny glasses up in the air, clinking them.

In the dimly lit coziness, Michael worked his way through a few whiskeys. Some jangly old Byrds tune about feeling lonely in the daytime played in the background. In his mind, he saw Mercer, handsome and unshaven, his calm blue eyes smiling at him.

Sitting at the far end of the bar with Tabor still drowsing and dreaming beside him, he watched people trickle in and thought back to happier times, before Mercer got sick. For a couple of years, wanting a break from St. Louis, they had lived on Mercer's family farm by Lake Wappapello in rural southeast Missouri. Set on sixteen acres, the three-story house had a sprawling wild garden that spilled out toward the lake. Michael worked as a chef in a steakhouse, Millers House of Angus, just down the road, owned by an old St. Louis gangster named Lefty Miller, who had done time for tax evasion, and his wife, Anita. They served surf and turf fare, mostly to locals who came in for their weekly steaks. Michael got along well with the owners, but they were drunks, and there was always some sort of drama going on.

At the end of the night sometime around New Year's Eve, Michael was tired and irritable. Someone had sent back a steak, complaining that she wanted it black and blue. Michael was squalling around the kitchen, when he heard a big crash in the restaurant and Lefty's wife, Anita, stormed into the kitchen. "Michael, I need you now," she shouted. "Come out here, you've got to get Lefty."

"I'm busy," he said. "Why do I always have to get him?"

"Because you're the only one who can touch him," she snapped, and stalked off.

When Michael had first walked into the restaurant looking for a job after seeing an ad in the local paper, Lefty hired him on the spot—and promptly anointed him the chosen one who was allowed to touch him when he fell.

Michael threw off his stained chef's whites and left them in the middle of the kitchen. He went out to the dining room, where he found Lefty flat on his face by the steps leading to the bar where he'd fallen, cursing and grumbling to himself. With his limbs splayed out all over the place, he looked like one of those chalk outlines of a dead body at a crime scene.

One of the young waiters was trying to help pick him up off the floor. "Don't *fucking* touch me," Lefty snarled, pushing him away. "Get King out here."

"I am here," Michael said, and scooped up Lefty. He carried him out to his Lincoln and drove him across the street to their house. Lefty was so drunk he was crying. Michael carried him inside and poured him on the couch and then left to get back to work.

When he was walking through the parking lot around the back of the restaurant, Michael heard whimpering and snuffling coming from under the dumpster. Crawling down on his belly to look, he saw a little dog, a fluffy brown thing that looked like a tiny bear cub with filthy, matted fur. He picked up the scared, trembling pup and took it inside with him while he closed up for the night. He decided to call the pup Angus after the steakhouse and brought the little thing home to Mercer.

They cleaned up the puppy and took him to the vet, where they discovered that he was a she, nearly fully grown and pregnant, possibly the reason she had been ditched. Michael changed her name to Aggie. When she had her puppies, they found homes for them among friends and family but kept Aggie and one of the pups. A few months later Aggie got out of the house and was hit by a car, so they renamed the pup that they kept Aggie Jr.

He'd always been glad that he'd saved Aggie and her puppies. Aggie Jr. had been a great dog and given him so much love. That was long ago, and now he had Tabor to look after. And he hoped that they would have a good long time together.

* * * * *

The next morning, Michael woke up blinded by the sun under a magnificent old magnolia. He caught a whiff of cotton candy mingled with salty air from the boardwalk, and glimpsing the shimmer of sea, he packed up and headed for the beach. But when he saw a bus going to Salinas about thirty-odd miles away, he hopped on so that he could show Tabor Steinbeck's hometown. Steinbeck was Michael's favorite writer. The way he wrote about broken America still rang true and meant something to Michael.

Rumbling along the highway through Steinbeck country, the wooded canyons, valleys, and vineyards stretching out all around, Michael had Tabor nestled on his lap, with her paws neatly folded over each other. Every so often, Tabor stood up or swiveled her little head to the window to get a good look at the new scenery. Her eyes grew large as the bus swept by the eighteen-foot-tall cardboard cutouts of farmworkers sprouting out of the fields like giants lining the highway.

When they got off the bus in the old downtown of Salinas, Michael walked down to Central Avenue, Tabor on his shoulder, to the house where Steinbeck grew up. Steinbeck's presence was everywhere, on the street plaques, stone monuments, the "Steinbeck ate and drank here" signs in bars and café windows. Strolling around this preserved sleepy hollow with its maze of pretty streets, Victorian houses, and ancient oaks, Michael talked to the cat on his shoulder, pointing things out to her.

After exploring Salinas, Michael found out from the locals that there was a bus going to King City, so he and Tabor slept in the bushes along a grassy median to not miss the bus. He had told Tabor that they would stop when they reached the first warm town, and that happened to be King City.

Chapter 12

King City:
Sweetheart of the Rodeo

A sleepy coastal town tucked among lettuce and strawberry fields, King City was a regular passage for Michael whenever he migrated down the coast to California. The whole place smelled of strawberries and summer, even in the winter. When they got there, the sun was shining and the temperature was in the 70s. The sweet scents and the warmth of the sun felt like Eden for the drifter and the cat with a vagabond heart.

On that first day, with Tabor perched on his shoulder, Michael wandered around the town center, an old-fashioned Mission-style shopping arcade. Taking in the myriad sights and scents, they passed artisan boutiques, folksy secondhand book-shops, and cute courtyard cafés, before settling in the shade of a lemon tree outside a grocery store to panhandle. The tree was in full bloom and shedding blossoms.

With white petals stuck in her fur, Tabor greeted the children and dogs who approached her like a world-class diplomat. She had to say hello to everyone, rolling over on her back and showing her white belly, which was becoming rounder by the day. The children chattered excitedly and squealed with laughter as they petted and cuddled the cat.

One little boy, dressed in a red cowboy hat and a plastic holster with a toy gun, told Tabor, "You've got patches like a cow. You're the sweetheart of the rodeo." Michael couldn't help but smile.

When the sun got too hot, Michael found a shadier spot outside McDonald's. A chubby perky young woman in denim cutoffs and flip-flops walked out of the store and right up to them and handed him a bag. "Here's a cheeseburger for you and a small cheeseburger for the cat."

Michael thanked her, but thought, *Some people just don't know.* He'd never feed the cat garbage like a greasy burger. He used to get annoyed at Stinson for trying to give Tabor french fries. Then the woman reached into her purse. "And here's twenty dollars to get whatever you want," she said, handing him a crisp note. "God bless you both." Michael thanked her again. He'd eat Tabor's small burger and replenish his stash of cat food for her with the cash.

The local population was largely Latino and religious, very generous to the homeless. Someone gave him a pocket Bible with a ten-dollar bill wedged inside. "Thank you, Jesus," Michael whispered as his benefactor walked away. The cat was a constant reminder of the goodness of people and he thought he would spend God's money on her.

"Tabor, we're staying here," he said to the cat who had rolled on her back again, a little distance from him, in a patch of winter sunshine. She gazed up at him, her eyes vertical black slits in the brilliant sunlight. "We're taking a vacation."

.　．　.　．

Michael and Tabor stayed in King City for two relaxing weeks—exactly what they needed after all the snow and hardships of Oregon.

One late afternoon, after washing his dirty clothes, Michael settled outside the Laundromat near a back alley creeping with flowering vines. On a bench under a grapefruit tree, he sat there happily reading the local paper, smoking a roll-up spiked with the local pot, with Tabor spilled across his lap. A minivan pulled up alongside them with a man and a small boy in the passenger seat. The driver rolled down his window and shouted: "Hey, how much do you want for the cat?"

This annoyed Michael. "I'll take the van and the kid," he said, stunning the guy into silence.

Moments later, a young woman with long, dark hair wearing a snug black sweater and ripped jeans stopped to say hello to Tabor. "Well, aren't you just adorable," she cooed, petting Tabor. "Don't you just love her?"

"Like crazy," Michael said, a cigarette hanging out of his mouth. He put down his newspaper. "She's a great cat. Some idiot just tried to buy her from me. He was expecting that I'd say twenty bucks or something. But the cat has no monetary value. She's priceless."

The woman patted Tabor and then asked where they were from. He told her the story of finding the cat and how she had appeared as if by magic in the rain. "From that very first night, Tabor and me got along like peas and carrots."

"Sweet," she said. "It's written in the stars. You two were probably meant to find each other."

"We're the perfect match. We're both mellow, and neither of us is ambitious."

"Do you mind me asking how you became homeless?"

"Well, I hit the skids," he said, suddenly glum. "It's just one of those things." He stared at the crack in the sidewalk, snagged on a memory of Mercer's face when he was dying. Michael had been working at the restaurant two blocks away when he got a call from the hospice nurse he'd hired to watch over him, saying, "Mercer's going, come home." By the time he got to his bedside, minutes later, Mercer was fading in and out of consciousness, so he slipped away before Michael got to say good-bye.

"I'm sorry, I didn't mean to pry," the woman said, seeing the despair on Michael's face. "We all have our issues and our sorrows. Don't lose hope. We can live for forty days without food, three days without water, and three minutes without air. But we can't live seconds without hope."

"Don't know about that," said Michael. Walter, his foster father, also talked about the importance of hope and always told him to expect nothing but hope for the best. It was a philosophy that Michael only partially lived by. "Hope is often cruel. . . . Food, water, beer, and cigarettes is usually enough," he said, smiling. "But I'm not doing too badly. I've got the cat. And the friendship and feeling between us is as deep as the Mississippi River."

Tabor stretched and hopped off his lap, giving him a look over her shoulder as she headed over to the flowering vines along the brick wall of a nearby alley. This struck a nerve, and the woman stepped back, tears streaking her mascara. "Your cat reminds me of my own little tabby," she said, and then pulled some money out of her handbag, stuffed it in his hand, and said he should buy Tabor something to eat before rushing away.

Michael was surprised to see that she had given him a fifty-dollar bill. The people with the saddest stories always seemed to be the most generous.

Now feeling a little low, he noticed that it was getting dark. Tabor came up to him silently, nuzzling against his ankles. She

smelled sweet and musky, and Michael noticed little white stars
of jasmine sticking out of her fur; she must've been rubbing
herself against the creeping vines of the alley wall.

"Let's go," he said, scooping up Tabor, who was still purring,
and swung her onto his shoulder. He headed for the nearest liquor store with the woman's cash. Minutes later, he'd got a bottle
of cheap sour mash whiskey, a six-pack of Rainier, and a pack of
American Spirit cigarettes.

. * . . .

The next day at dawn, cold and confused, Michael woke up,
unsure of where he was. He could make out a deserted alleyway
and a heap of sagging garbage bags, which had been ripped apart
by coyotes or raccoons. He felt wrecked, with a crushing head-
ache. Tabor was curled on his chest, paws tucked underneath
her, staring down at him sleepily. Trying not to disturb her, he
reached for his hat, a worn jade-green snap-brim he'd long ago
found in an empty cactus-strewn lot in the Southwest, and put it
over his face to block out the daylight. Then he fell back asleep.

A little while later he felt a strong hand grip his shoulder.
Michael moved his hat to peer up with glassy, unfocused eyes,
barely able to see anything beyond a blur of navy blue through
the haze of sunlight. A gruff, square-jawed policeman was standing over him.

"Goddamn it," he grumbled to himself, rubbing the sleepi-
ness from his eyes. He staggered up, dislodging Tabor, and fell
back onto the ground. Tabor scampered off to sit and watch, a
few feet away, beside the alleyway wall.

"You can't sleep here."

"I'm sorry, officer, I just passed out here."

"I'll have to fine you for blocking the sidewalk," he said, and
started writing up a ticket for loitering.

"I can't make myself invisible. . . . Wish I could."

The policeman asked for his ID and continued writing up the ticket. Michael, too hungover and groggy to think straight, took out a selection of state IDs and driver's licenses, including long-expired ones showing him with varying lengths of hair and beards. He picked out his Montana ID and reached up to give it to the cop.

"Montana," he said, looking down at Michael, "is this where you live?"

"Don't live anywhere."

The policeman handed back the ID with a ticket. Michael stared at the piece of yellow paper, stunned by the amount of the fine. "Um, seriously, $265 bucks for lying on the sidewalk? But this is an alley," he protested halfheartedly, pulling out his sketchpad, where he kept other unpaid tickets he'd received over the last few months, and added it to the stack.

"People still have to get through it."

"How am I s'posed to come up with that kinda money?"

The policeman looked down at him with a mixture of pity and exasperation and extended a hand to help Michael to his feet. "Let me give you some advice," he said. "Out of sight, out of mind."

"Okay, officer, sorry," he mumbled as he turned to walk away.

Tabor had stretched out in a sunbeam, half-veiled by the mesh of jasmine that splashed across the wall, watching quietly as the two men talked. When the policeman looked at her as he started to leave, she sauntered over, brushing against his legs, meowing to be picked up. She did her best to charm him, but he walked straight past her.

She turned her head toward Michael and let out a soft, sad little mew.

"I'm sorry, Tabor," he said, propping himself up against a wall only to slide back down clumsily onto the pavement. Empty cans, bottles, and cigarette butts surrounded him.

Tabor yawned wide, stretching her legs, then padded over. She leaped up onto his shoulder and nuzzled his cheek.

"This is no way for a lady to live," he said to her. Tabor gazed back at him as though she knew what he meant. "I'll try to do better."

She rubbed her head against his chin, purring loudly, her fur soft and warm from the sun, trusting that she was in the right place, with him, together.

Chapter 13

Bad Moon Rising

The rain was pelting down. The palm trees were bent over by the wind, and coconuts fell from the sky. Ron huddled behind the ruins of a stone house, clinging onto Mata and watching bits of wood and branches flying past. As the winds grew, lashing at them, Mata slipped out of his grasp and was swept away into the sea as he watched helplessly.

Ron's eyes snapped open. He was disoriented and drenched in a cold sweat. He heard a thud as Creto skidded across the wooden floor and out the bedroom door. He must have been scared off by Ron starting to awaken from his bad dream.

It was nearly eleven on a bitterly cold January morning. Every morning felt so bad and he struggled to get through each day, but the weekends were the hardest. He had fallen into the habit of not leaving the house for days at a time. His friends teased him that he was in danger of slipping into the murky twilight world of daytime TV and antidepressants or, worse, collecting guns. He lay there, dazed, staring at the three vintage black velvet Elvis prints on his wall, pondering the meaning of his dream. He felt as though he were being swallowed by his searing heartache and anger, which were sapping his energy.

Creto reappeared and jumped onto the pillow beside Ron's head, meowing. Ron stroked his furry cheek. *If it weren't for this cat*, he thought, *I wouldn't bother with anything. I'd probably end up like Brian Wilson and just live in bed.*

Not a moment too soon, Jim, a sleek chocolate-faced Siamese, jumped on his bed, too, meowing for breakfast. Jim belonged to his lodger, Steve. Ron had met Steve four years earlier when Steve, a struggling young musician, had just become homeless, along with his elderly cat, Lennie. Ron kindly took them both in without ever charging any rent, and after Lennie died, Steve adopted Jim as a kitten.

Ron went to the kitchen, his eyes red with fatigue, moving sluggishly toward the coffee machine. Creto and Jim dashed ahead of him and stood by their food bowls. Ron knew that Steve already fed the cats, but they always wanted more and acted like they'd been starving for days to cadge an extra meal.

While filling the cat dishes, he glanced out the window toward the house across the street, where Jack lived. Ron was convinced the guy was a drug dealer—he had a stream of wild-eyed and strung-out creatures going in and out of his house at all hours like it was a Chinese takeout. Just the thought of him made his blood boil. "Junkie loser," he mumbled, "I hope you die of an overdose."

As he put down the cats' second breakfast, Ron told himself he had to try to stop the loop of vengeful thoughts about his hateful neighbor. Willing himself to do something positive, he got on the computer and sent some money to his favorite feral-cat rescue charity, and then scoured the house for towels, blankets, dishes, and other items that the local shelter could use. Afterward he browsed on eBay for Stratocaster parts for his store, and he went on a vintage-guitar-buying frenzy. Then it was time to pack up the Christmas decorations. He turned on the golden oldies radio station, listening to Linda Scott sing "I've Told Every Little Star" in her sultry, sugary-sweet voice, as he took the lights and ornaments off the tree and boxed them. He tried to keep himself busy, because if he stopped, he'd start pining for Mata, and a cyclone of dark thoughts would spiral in his head.

That gloomy afternoon, it was dark by 5 p.m. Steve came home from work earlier than usual and invited Ron for happy hour at one of the local bars, but Ron was too upset to leave the house, so Steve went out for the night.

Creto was curled up under the radiator across the room. Jim nuzzled around his ankles and watched with wide-eyed wonder as Ron dragged the tree outside, trailing pine needles along the way. Then he lugged the boxes up to the attic.

Paneled with cedar, the attic resembled a sprawling sauna. To Ron it felt like a secret tree house, his hideout from the world. Sometimes he went up there to meditate to clear his mind or listen to music. Its slanting walls and dormer windows faced the front and back of the house. Boxes of vinyl LPs were stacked against one wall, a framed early-1960s poster of the Beatles in the electric blue doorway of the London Palladium above them. A vintage mike stand sat beside a small bookshelf with a red lava lamp. Peaceful coziness pervaded every corner.

An antique barber chair faced the rear window, and Ron collapsed into it after stowing the Christmas decorations in their designated space. Carved out of walnut, with plush leather upholstery and metal foot pedals, the chair had belonged to his grandfather who had owned a barbershop in St. Johns, a tiny quaint suburb in North Portland across the Willamette River. Ron had virtually grown up in that chair, a little chubby-cheeked, towheaded boy getting his hair cut in a military-style flat top at his granddad's dusty old-timey shop. With its traditional barber pole, vaulted ceilings, wood-paneled walls sporting yellowing photos of men's hairstyles, and colorful tonic bottles lining the counter, the shop had a warm, homey atmosphere. And it was always filled with pipe tobacco smoke as mustached men sat back, smoking, talking, and laughing.

His granddad's barber chair was like a time-travel machine. Every time Ron sat in it, his mind would wander back to being a kid playing under the misty-blue gothic arches in Cathedral Park beneath St. Johns Bridge. He had loved going to the neighborhood family-owned stores, some of which still existed: the Tulip Pastry bakery, where his mother took him for bear claw pastries and black-cherry soda after he got his hair cut; the cluttered comic book store with creaky hardwood floors, owned by a nice Iranian family who gave out Tootsie Rolls and where he'd spent all his pocket money; the old St. Johns movie theater where he first saw *Jaws* in the summer of 1975; the Lion's Den Man's Shop, the haberdashery whose funny name made him smile whenever he'd passed it.

Before he became a barber, his granddad had been a musician in a ragtime band in the 1940s. He had given Ron a harmonica and his first guitar and introduced him to everything from the old jazz greats to Buddy Holly and Bob Dylan. Swiveling around in the barber chair, Ron thought that now might be a good time to renovate the attic and build the small recording studio that he'd always wanted. It would be the distraction he desperately needed.

Ron turned toward the back window and looked up. It was completely dark by now, and a full moon lit the cold night air with a grayish tint. For a split second Ron mistook it for a blue moon. But the last blue moon had been in August, around Mata and Creto's third birthday, so another was unlikely to come so soon. To Ron, a full moon meant emotional upheaval. He certainly felt that and thought how the chill and bleakness of January reflected his own depression. His birthday—which he liked to tell people he shared with Elvis Presley and David Bowie—was three days away. He suddenly felt trembly and wondered where his youth had gone: he'd made a lot of wrong choices, chosen bad boyfriends, and missed a lot of opportunities. His life hadn't changed much from the way it was at twenty-five, except now he was alone, depressed, and living next to a sadistic sociopath.

In the glow of moonlight, bits of stray tinsel glittered on the attic floor. Ron got up to fetch a broom and dustpan and swept them up. Then he rummaged through a box, coming across Mata's unopened kitty stocking from the previous Christmas, the first time she'd strayed. Seeing the stocking still sealed in its red plastic mesh, as if frozen in time, he recalled those long cold days of last winter when Mata was lost and living wild in the woods.

He replayed in his head the details of the day he'd collected Mata from the Vancouver Humane Society. She was so skinny and sick with the flu. When he arrived at the shelter, the staff couldn't find her. She had been shunted into the back room, death row. She was only hours away from being destroyed because they had deemed her semi-feral and too ill to treat. The shelter kept animals for five days before killing them if they weren't adopted or reclaimed, while the feral and less friendly ones were sent straight to death row. A sympathetic kennel worker led Ron to the bleak, bunker-like back room that held all the condemned animals. It was the saddest, most heart-wrenching place he'd ever seen.

He walked in silence and in tears past rows of metal cages with terrified cats and kittens. Some cowered in their litter trays; others stood, crying with pleading eyes. The saddest ones had already given up and were quiet, hunched up in the back of the cages.

Mata was among them, hiding at the back of her kennel, her

head resting on her paws. But the moment Ron shouted out her nickname, "Honey Bunny," she pricked up her ears, looking up at him, and called back to him with a series of sad, plaintive little meows.

On the drive back home, Mata had stuck her paw through the bars of her cat basket and wrapped it around his finger. Ron wept remembering that he'd come so close to losing her.

Miserable, Ron went downstairs to grab his laptop to see if by some miracle he had any emails about Mata. Then he climbed back up to the attic with the laptop and posted on his Facebook page his favorite picture of himself cuddling Mata and Creto. He wrote: *Mata please come home. We're incomplete without you.*

He flicked his laptop shut, set it on the floor, and crumpled up in the barber chair again, burying his head in his hands. At that moment, he heard the light footfalls of a cat on the creaky stairs. He looked up to see Jim's head poke up over the top of the stairs. The big Siamese tom gazed at Ron intently, blinking his odd-colored eyes, one blue and one gold, repeatedly.

"Oh, Jim, Jimmy Jim Jim," he cooed to the cat. "You're such a sweet boy."

When Ron spoke to him, Jim said, "mrrr" mournfully with his rusty meow. He sauntered over—his coloring made him look like he was wearing brown tights—and hopped into his lap like a little gymnast. He gazed up at Ron with his mesmerizing David Bowie eyes. Then he head-butted Ron's face and patted his leg with his paw.

Jim's pure heart and silly kittenish ways brought Ron around and made him smile.

Ron heard keys jingling on the front porch as Steve came home. He didn't want his lodger to see him in this state. He lifted Jim as he stood up and turned to set the cat down on the barber chair behind him. He turned off the lights, took a deep breath, and wiped his tears with the sleeve of his sweater. He heard Steve banging around the kitchen for a late-night snack.

He needed to pull himself out of this gloom in case Steve staggered upstairs. Flipping through his boxes of vinyl, he put on the Modern Lovers' punky anthem "Roadrunner." He could happily listen to its gleeful, clashing guitars and drums forever. Music had always carried him along through the best and worst of times.

Somehow, he thought, he had to keep it together and get through this winter. He had to believe that he would find Mata and bring her home again.

Chapter 14

Ventura, California:
Good Vibrations

In the middle of January, Michael took a local bus headed south out of King City. Then he hitchhiked, with Tabor riding on his backpack, down the coast. Almost immediately they were picked up by a kindly old man with a white mullet and plaid Western shirt, who was going to Santa Barbara for cancer treatment. He had a huge, gentle German shepherd in the backseat. Tabor, who always seemed to get along with dogs, just fell asleep all the way there. It turned out to be a smooth ride—a straight shot down the 101 Freeway to Santa Barbara. After their ride let them off on a coast-curving stretch of highway that tightly wound around the Pacific, Michael could see a sparkling inlet dotted with surfers. The waves tumbled end over end toward the beach, and the breeze carried the smell of warm creosote and salt.

"Come on, Tabor," he said, walking down to the beach the moment they were dropped off. "I wanna show you the ocean."

As they approached the water's edge, Tabor looked ecstatic. Her jewel eyes were wide, and her nose quivered as she took in all the sights and smells: the crashing waves, the line of birds along the surf, the salty sea air, the blue vastness of the ocean. The moment Michael set her on the sand she crouched down and dipped her paws in the sea foam. She had no fear of the roaring waves or of the water lapping at her feet.

"Tabor, you're so weird," he said, grinning. "Cats aren't supposed to like playing in the water."

Tabor spotted a flock of seagulls landing along the shore. She crouched and locked her eyes on the birds, her whiskers twitching, rocking back and forth in hunting mode, ready to pounce. She spent a good half hour chasing seagulls and came away covered with sand and seawater, so filthy that he took her to the local pet-grooming parlor in town for a shampoo.

They stayed in Santa Barbara for a couple of days and hung out with some homeless friends, who couldn't believe that Michael was traveling with a cat. Tabor became a big hit on the streets of Santa Barbara, riding on Michael's shoulder and greeting people wherever Michael panhandled on the sidewalk.

But Michael wanted to move on, so they scored a ride to Ventura, a peaceful community that stretches from the ocean east into the California Coast Range. Michael headed to an old favorite camping spot in a secluded cove under some acacias, just down from the highway and out of sight of motorists. It was also hidden from anyone on the beach but was close to the center of town. He was relieved to find that it looked just as he'd left it last winter, which meant that nobody else had discovered it. And he intended to keep it that way, so he made sure to hide his campfire. He had to avoid being seen coming and going by the local "home bums" who might rob him or by residents who might call the cops, even though he wasn't doing any harm. He hadn't forgotten the words of the cop who'd given him a ticket for loitering: "Out of sight, out of mind."

Under the acacias, Michael wasted no time building their little house by the sea. He built a squat from driftwood, a mishmash of battered plywood, splintered branches, and plastic flotsam. He had learned to make squats in Brookings, Oregon, on the Winchuck River (which Michael called the Woodchuck River because so much wood piled up on its shores). It was a necessary skill, because the ocean acted essentially like a wind tunnel, and a shelter would protect him from severe wind chill. Yet even a good squat looked like it had been built by someone who'd survived a shipwreck.

That first day on the beach, Tabor seemed to love her new turf—spending a good long while lying on her back, flipping rapturously from side to side. She climbed into Michael's lap, with a rumbling purr, resting on her curled-up forepaws like a roosting hen. Stroking her, he shaped up the soft, velvety fur between her ears into a little cat Mohawk, and she purred contentedly. As the sun dipped below the horizon, Michael felt something close to happiness.

∘ ° ∘ °

On most mornings, Michael and Tabor would rise before the sun to the cooing sounds of mourning doves. At night, they huddled together in the sleeping bag next to the pile of driftwood. During the day, Michael filled the long hours listening to LA radio talk shows, scribbling in his crumpled notebooks, and reading the mangled paperbacks he had found on people's lawns among other castoffs. Besides Steinbeck, he liked classic American literature and books about American history.

While Michael was reading or doodling in his sketchbook, Tabor kept herself busy, often sitting on the low-lying branches of the tree above his head or playing alone beside him. She had become quite good at making her own toys out of leaves, feathers, and wine corks that Michael found on the beach for her. Tabor behaved like she owned the place, and she would sit for hours with her front paws crossed, gazing toward the sea like a lioness surveying her wild and infinite kingdom. She never ventured far from Michael, but he always kept a watchful eye on her as she swatted dragonflies or stalked tiny lizards and crabs.

In the late afternoon, when the silver-green surf was quiet and empty, they walked the beach, Tabor on her leash, Michael looking for sand dollars, seashells, and wood for the campfire. It was a simple, reassuring routine that kept at bay the crush of Michael's depression, which was always threatening to flood in but never quite arrived.

One day, when Michael tried to clip on her leash, Tabor wriggled away and ran off. After she was safely a few yards away, she looked back at him playfully, mewling. She waited until he caught up and then scampered across the sand. He ran after her, stumbling, half laughing, and murmuring to her, "Oh, Tabor . . . come back."

Michael couldn't recall the last time he enjoyed himself this much without drinking. Anybody watching would have thought the bearded homeless guy had lost his mind chasing a cat down the beach.

When she'd tired herself out, she leaped on his shoulder, expecting him to carry her home.

On a few days when Michael woke up, he found Tabor playing in the surf. Then he'd whistle and she'd run back to him. But one morning when he had turned his back on her to light a fire and make himself coffee, Tabor disappeared. She had no idea that her little walkabout in the wilds could end in her sudden death in the jowls of a bobcat or coyote. He walked up and down the shoreline, looking for small cat-paw prints in the sand and desperately calling her name. Just as he began to panic, he heard the squawking of seagulls and a faint, faraway MEEEEEOOW and spotted her even farther down the beach, stalking seagulls.

She was crouched, her tail flicking back and forth, and creeping up on one big unsuspecting seagull at the edge of the flock. Michael panicked, knowing that seagulls could be aggressive and attack cats and small dogs by dive-bombing and raking their heads with their hooked beaks.

He rushed toward her, shouting, "Tabor, whaddaya doing? Tabor! NOOO!" Tabor understood *no*, but she just looked at Michael and plowed through the sand, toward the enormous seagull, who flew off along with the rest of the flock.

"Tabor, leave 'em alone. Their lives are hard enough without you harassing 'em!" Michael said as he caught up to her and swooped her into his arms. She let out a small rumbling growl, angry that he'd disturbed her ambush. As he clipped on her leash, she hissed, furious. It was the first time she had ever hissed at him, but she needed to wear the leash for him to be able to protect her from predators, being swept away by waves, and a million other things. When he had first tried to train her to walk on a leash, she'd lie down and refuse to move or leap onto his shoulder. But she had found comfort in their ritual walks on the beach and she followed him to their camp.

But when they got back to their home beneath the acacias, Tabor turned her back to Michael and sulked, thumping her tail. When he tried to stroke her, she'd turn around, pausing only long enough to give him a look of disgust before scurrying away with a cranky little *aieou*. But by lunchtime, when he served her favorite dish of Fancy Feast chicken, she shoved her face in her bowl and forgot her anger.

Michael liked to think Tabor had a conscience about things, although that didn't always stop her from doing things she shouldn't. At the same time, he adored her mischievousness, which only added to her many charms. Sometimes she would rebel and run off on some secret mission. He tried to follow her without being intrusive, but she would usually sense him looking and turn around to mew with a trilling, birdlike call that kittens make when calling their mothers.

Late one morning, he trailed Tabor to a parking lot adjacent to the beach. He managed to keep her in sight until she slipped inside an open camper van. It took him a few minutes to walk over to peer inside. Through a fog of marijuana smoke, he made out a couple of surfers in youthful drift. A good-looking young guy in wet denim cutoffs, with cheekbones like cliffs and scruffy sun-bleached hair, looked up.

"I think my cat went in there," Michael said.

"I think you're right," the surfer replied, smiling and pointing at the cat behind him. Tabor was stretched out, belly up, on a stack of wetsuits. She turned her head lazily when she heard Michael's voice. "She's chilling," he said. "Wanna come in? Think she's too stoned to move."

"I hope not," Michael said as he stepped inside the van, which was filled with a blue haze. Back in Portland, he'd gotten angry at a couple of the street kids who had blown pot smoke in Tabor's face for a laugh. "Take all the frickin' drugs in the world if you want," he'd yelled at them. "But don't *ever* get the cat high. I have to deal with a stubborn adult cat; I don't want to deal with a high adult cat."

"This cat's the real deal," the surfer said, puffing on his joint. "She came in here, climbed on my chest, and started licking my eyeball. I'm like, 'Oh, my God, cat, really . . . we're not lovers, I'm just chilling with you, dude.'"

Michael laughed as he picked up his errant cat. "She does that. Once while I was panhandling, this police officer comes over and says, 'You can't do that here.' And the cat goes up to him and climbs up his leg because she's used to whooshing up my leg and thought she could climb up anyone. I said, 'No, Tabor, no. That's a policeman.' I had to pull her off him. I told him, 'Sorry, officer.' And he said, 'Yeah, that's not a good idea.' There was something about that cop the cat liked. But she's like that with some people."

On the way back to their tree squat, Michael found a crumpled *Los Angeles Times* sticking out of a trash can and snatched it up. On the front page was a story of an LAPD ex-cop who had gone on a revenge-fueled shooting spree in the snow-covered woods of Big Bear. He was still at large in the San Bernardino Mountains, which, luckily, were about three hours away.

Fugitive serial killers were the least of his worries. But the most pressing danger Michael and Tabor faced was not from cops, crackheads, or home bums, but the local coyotes. Michael could hear them at night and feared that sooner or later they would try to snatch Tabor. He'd already spent several terrible nights wide awake, as he and Tabor lay bundled together in the sleeping bag, listening out for every sound. He had even worked out an escape route. He had broken branches off the tree trunk to create handholds and footholds so that if the coyotes got too close, he could just grab the cat, push her into her carrier, and climb with it into the tree. They'd even practiced the route a few times, like a fire drill.

Michael had to be vigilant, but constantly watching out for Tabor and trying to teach the cat that there were real dangers out there made him anxious. He started drinking more to calm his fears. A pair of red-tailed hawks that occupied the neighboring tree also worried him. They would fly about ten feet above their heads, mostly hunting mice, but one evening, he had seen them kill a squirrel and drag it up to their nest.

Several times a day, Michael would say: "Look up, Tabor, look up," pointing upward, and she'd turn her sweet little feline face to the skies. He even taught Tabor to come when he whistled— what he called "the Tabor whistle." *In a sense*, he thought, *it was like having a child: you feed them, protect them from bad things, do your best to educate them, and hope for the best.*

Teaching animals felt like a natural instinct for Michael. When he and Mercer were living in the row-house apartment in St. Louis, Michael had trained the landlord's bullmastiff show dogs.

One evening, while sitting beneath their tree squat, Michael saw a lone coyote on the edge of the bluff by the highway, his silver-tinted coat glinting in the moonlight. A few nights later, a coyote came out of nowhere on the beach and moved steadily toward them, his sly, slanted amber eyes glowing in the dusk as he edged closer. Another two joined the first, and they all started circling Michael and Tabor's camp. Michael, at that instant, snatched up Tabor, stuck her in her zip-up carrier, grabbed a couple of cans of cat food, and scrambled up the tree. Once he was high enough in the tree, he threw a can at the largest coyote, who seemed to be the alpha, and nailed him right on the snout. The coyote yelped and growled, but didn't budge. Michael felt bad hurting the animal, as the coyotes were just doing their best to survive in a hostile world, but he had to protect Tabor no matter what.

After a while, the coyotes wandered off. When Michael was sure they were gone, he climbed down, hoisted on his pack, grabbed the carrier, and took off, too. That night, he and Tabor camped outside the Bank of America doorway in the center of town. But Michael was unsettled and kept thinking, *I've been traumatized by wild dogs. I'll never be able to sleep again.*

In the morning, Michael bought a hard plastic carrier at a

PetSmart. The mobile home would give Tabor more protection from wild animals. He also got another, longer, twenty-foot leash so that Tabor could walk around but stay safely connected to him. Even with this new protective gear, he decided they should relocate to Thousand Oaks, another town nearby in Ventura County, at least for a few days to put the coyotes off their scent in case they returned. Thousand Oaks had a shopping mall and a senior citizens center with lots of foot traffic, and Michael hoped that they would be able to beg for enough money or food to get by. Across the road from the mall, there was also a wide grassy area dotted with palm trees where they could sleep at night and Michael could drink in peace, undisturbed by the cops or anyone else.

In Thousand Oaks, Michael quickly established a routine. Every day by 6 a.m., with Tabor on his shoulder, he made his way from the palm-fringed grassy knoll to the main street in town to get coffee. On his way there, people would notice Tabor, pull over, and get out of their cars to pet her and hand him money. They all seemed to have the same questions: "How'd you get the cat? How'd you train it to stay on your backpack? How'd you become homeless?"

After having his coffee, he would put Tabor on his shoulder and go to the shopping mall and set up near the senior citizens center. He put out his cardboard sign asking for spare change, and almost every day someone gave him a bag stuffed with cat food or a coffee shop gift card. One genial, cat-loving old gent even bought Michael new clothes and invited him around his house to take a shower. At first, Michael thought it was a bit weird going to some guy's house for showers. Turned out he was a widower with three rescued cats of his own and was just happy to help.

Around noon on the third day, an old lady with a cane teetered toward them. Michael wanted to rush over and help her but thought she might take offense.

The old lady stooped to pet Tabor. "You've got such a beautiful cat. What's her name?"

"Tabor."

She looked surprised and her eyes filled with tears.

"Why are you crying?" Michael asked.

"That's my name, too," she said. "I'm Linda Tabor."

Michael thought, *Holy cow, Catwoman.*

"Did you just arrive here?"

"I've been coming to Ventura for the winter for about four or five years."

"How come I never noticed you before?"

"I didn't have a cat then."

"Oh," Linda said, leaning on her cane, thinking about this. "I'll be right back." She shuffled back to her car and, a few minutes later, returned with some cash. "How would you like to try some of my casserole? I'll come by again tomorrow. And I'll bring some food for the kitty, too."

Michael was touched by this unexpected generosity, and his eyes misted. He struggled to say something, but all he could manage was "Thank you."

Linda told him her story. Almost forty years ago, after her husband had died unexpectedly, Linda had started drinking heavily. She had kids and an elderly mother to look after but stopped caring. Often too drunk to drive, sometimes she couldn't even get out of bed. She knew she was losing control of her life and decided to call Alcoholics Anonymous, which she found in the Yellow Pages. When she called, somebody asked for her address, and shortly after a woman named Pat showed up at the door. She took Linda to an AA meeting, spent the day with her, and then dropped her back home. Linda never had another drink, nor did she see Pat again—whom she called "the most important stranger I've ever met." She'd been looking to pay back the debt ever since.

For the next few weeks, Linda met Michael at the mall once or twice a week, bringing him all sorts of delicious home-cooked casseroles. She brought Tabor roast chicken, cat food, and other treats. She also gave Michael clothes and a little money. Michael wished he could pour all the extra cash into booze, but he restrained himself to the odd six-pack of beer, since he worried constantly that someone would see him drunk and try to take Tabor away from him.

One day Michael noticed the store windows along the strip were decorated with big red cardboard hearts, paper roses, and metallic balloons. It was February, and Valentine's Day was coming up. He became emotional, saddened by a childhood memory that suddenly resurfaced. His second-grade teacher, Sister Maureen Teresa, had given him colored paper and crayons to make homemade cards for the other kids in the class to exchange on Valentine's Day because she knew Michael's family was too poor to buy store-bought cards. But when he showed them to his mother, she snatched the crayons and paper out of his hand, put them on top of the fridge, and told him, "You're not making cards for anyone." He felt humiliated all over again at the memory of being the only kid without cards to give.

Sister Maureen Teresa died just a few years later. Michael had dressed up to attend her funeral, but his mother wouldn't let him go. These sad memories were made even worse by another: around the same time that Sister Maureen Teresa died, one of his classmates was molested by a priest and hanged himself in his parents' house.

Michael thought how strange it was that particularly crushing memories always stay with you—linked together indelibly.

That afternoon, Linda arrived with a poem she had written on a Valentine's Day card. She handed it to Michael with a casserole. He opened the card and read the poem:

My new friend Michael makes me smile,
as he walks with kitty Tabor for miles and miles.
She's cozy and snug 'cause she knows she's well loved
by her daddy Michael and the angels above.

Michael was so touched by the card and, again, at a loss for words. "Thank you," he murmured, looking up at Linda, his blue eyes teary. He got up and gave her a hug.

That was a good memory that would be marked indelibly on his heart.

Chapter 15

The Stars Are Out Tonight

On an unseasonably warm Saturday afternoon in March, Ron mustered the energy to do a little gardening. Across the street, Jack was loading furniture into a moving van with his neo-Nazi buddies. All three had the same severe Hitler Youth haircuts with shaven undersides, and one was wearing a Confederate flag T-shirt and jackboots. When he spotted Ron, Jack stood on the curb, puffed out with alpha male righteousness, and started shouting abuse at him.

Ron was on his knees pulling out weeds, listening to *Rubber Soul* drifting out his kitchen door. He simmered silently and ignored his clichéd homophobic slurs, suspecting that Jack was looking for a fight just to show off in front of his thug friends. But minutes later, the van screeched up alongside Ron's house, and Jack stuck his head out the window. "Bet you're glad to see the back of me, faggot. You better stop spreading lies about me . . . you fat fishwife."

Ron glanced up. "Look," he said curtly, "I accept your story, but I don't believe you. I don't want to fight with you anymore."

"Keep talking, bitch, and Creto's gonna disappear. You'll

come home one day and he'll be gone." And with that, the van sped off and ran the stop sign on the corner.

Later that night, Ron was awakened by a loud crash. He crawled out of bed and went to the living room. Broken glass glistened all over the floor, surrounding a brick that someone had hurled through his window. He went outside and saw that FLAMING FAGGOT had been spray-painted across the front of his house, and all the tires on his car were slashed. Ron called the police, who escorted him, Steve, and their two cats out of the house to friends' places for the night.

After returning home, they kept Creto and Jim locked indoors. When Ron went to work at his guitar store and Steve wasn't home, he took Creto and Jim with him. Every night he slept with his phone on the pillow and a baseball bat by the bed. He was so shaken by these latest attacks, and he became more and more anxious. His growing unease made him think about moving to another house or leaving Portland altogether. But he couldn't leave without finding out what had happened to Mata.

Talking to Ron on the phone after the vandalism and hate crime, his friend Miguel persuaded him to visit him and his partner on Sauvie Island over the long Easter weekend. He could bring Creto with him, and they both would benefit from a change of scenery.

Less than an hour away from downtown Portland, Sauvie Island was a world apart—a place of reedy cliffs and winding country roads flanked by fields of roses, corn, pumpkins, and apple and peach orchards. George and Miguel lived in an old farmhouse on a grassy bluff overlooking the Columbia River. Their house, a weathered cedar-shingled former country inn, was surrounded by lush rolling pastures. They had a small vineyard, grew their own fruit and vegetables, and kept pet chickens and turkeys, who all had names.

Carrying Creto in his basket, Ron arrived at George and Miguel's on the afternoon of Good Friday. He found Miguel in the backyard feeding corn and grain to his flock of fifty hens and five turkeys—his girls, as he called them. He sold small batches of their beautiful blue eggs to the local farmers' markets. Ron had met Miguel, an unassuming, thirtysomething man with dark almond-shaped eyes and smooth bronze skin, on the island twelve years earlier. His partner, George, a stylish silver-haired gentleman in his sixties, was a vintner and wine broker and sold his homegrown boutique wines to high-end hotels and restaurants across the West Coast.

George was out, so Ron and Miguel left Creto asleep in the house and took a long walk past surfers and rusting little boat wrecks along Warrior Point's beach, a shimmering strip of sandy shore. They wandered toward the small white Warrior Rock lighthouse on the island's northern tip and stumbled on a tiny rustic inn with a dining room for lunch. They took a window seat and ate fish and chips, comfort food that reminded Ron of summer holidays on the island with his granddad in the '70s, when it was just a rough-and-tumble patch with a few fishermen and farmers. They would fly kites on the beach and afterward get seafood from a surf shack. Ron used to feed his fries to the gulls.

Ron and Miguel walked back to the house before it got dark. George had just come home, and the three of them settled into the family room on the second floor, facing a row of glass doors that opened onto a sundeck. There, they could hear the seabirds and the rustling of trees, and see deer feeding on the wild brush and long grasses. It was its own little paradise.

George had set out a couple of bottles of his special reserve wines and a cheese platter, with melon and strawberries, to nibble on as they drank. In spite of the peace and beauty around him, Ron worried that his house would be vandalized and broken into while he was away. Steve had gone to his sister's for the weekend and taken Jim with him. Ron kept shifting restlessly on the sofa and glancing at his phone. Creto lounged on the sofa beside Ron, wearing his kitty harness, which was attached to a leash in case Ron needed to keep him from getting too close to Miguel's birds.

Miguel noticed that Ron had dark shadows under his pale eyes and tried to allay his fears.

"I don't know what to do," he said, looking toward the windows, tense and distracted. "I mean, how do you even begin dealing with a criminally insane person? I feel like a fugitive in my own house, with bricks coming through the window. But what really scares me is him threatening to take Creto."

"You're doing the only thing you can do, keeping Creto close," Miguel said, topping off their wineglasses. "He's gone now."

George said, "You know you're welcome to stay here as long as you like."

Suddenly they heard a knock at the door and turned to see a chicken squawking on the other side and banging the glass door with her beak.

"That's Lucy. She wants to come in," George said as he got up to slide the door open for the fluffy iridescent-black hen. "Every evening, at sundown, she climbs up the outside staircase and pecks at the glass." Another smaller rusty-red hen with a bouffant hairdo and flared, feathery boots followed closely behind and hopped inside after her. "And the little red, that's Helena. She's blind. It's interesting how the others know this and look out for her. They all make sure she gets her fair share of feed. They guide her and curl up around her protectively."

Helena was chirping away as George talked to her and told her how pretty she was. She wanted to be held and petted, so he scooped up the little blind chicken, clutching her to his chest, and plopped back into his armchair.

"Some of the girls are ex-farm factory hens that we rescued," George said, feeding Helena bits of melon. "But amazingly, they usually end up being the friendliest and most affectionate."

Still attached to his lead, Creto stood politely on the sofa, observing the strange clucking creatures. Lucy cocked her shimmery black head to give the cat a quizzical stare and then followed Miguel as he went to get more wine.

When they returned, Lucy came closer to the sofa, clucking and angling her bright copper eyes toward Ron and the cat. Creto had never seen such a large bird before and, a little in-timidated, bolted to the other end of the sofa, as far as his leash would allow him. Miguel went over to pick up the frightened cat and cradle him in his arms.

"Ever since he was kicked in the face last year, Creto's become scared of everything," Ron explained.

"Was it that creep across the street?"

"I'm pretty sure it was him," Ron said. "All the cats and kids on our street are scared of him. One day I was talking with Ann from next door about the crow man, this elderly man who feeds crackers to the crows. The crows follow him up the block like the pied piper. It got us talking about people who like animals and people who don't. These two kids who were hanging out on their bikes and petting Ann's cat, Gordon, said: 'That man with the beard and all the metal on his face across the street is real mean and hates cats.' Ann goes, 'Why?' And they said, 'Because we've seen him chasing Gordon off the property, and shouting, 'Get outta here.'"

"Poor Creto," Miguel said. "I hate people who hurt animals."

Stroking the little blind chicken in his lap, George looked up and said, "Maybe it's time to leave Portland."

"With all the upsets, I'm starting to get sick of Portland. But I don't think I'll have any more trouble from that psychotic pimp. He's safely tucked away in another drug den somewhere else."

Ron bent down to stroke Lucy where she was still standing by the sofa. She jumped onto his arm, so he scooped her up. She fluffed out her feathers and burrowed into his lap as though she sensed he was troubled and was trying to soothe him. As he held her, he could feel her tiny heart beating against the palm of his hand. Her soft clucking and warmth were calming, and he allowed himself to think about moving to the coast. He imagined himself in a little fisherman's cottage with roses at the door, a big garden for Creto, and chickens wandering in and out of the kitchen. Sitting there in the hushed quiet, with the stars coming out, it was easy to forget about Portland and all his concerns.

Mata was still on his mind, though—and as long as she was gone, he knew he had to stay in the home that she knew.

Chapter 16

Yosemite: Walk on
the Wild Side

In late April, Stinson, Michael and Tabor's old pal from Portland, arrived in Ventura to pick them up to go back to Portland
for the summer. Stinson also brought along a girlfriend from
Mississippi, a pretty dark-haired mellow pixie of a girl named
Madison who traveled with an acoustic guitar and a caramel pit
bull mix named Bobby. Sweet-spirited, the dog got along fine
with Tabor right away. Stinson had driven Madison and Bobby
all the way from the Deep South.

The day before Stinson and Madison were to arrive, Michael
packed up camp and stopped by Linda Tabor's house in Thousand Oaks to tell her he was leaving. She asked to hold Tabor
one last time, and they promised to stay in touch. Then Michael
and Tabor walked back to Ventura to wait in their old camp
under the acacias.

Michael and his wandering friends would split for months
at a time and then reunite in some wild part of California or
the gritty backstreets of Portland. Stinson, like Michael, was

restless. A wanderer and a slacker, he had spent time in the navy, which made him realize he wasn't keen on rules and routines. He valued his freedom, even if it meant scraping by. He saw no point in being miserable working long hours to buy things he didn't need.

When Stinson and Madison arrived at the beach squat, they told Michael that they wanted to squeeze in a side trip to Yosemite before heading north and talked nonstop about how beautiful it was. After that, they wanted to head to Mount Shasta.

"You can show Tabor the world," Stinson told Michael, though he didn't need much persuading.

For her part, Tabor was excited to see Stinson again. She had greeted him enthusiastically and kept crawling into his lap over and over again to purr and pull on his beard.

After a couple of days on the beach drinking, listening to some beats, and trading road stories, Michael agreed that he and Tabor might as well get back on the road. He thought since she'd loved their time on the beach, she'd likely enjoy the mountains, too.

They began the long, slow drive up the coast. Their first stop was San Luis Obispo, a romantic old mission town on the Central Coast tucked between the Pacific Ocean and wine country. There they visited a spirit's cove, and Michael got another ticket for panhandling.

The next morning they set off early and finished the four-hour drive to Yosemite National Park by lunchtime. The May snowmelt had swelled the rivers, and the park was filled with campers. They found a quiet spot surrounded by the granite monoliths and giant trees on the edge of a campground, someplace half-hidden by bushy foliage and scrub but close to the road where they parked. They hoped to avoid run-ins with wildlife like big cats and bears by staying near the road.

With the afternoon sun behind him, Michael tossed off his

shoes and rested his back against a rock. Tabor stretched out to snooze beside him, and Bobby lay at his feet.

Stinson took a picture of the three of them and said, "Did they even have cameras when you were a kid?"

"Yeah, back in the seventies, they were the size of Rhode Island."

A group of girls setting up in the neighboring camp couldn't believe Michael and his crew had brought a cat into the wilderness, let alone that the pit bull and cat were friends. Michael convinced himself that it couldn't be too dangerous to have a cat in the park with so many people around.

On the second morning, Michael was excited to introduce Tabor to the soaring sequoias and sugar pines, figuring since she enjoyed hanging out on the acacias in Ventura and had probably never seen such giant trees she would love them. But she didn't seem to notice. She was lazing on the grass sunning herself, watching and yawning, as Michael and Stinson strung up a couple of hammocks. As soon as Michael finished stringing his, she instantly hopped on and hogged it, as if it was entirely for her. While Madison took Bobby for a long walk, they spent the afternoon lounging among the trees with Tabor. From their hammocks, they could see the rocky stream of the Merced River, the serene golden meadows beyond, and, further in the distance, El Capitan and other rock formations rising above Yosemite Valley, as well as teams of climbers working their way up and down the sheer granite-cliff faces.

Michael lay in his hammock with Tabor on his stomach, her leash wrapped around his wrist. The other campers had made him paranoid about the presence of coyotes, bears, and mountain lions, so he wasn't going to let her out of his sight.

Tabor craned her neck staring up a tree with fierce intensity, making a crunching *ack ack* sound.

Hunched among the sugar pine branches, a pair of ravens turned their silky black heads toward Michael and Tabor, *kraa*-ing and croaking, their bright gazes unyielding and intense.

Smiling at the cat, Michael said, "No way you're going up that tree. I'd need a crane to get you down and those birds would kick your ass."

She seemed to understand and curled up in defeat. While half reading *The Grapes of Wrath*, he watched her dozing off, her head slowly slipping onto her paws.

"You know the Native Americans believe ravens are sacred . . . shape-shifters and the creators of all living things," Michael said to Stinson, who wasn't listening.

Tabor woke up to wash her face, pausing now and then to stare at Michael with her intense gold-flecked green eyes. She pushed her head against the book and tugged at the pages. When he ignored her, she stretched out a paw to swat at Michael's face. He laughed and began reading out a passage to her about the main character, Tom Joad, hitchhiking his way home to the family farm from prison. "See, Tabor, he had to thumb rides like us. And he drank whiskey and liked little animals. He rescued a turtle on the road from being run over."

Stinson cocked an eyebrow. "You turning into a crazy cat lady reading to cats?"

"Tabor understands, but she prefers books with pictures in them." Michael felt as if he and the cat shared a private language. She seemed to read his moods and his mind with supernatural ability. Sometimes Michael would test her: he would imagine her doing something—like jumping on his shoulder—and he'd look into her eyes, and she would do it.

"Maybe you should start a school for gifted cats," Stinson teased.

"Cats don't wanna learn. They wanna have fun. Tabor's very

complicated and clever and smarter than a lot of people I've met."

"That's not saying much for Tabor."

Closing his book and marking the pages with a leaf, Michael was distracted by a group of guys rappelling down the mountainside across the stream. Out of the corner of his eye, he caught sight of something dark lumbering out of the woods behind them.

Stinson was looking toward the woods, too, and shot up from his hammock yelling: "There's a bear behind you . . . a bear . . . get outta the way!"

When Michael turned to look, glimpsing a huge bear ambling out of the sugar pines, he snatched up Tabor and stuck her in her carrier. He and Stinson were already sprinting toward Stinson's car when a big, butch guy with a buzz cut and beefy bulldog jowls from one of the nearby campsites charged the bear. He ran like a madman, waving his arms about, yelling and screaming. The bear froze, then wheeled around and ran away back toward a grove of low brambly trees.

"What's he doing?" Michael asked, shocked. "Is he trying to catch that bear?"

"I guess that's the way to get rid of it," Stinson said, watching the big guy tearing after the terrified animal.

According to Michael, black bears hardly ever attacked people unless they were surprised or protecting their cubs. They were just curious and only came near them when raiding campgrounds for food. So after a little while, Michael and Stinson returned to their camp spot.

When Madison and Bobby came back from their hike, though, they decided to retrieve their hammocks and relocate. They found another secluded sliver of wilderness just off the road where they could stretch out on a wide, flat boulder on the edge of a clearing. With their backs to the woods, Stinson and Madison sat on the rock, and Bobby, tired out from his long walk, was curled up on the grass at Madison's feet, napping and snoring loudly.

Michael set out cat food and water for Tabor, then ripped open a can of Steel Reserve and settled next to the cat.

Tabor looked up from her dish, her ears flickering, and sniffed the air. Suddenly she arched her back and all the hair on her body stood up, and her tail puffed into a brush. Michael looked over his shoulder in the direction where the cat was looking. He saw the brush shaking, the leaves rustling, but couldn't see what Tabor saw. When he looked again, some fifty yards away, a big brown bear had surged out of the thicket of big old oaks and pines. A cinnamon-colored sow with paws the size of dinner plates, she fixed her golden-brown gaze on Michael and the cat and lumbered toward them.

Facing Michael on the rock, Stinson was absorbed with rolling a joint and didn't notice anything.

Michael sat perfectly still but exchanged fearful looks with Madison, who had turned to see the bear, too. He whispered to Stinson, "There's a bear behind you."

"I'm not turning around," he said, laughing. "I know you're lying."

"No, dude, it's a bear."

"Yeah, Groundscore, shut up."

"No, Stinson, there's a fucking bear."

Madison, with her eyes fixed on the bear as it neared, leaned over to Stinson, and whispered, "He's right behind you."

Stinson spun around and then leaped to his feet. "Oh, shit, there's a bear."

As the bear came closer, Tabor started hissing and spitting, trying to scare it away. Bobby, roused from his sleep, was all riled up and started barking, too. Madison grabbed him by the collar, and they ran for the car.

Michael scooped up the cat and stuck her in her carrier again. Even though Michael knew he shouldn't show fear and flee from wild, predatory animals, fear and instinct kicked in and he scrambled to the car again, Stinson on his heels.

From the relative safety of Stinson's car, they watched the bear look in their direction, finish Tabor's meal in one swift scoop, and then amble off back into the trees.

"Shit, that bear must've woken up from hibernation and hungry as hell," Michael said. He realized it had been a stupid idea to feed the cat, as bears could literally smell food from miles away.

In fact, he realized, they had violated almost every park rule about safety. They had not stayed in the picnic areas to eat; they hadn't used the park's metal food-storage bear boxes; and they had brought a house cat into the wilderness.

They packed quickly and moved to another campsite for the night.

· · · ·

Waking up in the predawn haze the next day, just before 6 a.m., they all piled into Stinson's car and drove back to the coast. But over the next two days they had two flat tires and had to stop over in King City to get the tires fixed before getting back on the road. Tabor and Bobby, usually cuddled up together, slept through the breakdowns and everything else.

Once they were on the road again, they decided their next stop would be Mount Shasta. Revered as a sacred place where heaven and earth conjoin, Mount Shasta is a pilgrimage for spiritual seekers from around the world. The fifth-highest peak in California, the mountain is a dormant volcano and also a destination for outdoor adventurers and rock climbers.

It was warm and sunny, and the park was crowded with campers, but just before sunset they found a quiet, shady spot near the edge of Castle Crags State Park.

Stinson built a fire and grabbed a six-pack from the car for the three of them. Michael let Tabor loose so she could play with the dog, while Madison fixed a modest picnic of bread, cheese, Doritos, and beer. As Madison broke up the crumbly block of cheddar, Michael saw that there wasn't enough for all three of them—and barely enough to feed a family of mice.

"I'm not that hungry," he said. "I'll just have my beer."

"You can't go around with an empty plate," Stinson said, knowing that Michael was starving and just being thoughtful.

"It says not to feed the wildlife," Michael said, laughing. He pointed to a sign tacked to a tree behind Stinson and Madison: DO NOT FEED THE BEARS AND WILDLIFE IN THE PARK.

Michael sat back against a tree, guzzling beer and doing a crossword from the *Los Angeles Times* that he had pulled out of the trash. He'd been controlling his drinking, after the campers in Yosemite had warned he'd need to look out for his cat in the park, but he figured he and Tabor were safe now. He looked up periodically, keeping an eye on Tabor and Bobby chasing each other through the brush and trees. The cat would wait on one side of a tree, the dog on the other, and then one of them—usually Tabor—would dart away and they'd be streaking through the undergrowth like amphetamine-doped racehorses.

Finally they collapsed together, and when Michael glanced up again to check on Tabor, she was curled up with Bobby, napping in the twilight with their heads together and paws tangled around each other. Michael took another big slug of beer and felt a kind of wild joy. The faint sounds of chatter, laughter, and music from the surrounding camps mixed with the booze and the buzz of crickets lulled him to sleep—a short, but very deep one.

When he woke from his snooze with a start, he wasn't sure how much time had passed, but it was now dark. Stinson and Madison were chatting on the other side of the fire, and the dog sat alone beside the tree where he had been sleeping with the cat. But Tabor was gone.

"Did anyone see Tabor?" Michael asked.

Stinson glanced around. "Thought she was with you," he said.

Michael rose stiffly and walked around the campfire. "Bobby, where's Tabor?" he asked the dog, who looked up at him with his gentle butterscotch eyes. He cocked his head thoughtfully, then shifted his position, lay his head on his paws, and went back to sleep.

Panicked, Michael staggered into the woods, scanning the brush around the towering ponderosa pines for the cat. "Tabor, where are you?" he called out. Still nothing. "Tabor, come on, girl, where are you?"

Madison and Stinson joined the search, and Bobby woke up to trail behind them. They went off into the woods, calling and listening for Tabor.

After about forty-five minutes, they met back up at their campsite.

"What was I thinking bringing her here?" Michael said, desperation in his voice. "I just wanted Tabor to see the wilderness, to understand that the world isn't all street corners and freeways."

"I was worried about bringing Bobby, too," Madison said. "This place is full of cougars and bears."

"*Damn it*," Michael said. He hadn't thought about cougars. "This is *sooo* messed up."

Stinson went over and put a hand on his back. "Calm down, Groundscore. She's around somewhere." Stinson was good that way; whenever Michael got mad or wound up, Stinson could talk him down. "But we better start looking before something eats her."

The three of them split up again. Under the light of the moon, Michael saw large paw prints in the dirt, too large for a house cat. All around him he heard rustling in the bushes and trees, and he thought he caught glimpses of unidentifiable creatures melting into the dusk. In a sense, he felt like he was being punished for running away from home so many times when he was a kid. The difference was that his parents didn't care nor want him back, but Tabor was everything to him.

As he went deeper into the woods, the blackness engulfed him. He had no flashlight, and his eyes hurt from squinting into the dark. He kept tripping over tree roots and rocks.

"Howdy," said a voice on the path in front of him.

Michael looked up to see a stocky little man in a Stetson being tugged along by a chunky chocolate Labrador. A cartoonish cowboy, he looked like Yosemite Sam with caterpillar eyebrows and a bushy mustache.

"I just saw a huge cougar on the trail, and we've heard coyotes out here," Yosemite Sam said. "I really hope you find your dog tonight."

Michael didn't respond. There was no point correcting the man or getting into a conversation. It had been nearly two hours, and he was worried sick about Tabor. Owls were hooting above his head, and there was constant rustling around him.

Twigs crackled and branches snapped and a hand took hold of his shoulder, startling him. It was Stinson. He led Michael back to their clearing. On the way, Michael saw a sign: WARNING COUGAR SIGHTINGS ON DEER TRAIL.

Madison was already there, sitting on a rock by the fire, petting Bobby. "Nothing," she said, looking up at them, her dark eyes wide with concern. "I really hope Tabor's all right and just hiding somewhere."

Stinson lit up a cigarette when they got back and after a few drags, stamped it out with his shoe, and said, "We'll find her. Come on, let's go back out again."

Michael imagined how scared Tabor must be. "I can't believe this," he said. "I've been drinking less for months now because I didn't want to have Tabor taken away from me. Instead I lose her in a national park."

"It'll be okay," Madison said, trying to calm him.

"No, it won't," Michael said, his voice tired and ragged. "She's all I've got."

High above them, a bird let out a warning squawk. The bird squawked again.

"Ssshh, hang on," said Stinson, glancing around and listening intently. "Did you hear that? It sounded like a meow."

Stinson shone the light from his cell phone up into the trees. The beam skimmed off branches and caught a pair of glowing eyes. It was Tabor, perched on the bough of a tree, lazily looking down at them. Her drowsy gaze made it obvious she'd been up there the whole time, asleep.

"She has a wicked sense of humor," Stinson said, laughing.

"Yay! Stinson saves the day again," said Michael. It was Stinson who had picked up Tabor that rainy night in Portland. All he could feel was joy. At that moment nothing in the world mattered except this cat.

When she climbed down, Michael scooped her up and pressed his face into her furry cheeks, which smelled like spring leaves and earthy bark. "Oh, my God," he said. "You're all right." Tears shone in his eyes. He was relieved that nothing had happened to Tabor, and happy to have her back, but he was also disappointed in himself: he hadn't pulled himself together enough to look after her properly. This was the second time his carelessness had put her in danger.

He told Tabor that he loved her and she head-butted him and licked his face with her sandpapery tongue. "I'll get it together," he whispered into her fur, and meant it. "You'll see."

. . . . .

The following morning they drove to downtown Mount Shasta for more supplies and then continued south on to another campground near the Buddha Hole on the south fork of the Sacramento River.

Following the barely marked byzantine park trails, they walked deeper into the forest and found a hidden, sun-drenched nook. Dipping down the rocky incline, they settled on a brushy knoll along the riverbank. The Buddha Hole was a crystal-clear emerald swimming hole fringed by a tumble of boulder fields, cedar, and pines. This particular stretch was where all the hippies came to go skinny-dipping en route to the Burning Man festival in the desert.

While Stinson and Madison started pitching camp, Michael put on Tabor's long lead and tied it to a slender sapling. Tabor, stretching her legs and yawning, moved into the shade beneath a lacy tuft of fern, where Bobby had already made a cozy nest, and plopped down beside him for a long nap. That afternoon, as Stinson and Madison swam and splashed around in the shallows, Michael sat and read alongside Bobby and Tabor, wary that the cat would be snatched away by cougars or coyotes.

Later the three of them smoked a bit of grass, drank, and talked into the night. After all the stress and drama of the previous day, Michael thought he could do with a couple of beers, and although he could sometimes go weeks or months without touching a drop, he got carried away, since he was stoned.

As he tore through another six-pack, Michael launched into one of his road stories: "Last summer I met this woman on the sidewalk and she said to me: 'You drink beer, then?' I said, 'Yeah.' She said, 'How many beers do you drink a night?' I said, 'Dunno, about six.' And she said, 'How many years have you been drinking beer?' I said, 'About thirty years.' She said, 'Do you realize if you didn't drink beer and you'd put all that money away thirty years ago, every month in a high-investment account, you'd have enough money today to buy an airplane?' I said, 'Fucking hell . . . that much.' So I said to her, 'Do you drink beer?' She said, 'No.' I said, 'Where's your fucking airplane then?'"

The wind blew in from the Sacramento River and it got chilly, so Michael built a campfire, got out his camping stove, and fixed them something to eat. When the fire burned out, he started another one.

Winding down by the fire, Michael watched Tabor collapse into a deep sleep. He carefully lifted her off his lap, wrapped her body in her fleece blanket and put her in her mobile home. Stinson and Madison had already passed out cold. Feeling chilly, Michael crawled into his bag, still wearing his clothes and shoes, and without meaning to fell asleep before the flames had died out.

Michael woke up to the sound of Tabor wailing in her carrier, where he'd tucked her in for the night. She'd been desperately trying to rouse him. He smelled smoke and when he looked down, the bottom of his sleeping bag had burned away up to his knees.

Tabor's yowling and screeching woke Stinson, too, who sprang up when he saw the smoldering sleeping bag and shouted, "You're on fire!"

"Yeah, I can see that," Michael said, still drunk and strung out, moving his legs and thumping them on the ground to put out the fire in the dirt.

The fact that he could have been severely burned hadn't quite sunk in.

. ° . . °

The next morning, though, Michael was rattled. He'd almost lost Tabor and he'd woken up in a burning sleeping bag. Michael thought about how he'd spent much of his recent adult life blacking out and blocking out bad memories. Except now he had a cat who depended on him and loved him wholeheartedly, and he was endangering her. He decided he would stop drinking for the homestretch from Mount Shasta to Portland.

Chapter 17

Big Sky Country: Devils & Dust

A couple of weeks after leaving Mount Shasta and arriving in Portland, Michael realized that he needed to visit Walter in Montana. Walter was the closest thing he had to family. Whenever Michael was desperately hungry or cold, he could count on Walter to wire money for food or a motel room. When Michael got arrested for vagrancy or public drunkenness, he paid the fines or bailed him out of jail, usually grumbling, "I'd like to be sitting under a tree doing nothing, with my personal banker on speed dial."

Walter reminded Michael that he wasn't worthless, that he was loved.

Soon after returning to their squat in the UPS bay on Hawthorne, Michael invited his friend Kyle to go to Montana with him and Tabor. Just nineteen, brash, tough, yet vulnerable, Kyle was a lot like Michael had been at that age. Kids on the run usually won't listen to adults, since most of the adults they knew had mistreated or abused them. But Michael was a drifter, too, so in some ways, he was a father figure to Kyle: a guy who'd seen a lot of ups and downs and was willing to listen and dispense his bits of wisdom.

Michael and Kyle shared a fascination for wild places. In Montana, the blue skies went on forever, and the sweeping alpine valleys and raw, rugged prairies were almost otherworldly in their wild beauty. Wildlife—moose, bighorn sheep, and bison—could sometimes be seen from the road grazing in the valleys and roaming through carpets of bright yellow glacier lilies.

Michael knew from previous trips that passing through Idaho would be their biggest nightmare. Hitchhiking there was illegal. So, before leaving Portland, Kyle posted their photos and a "ride wanted" message on Craigslist Rideshare. Having already spent weeks on the road with Stinson and Madison, Michael hoped to get to Montana quickly without lingering anywhere. But when they didn't get any responses to their posts, they decided to set off anyway. They could check in on shares from the road.

Barely four hours after leaving Portland, they were left off in Hermiston, an eastern Oregon farming community widely known throughout the Pacific Northwest for its watermelons. The back roads were lined with dried grass, telephone poles, and homemade farm signs for raspberries, rhubarb, and fresh eggs. They were stuck on the dusty roadside under the power lines of Hermiston for half the day.

Seeing Kyle getting anxious and occasionally moaning, Michael tried to reassure him: "The roads are kinda slow."

They were forced to walk six miles to Stanfield, another rural outpost, to look for a better hitching spot, and settled at a promising crossroads that had a decent amount of traffic, mostly truckers, motor homes, and a few hippie vans. After a depressing hour of flashing various signs—EAST, MONTANA, HELENA—without success, they made a new one, DESPERATE FOR RIDE WITH CAT. But no one stopped.

It was Kyle's first long-distance hitchhike, and he was unprepared for the hard stretches of waiting, the sheer exhaustion, the monotony, and the boredom. He had brought his skateboard, so he broke up a few afternoons on it, but it was so hot, with temperatures in the 80s and no shade, that he couldn't keep it up. After sitting on the road in Stanfield for three dismal days, staring at the sky, kicking rocks, and seeing cars blow by, they were both frustrated, their spirits worn down.

Kyle finally had had enough. "This is a drag," he said, standing up and flinging on his pack. "I'm heading home if we're not getting any rides forever." He crossed to the other side of the road.

Michael was just as fed up but didn't say anything—he'd learned to be patient with street kids, just as he had learned to be patient with Tabor. Before he had Tabor, he wasn't too bothered about being stranded on the side of the road. But now he worried about the cat getting stressed from the heat. He always kept her shaded with his snap-brim hat or inside her carrier during the hot parts of the day. Fortunately, Tabor was remarkably laid-back, content to just snuggle on their laps during the day and in their bedrolls in sleep-outs beneath the underbrush at night.

On the other side of road, Kyle got a ride right away from a scruffy guy who looked as if he lived out of his car. But the ride seemed to take him farther into a desolate rural wasteland, with nothing but dry grass for miles, so Kyle bailed and asked to be let out. He crossed over the road again, and right away another car pulled over for him.

About an hour later, as Michael gazed at the glaring noon sun, which was getting brighter and hotter, thinking about walking to the next town, he saw a car moving slowly toward them with Kyle in the passenger seat. They picked up Michael and Tabor at the same crossroads where Kyle had left them. Together, they made the three-hour drive all the way to Idaho.

Their ride dropped them off at a rural exit somewhere just northwest of Boise in the late afternoon. Michael, Tabor, and Kyle now found themselves in the Idaho high desert. After walking a couple of miles, they were desperate and almost deranged from the heat. Even in her carrier, Tabor was visibly uncomfortable. They found some spindly trees and shrubbery to shelter under as the sun faded and prepared for another roadside sleep-out. Early the next morning, Tabor broke out of her carrier, ran over to Kyle in his sleeping bag and started pulling his hair. Michael woke up to Tabor's loud meowing and Kyle yelling, "Go away." When Tabor saw Michael's eyes open, she rushed over to him, jumped on his chest, and began pulling at his beard.

"C'mon, it's four a.m.," Michael groaned, brushing her away from his face. "No, Tabor, no . . . stop!"

But she wouldn't stop, so they decided to make an early start before the sun came up. Michael fed the cat and packed up camp. As they headed off, Michael told Kyle that nomads navigated their way around the wilderness using the sun and the stars. But somehow the two of them got lost in the dark and wound up way off the road to Montana, in some tiny town that looked like an abandoned Western movie set, with dusty storefronts dating from the 1800s. The side streets were lined with sagging, wood-framed houses and shotgun shacks that had NO TRESPASSING signs posted on the front doors.

All morning long they wandered along the town's hot, dusty roads, looking for shade, clinging to the storefronts' shadows to avoid the white, burning sun. Sweat dripped down Michael's face, and his head was pounding. Tabor was panting in his arms. He worried that she would overheat, as cats can only sweat through their tongue and paws, so he frequently poured water into his hands and wetted her fur to cool her down.

At the end of Main Street, Michael saw a spot of shade outside a deserted antiques store. A wooden structure with a patchy corrugated metal roof, spread over three stories with a widow's walk on top, it looked like a wrecked ship salvaged from the bottom of the ocean.

"We've reached the road to nowhere," Michael said, and collapsed on a chipped, sea-green metal garden chair, stretching out his long legs. He took a look at the vintage signs for Coca-Cola, Virginia Slims cigarettes, and railroad crossings that were strewn around outside. Suddenly Tabor leaped out of his arms and shot into the shuttered store through a hole in the wall.

Exhausted and hot, Michael could only shrug. "Oh well," he said, and put his feet up on the edge of a claw-foot bathtub. "Guess we're stuck here for a while. At least she's still attached to her leash. She can't go too far."

Kyle looked at him with a worried expression and asked, "How are we going to get her out?"

"She'll come out when she feels like it, probably when she gets hungry. She's having her siesta. Just leave her to it."

While they waited, Kyle roamed the junkyard, which was piled high with antique road signs, rickety bicycles, rusting car parts and farm machinery, an art-deco-era turquoise Spirit of 66 gas station pump, and other curiosities.

"I've never seen such weirdness," he said, browsing around the bric-a-brac, then walking up to the building to peer through the cloudy, dirt-encrusted windows. He circled the building, looking through every crack in the wall, trying to catch sight of Tabor in the junk-filled darkness.

"She likes poking her nose into everything," Michael said, unraveling the brown bandanna beneath his canvas hat and using it to wipe the sweat off his sunburned face. "She just wanted to escape the sun and cool off. We can't always go where we want if she doesn't want to move. She's a female cat, so I have to treat her like a female cat and always let her decide."

About half an hour after she'd vanished, Tabor stuck her head out of the splintered, sun-bleached planks, as Michael had predicted she would. He tempted her out with some Fancy Feast, then blocked the hole with a washboard and kept a tighter hold of her leash.

Sun-flushed and wilting with fatigue, Kyle worried they might be stuck there all day. "This really sucks," he said, sitting cross-legged and leaning against the building in the only sliver of shade he could find. He mindlessly tore at the weeds and dandelions sprouting next to it. "Didn't know it was possible to stay alive in these temperatures." His mouth was dry, and his lips were burned. Michael had used all of their water to help Tabor cool off. "It's like being on another planet. Venus or something."

"Idaho might as well be another planet," Michael said, half listening, his eyes fixed on a sun scorpion scuttling past his feet. He didn't want to draw Kyle's attention to it and alarm him, but he had to make sure it didn't go near Tabor, whose face was buried in her dish.

The second Tabor finished her lunch, Kyle was up in a flash and halfway down the road. Michael picked up Tabor, boosted her onto his backpack, and followed.

A couple of blocks down the strip, they stopped outside a rickety old country store and café that looked like it was still in business. A handful of locals were going in and out.

Michael tied Tabor to the bench on the wraparound porch outside the store. "Anything you need?" he asked Kyle, who flopped down on the bench.

"Water."

"Anything you want?"

"Water."

Michael went inside, while Kyle waited on the porch with Tabor. Michael was glad to have a traveling companion, someone to help keep an eye on Tabor. Usually when he went into a store, he'd run through the aisles anxiously and get antsy at the checkout, afraid someone would take the cat. He also couldn't leave Tabor for too long or she would start caterwauling and crying like a baby until he came back, which could attract unwanted attention.

Michael filled their water bottles in the bathroom and took them outside to Kyle, then ran back inside the store to get provisions. He bought beer and tobacco, Skippy peanut butter, a block of orange plastic cheese, a loaf of Wonder Bread, and one lottery scratch card—what Crazy Joe called trailer-trash essentials.

"That was quick," Kyle said, in a better mood now that they had food and water.

"I don't mess around," Michael answered. They ate lunch on the porch, and then Michael put Tabor in her mobile home to escape the sun. They walked for a few hours, making it to the outskirts of Boise. Following some train tracks south, they stumbled into another dead mining town, even more haunted and forgotten than the one with the country store. An abandoned strip mall held a few gutted buildings, the skeletal frame of a gas station, and a couple of dusty boarded-up hotels covered in graffiti. In the barren landscape, scattered among the sagebrush, were a dried-up old boot, blown tires, and broken bits of green and brown glass that glittered in the sand. Windblown bags hung from cacti and drifted around like plastic tumbleweed.

"Guess this is where plastic bags go to die," Kyle said.

"Or hitchhikers who can't get a ride out of here," Michael said, pointing at a little homemade wooden cross set into a heap of stones, with some dead flowers and a pair of crumbling sneakers on top.

They eventually hitched a ride into Boise and got left off at Boise Stage Stop, a fancy truck stop set in a Tudor revival building with an old stagecoach parked out front. The temperature was creeping into the 90s.

Dazed and sunburned, they slid in the turquoise-vinyl-upholstered booths in the farthest corner of the brightly lit cafeteria-style diner. A food-and-fuel pit stop for truckers, the diner was full of good old boys in denim, Stetsons, and scuffed cowboy boots—men who spent much of their lives outdoors, with weathered faces and callused hands cured in the sun like saddle leather.

The two drifters and the cat languished in the air-conditioning, over iced water and watery iced coffees, while waiting for their phones to recharge. After cooling down, Kyle and Michael, with Tabor riding on his backpack, headed back outside. Michael knew it was pointless hanging around—as a rule, truckers rarely ever picked up hitchhikers anymore because it was against their company insurance policy. They walked down the road to a busy junction near an off-ramp of I-84, a multilane highway, and sat on the roadside with their sign for Montana, while Tabor, who was attached to his bag, stretched out beneath sagebrush. Michael picked a few sage leaves, rubbing them between his hands and breathing in the refreshing green scent, and then started eating a cheese sandwich.

A battered old black Chevy Avalanche pickup truck that was hurtling down the road screeched to a halt in front of them with a spray of dust and loose gravel.

The cowboy behind the wheel leaned out the window. "Where you folks headin'?" he asked in a slow, syrupy drawl.

Simultaneously Michael said, "Anywhere," and Kyle said, "Montana."

"Can't take you that far, but I can getcha going," the cowboy said, and jumped out to help with their gear. Standing just shy of six feet tall in baggy blue jeans, he was a broad and ruggedly handsome mountain man, with hair like corn silk and a trim beard and mustache.

"Can we hang on a sec?" Michael said, hurriedly finishing his last bites and grabbing Tabor's leash.

"No rush," said the cowboy, leaning against the truck to light himself a cigarette, who, with his bright fire-blue eyes blazing beneath his weather-beaten Stetson, looked like the Marlboro Man.

Kyle climbed into the backseat, and Michael handed him their backpacks. But when he turned around to get Tabor, she refused to get in the pickup. She looked up at Michael, her eyes full of defiance, and tugged at the leash to try to make a getaway. He thought he had a firm grip on her lead, but when he bent down to pick her up, she broke away and bolted along the busy feeder road, her leash trailing after her.

"Oh, God, not now," Michael said, pursuing the cat as cars flashed past them. Out of the corner of his eye, he could see wary drivers slowing down and swerving away from the cat.

"Tabor, *no*!" he shouted. "Tabor, come back!"

She raced away from him as if she knew he was taking her somewhere she didn't want to go, or for her own inexplicable reasons.

"Don't do this," Michael pleaded, walking after her quickly. He knew never to chase or corner a scared cat, as it only makes them more stressed and anxious. Big rigs roared past, blasting them with a rush of air. Tabor slowed to a trot along the white line. Then she stopped, turned, and looked at him with a fearful, anguished expression.

Michael stopped, too, and slowly edged closer to his scared, helpless cat, his heart pounding wildly. He talked to her in a low, calming tone, "It's okay, Tabor. . . . It's okay."

Tabor looked him straight in the eye and meowed.

After a tense minute, Michael was able to walk up to her slowly and scoop her into his arms.

"Bad girl, Tabor, bad," he scolded her as he held her close.

The cat flinched and flattened her ears but leaned into his chest.

"How could you do this?" he asked as he jogged back to the truck. Kyle and the cowboy had been watching them from inside the cabin.

"She's some wildcat, ain't she? Got the devil in her heart," the cowboy said to Michael as he climbed into the passenger seat, still keeping a tight hold on Tabor. "Thought for sure she was a goner."

"She frightened the life out of me," Michael said. He was so shaken his hands were trembling as he stroked her head. "I can't ever let anything happen to this cat. She's like a princess in my bag."

The cowboy flashed a wide smile, and they rolled out the ramp onto the highway, the hot midday sun piercing the windshield. He was a rancher. He'd also been a felon and just got out of prison. He glanced over at Michael, smiling, his fire-blue eyes blazing in the sunlight, and asked, "What's with the cat?"

After Michael told him the whole saga of finding Tabor and traveling down and up the West Coast with her, he broke into a deep, hearty laugh. "Boy, that's one helluva crazy story."

The cowboy turned off the highway to make a quick stop at his house. Cigarette between his fingers, he ripped along the bumpy rural roads, past patchy fields and tiny quaint towns with Western storefronts, crunching gears all the way. The air was thick with the smell of horses, wood smoke, and wildflowers. Hardscrabble ranches and grassy pastures dotted with cows and horses flicked past.

Leaving Michael, Kyle, and Tabor in the truck, he returned moments later, with bags full of food and some barbecue charcoal and lighter fluid for them. Then he dropped them near the Indian Creek Reservoir, a gorgeous wetlands area on the way to Montana with miles of hiking trails and meadows.

As he helped them get their gear out of the truck, the cowboy asked, "Do you smoke weed?"

"Yeah," Michael replied.

As a parting gift, he gave them a big jar of weed, along with rolling papers and a plastic lighter.

In the park ahead of them, the sun-bleached buffalo grasses stretched into the horizon and rippled in the wind, making waves in all directions like a stormy sea. Tabor streaked ahead on her twenty-foot lead, dragging Michael behind her, in a mood to explore. She slowed to sniff wild roses that were blooming along the path, which made Michael wonder whether she was maybe homesick for Portland and the roses that grew throughout the city there.

The guys decided to stay in the park for the night to catch up on sleep before getting back on the road again. They stopped, removing their packs, to sit and rest a bit in a field of swaying grasses, and Michael tied Tabor's long lead to his bag. She immediately started skulking around the tall grass, flushing out mice and shrews, while Michael and Kyle sprawled out on the ground. She sidled up to Michael with a cute, big-eyed deer mouse in her mouth, who was squeaking its little furry head off. She looked up at Michael and gently dropped it at his feet to show off her hunting skills.

"Oh, Tabor," he said, watching the deer mouse scuttle off and disappear back into the long grasses. "You scared that poor little mouse half to death."

They pulled up the tether, picked up their packs, and walked up an isolated, pine-fringed slope to pitch camp. They watched the sun melt into the lake. Red-necked loons and gray moorhens swooped down on the shores, and dusky grouse chattered from the fir trees. As they looked out across the fields, Michael identified all the waterbirds for Tabor and Kyle as they flew in to roost among the reeds along the shore for the night.

When it grew dark, Michael lit a fire and cooked the food the cowboy had given them: salmon that he'd caught himself, straw mushrooms, new potatoes, and warmed up a homemade peach cobbler.

As he cooked, Michael told Kyle how he got his first kitchen job. It had been on one of his runaway trips in 1979 when he was fourteen and sleeping along the railway tracks in his hometown. "I'd eaten hash browns and toast at Webster Bar and Grill," he recounted. "I opened the old screen door and was gonna dine and ditch, thinking there's no way the fat lady behind the grill can catch me. But there she was right at the door. 'Where you going?' she asked, blocking me. 'You planning to skip out on the check?' I was like, 'Yes.' And she asked, 'You got any money?' I told her 'I got nothing,' and she said, 'You wanna wash some dishes or you want me to call the cops?' I decided to wash dishes to pay off my debt.

"The lady happened to be the owner. I was good at doing dishes, and maybe she felt sorry for me. She ended up hiring me that day. I washed dishes for a while, and then she moved me up to line cook, flipping eggs and making biscuits and gravy from scratch. That's how I got into the restaurant business. I always wanted to become a chef as a kid. I knew how to make grilled-cheese sandwiches and peach cobbler when I was eight."

"It smells good," Kyle said as Michael handed him his dish.

"Oh, man, we're gonna eat really good tonight."

Tabor was ravenous, too. Before starting on his own plate, Michael filled up her bowl with Fancy Feast, but she ignored it and went straight for his salmon. Even though he liked to keep her on the same food to maintain her routine, he gave her half the filet, which she gorged herself on. Then she slipped into a shallow sleep, her fluffy little head resting on her folded paws, whiskers twitching.

Watching Tabor passed out after her big meal, he thought that life could be so lonely and monotonous, but finding someone to help you through it made it worthwhile.

Michael and Kyle stayed up late talking and smoking weed until the mosquitoes became too much. Michael put Tabor in her mobile home and took her and his half-burned sleeping bag to a small rise under a big pine, which would absorb the morning dew and keep them dry as they slept.

· · · · ·

Michael woke up the next day at first light and released Tabor from her carrier. After giving her breakfast and brewing coffee for himself and Kyle, he packed up camp. They smoked more of the weed and left the rest of the jar in a bush for someone else to find. It was a prison time's worth of weed—you could get two years or more just for possession in Idaho.

When they got back to the main road, they started hitching, trying to look friendly and nonthreatening to passing drivers. Idaho was hostile not only to hitchhikers but panhandlers, too. Some rural, red-state towns had particularly scary and surly guys who would put a hole in you if you looked at them the wrong way, and probably skin the cat, too. After almost a full day of not scoring a lift, they walked back into the park for the jar of weed, ate the rest of their food, and crashed out at dusk beneath a cluster of trees off the road.

· · · · ·

At the crack of dawn, they set off again and walked a whole day to reach Mountain Home. Wedged between the desert and the mountains, the town had an air force base, a few dozen churches, a rodeo, and an annual country music festival. Consistently ranked among the worst places to live in Idaho, it had extremely hot, dry summers, constant wildfires and a high unemployment rate, but also plenty of traffic passing through.

Michael and Kyle swung by several gas stations to try to wrangle a ride. That way drivers saw them on the way in and had time to consider giving them a lift as they paid for gas. They would fill up their water bottles, charge their phones, and sit outside with their sign and Tabor on her leash, playing cards to pass the time, until it got too hot to wait by the road. They could only hitchhike in two-hour stretches very early in the morning and late in the evening, because they had to spare Tabor from the searing heat. They were drinking too much, eating too little, being bitten by bugs, and crashing under trees in empty lots. Five days passed—and they were still waiting for a ride out of Mountain Home, where everything looked dusty and colorless, bleached out by the hot, relentless desert sun.

On the sixth day, as they sat outside a gas station in the morning sunlight, drinking burnt gas-station coffee and breathing in diesel fumes, Michael felt depleted. Of all the cross-country hitchhiking trips he'd taken over the years, he couldn't remember a harder one.

When it got too hot for Tabor, they moved over to a nearby strip mall, which had more shade and foot traffic. In a shady spot in the parking lot near a Walmart, they rested and charged up their phones. Kyle checked for any responses to their post on Craigslist Rideshare and updated their location.

Michael grabbed a piece of cardboard that he'd slept on the night before and used Kyle's Sharpie and his colored markers and made a new sign that read: FATHER, SON & CAT NEED RIDE TO MONTANA.

Tabor didn't seem too bothered about being stranded—she mostly slept through it all. Lying on her back contentedly, she turned her fluffy face like a sunflower toward the sun. Her eyes shut, her front paws curled, she looked so cute that Kyle snapped a picture and posted it on Facebook: *Tabor in Mountain Home, Idaho.* And as an afterthought, he wrote: *Fuck you Mountain Home. Been here for six days with no rides.*

For the rest of the afternoon, they sat, smoking and sharing small talk with the people who stopped to swoon over Tabor. As the heat mellowed, Tabor woke up in a feisty mood.

She looked up at Kyle playfully, with her intense green eyes, flecked with big-cat yellow, and she plunged her front paws into his open bag again and again, with a kittenish trill. Kyle stuck his hand in the bag and then pulled it out, waving it at her, letting Tabor know they could play. She slunk down, looking fierce, and focused on his hand as if it were a cornered mouse. She sprang up and started nipping at his hands and wrists, play-wrestling with him.

"Ow . . . ow . . . owww, Tabor, that hurts," Kyle said, trying to pull his hand away from her tiny needle-sharp incisors. "Tabor, let go."

"I told you she'll cut you open. She doesn't know the difference between bite and scratch," Michael said. Kyle tended his bleeding puncture wounds. "She's been traumatized. That's probably why she's tough and stood up to that bear. If it weren't for Tabor, that bear could've come over and eaten Stinson."

Michael rolled a cigarette, sprinkling tobacco along the paper and sealing it with his tongue.

"We should just start walking," he said, rising to his feet. "Don't want to spend the rest of my life here." The light was fading fast, and he wanted to find some shelter.

"I think we should hop on a freight train somewhere," Kyle said.

"Sure, I'll rustle one up with my magic wand," Michael said, assembling his pack, getting ready to leave.

Just as the last sun raked the parking lot, a stranger approached them. His head was shaved, he wore silver skull rings on his fingers, and he was dressed in short shorts and what appeared to be a white burlap sack. Tattooed blue serpents swirled up his meaty legs. A gun belt was slung around his waist with a six-shooter on each hip, a nine-millimeter was strapped to his thigh, and an intimidating blue-gray pit bull walked by his side.

"You the guys on the Internet?" he asked.

Thinking he must've recognized them from the photos he'd put on Craigslist, Kyle hesitated and said, "Um, yeah . . . that's us."

"Well, my name's Jesus Christ, and today's your lucky day. Got a ride for you," he said, and then walked off.

As soon as he was safely out of earshot, they both keeled over laughing. "What was that?" Kyle asked.

"Dunno," Michael said, "but wasn't that scary?"

"I've never been more afraid in my life."

Michael wasn't sure whether the guy was trying to be ironic or was some sort of armed roadside evangelist. In any case, he was wary of religious people after attending Catholic schools crawling with predatory priests. But, about ten minutes later, as they were packing away the last of their stuff, a blue four-door Corolla pulled up in front of them.

Jesus Christ leaned out the passenger window. "Here's your ride," he said, nodding at the disheveled, hollow-cheeked driver with dirty, lank hair. "He's going to Dillon, Montana, tonight."

"Man, that'd be great," Michael said. His twin, JP, the only sibling Michael erratically stayed in touch with, lived in Dillon, which was only a couple of hours' drive from Walter's house.

Kyle was a little reluctant, but after a moment, grabbed his pack and followed Michael and Tabor up to the car.

Michael thought Jesus's disciple looked like an old dopehead, and Jesus himself looked like he was getting ready to murder someone, but he figured, *What the hell . . . anything to get out of Idaho.*

Jesus's pit bull occupied most of the backseat and didn't look too happy to see them. He glared at Tabor through the car window, but she glared back, unflinching, from her perch in Michael's arms. She had a lot of dog friends in Portland, and Michael could only remember once when she hadn't liked a dog. That dog had learned to stay clear of Tabor. But now that she was a badass road cat, even pit bulls didn't scare her.

Jesus pushed the dog up into the front seat and swept his arms over the backseat to clear it of empty energy drink cans and candy bar wrappers. A dirty glass pipe was lying on the floor.

As they loaded their gear into the car, Michael said half-jokingly, "So are you gonna kill us or give us a ride?"

"We're not gonna kill you. But if you wanna ride, you gotta hustle," Jesus said. The guns were for protection, he explained, since he usually traveled alone. He had to cover the weapons with the burlap top in order to get into Walmart.

Jesus was just hitching a lift back to his own car, which he'd left two blocks away outside a huge monolithic white church. The tall neon-blue cross on top of the church shone like a beacon in the fading early-evening light. A gleaming mint-green, vintage Cadillac was parked in front. The license plate read: JC.

"Creepy," Michael mouthed silently to Kyle.

As they glided up next to the Caddy, Jesus said, "My friend here will get you where you need to go." Then he and his pit bull got out of the car.

After Jesus and his hellhound left, the guy twisted around to talk to them over the front seat, asking the usual stuff, where they were from and about the cat, and mumbling bits about himself. He claimed to be a farmer working in Idaho and heading back to Montana to visit his wife.

He didn't look like one. Michael was sure he was a meth head—he had a tick, bloodshot eyes, and messed-up teeth—and they had some three hundred miles ahead of them. Michael told him they had been stuck in Mountain Home for nearly a week, but that their last ride had given them some weed.

The tweaker got excited about the weed. "We can all have a smoke first," he said, his eyes darting furtively around the backseat. His manic intensity reminded Michael of a local addict he knew in Portland who'd snuck into people's gardens and cut poppy plants open to get the seeds for opium.

Michael handed the tweaker the nearly empty jar. He rolled and lit up a fat joint, took several long puffs, spilling ash across himself, and then passed it back to him and Kyle.

"Blow all the smoke outside," Michael said to Kyle, reaching over him to open his window. "I don't want a stoned cat."

After they finished the joint, Kyle moved up to the passenger seat, and Jesus's drug-fiend apostle screeched away. He raced over back roads through the rolling farmland of white-tufted potato fields before accelerating onto the highway.

Thirty miles out of Mountain Home, the guy realized that he only had a third of a tank of gas left and would have to drive through mostly desert, so he made a hasty U-turn and went back into town to fill up. When he returned to the two-lane highway, he weaved recklessly around trucks and other vehicles. Michael gripped Tabor closely, even though she dozed away on his lap somehow undisturbed by all the swerving and the smell of burning tires.

"You know Jesus was homeless, too," the tweaker said, looking at Michael in the rearview mirror. "He was out in the desert for forty-four nights."

"I'm the guy who's out here 24/7," Michael said. "Not that I'm comparing myself to Jesus or whatever you believe in, but I've been out here for forty-thousand frickin' nights for sure."

The tweaker turned his head around to face Michael in the back as he drove. "I think, like sheep, we've all gone astray."

"Look out," Kyle shouted, "there's a rabbit."

Instead of avoiding the animal, the tweaker deliberately swerved toward it, crossing lanes on the dark highway. When he spotted another rabbit on the other side of the road, he steered toward it, with a jerky swing of the wheel, to try to hit it.

As someone who had hitched alone over thousands of miles, Michael relied on his instincts and had rarely felt in danger. But once his buzz wore off, he thought, *What the hell was I thinking?*

Kyle was sure that he was going to kill them, and seeing how scared he looked, Michael said, "Hey, you want me to take a stretch at the wheel? So you can rest?" He hadn't driven in years, after getting a couple of DUIs in both Montana and Missouri, but he wanted to prevent the tweaker from killing the local wildlife—and all of them.

The tweaker seemed relieved, slammed on the brakes, and skidded onto the gravel shoulder, leaving the car running. He got out of the car, crawled into the back, and collapsed across the backseat. Michael handed Tabor over to Kyle, then slid into the driver's seat. Sitting behind the steering wheel felt awkward at first, like something from a past life, but he slowly merged back onto the lonely two-lane black highway and drove the last two hundred miles through the desert.

The drive took him back to the only family holiday he ever

had, one summer in the mid-1970s, driving with his parents, his sister, and his three brothers in a VW van through the muggy South. They'd driven through Louisiana's moonlit bayou country to wake up in the Florida sunshine at dawn. When they'd left Missouri behind, it seemed like everything ahead might be better, but when they arrived, nothing had changed: his mother was still severe and his father distant. But he had never forgotten the feeling, the promise that travel could somehow change things.

Along the I-15 freeway, the mountainous Idaho desert turned into high plains and then into forests of beautiful centuries-old trees as they crossed the Montana state line. Moths flickered in the headlights. Kyle held Tabor asleep on his lap, her paws and whiskers twitching, as she dreamed her adventure-cat dreams. A warm wind drifted through the window.

Michael turned on the radio to Bruce Springsteen's "Devils & Dust," a mournful, meditative tune that somehow at one in the morning sounded surprisingly happy. It felt good, like what a family road trip should be like, at least if you ignored the meth addict passed out in the backseat.

Shifting over to the MT-41 highway, they rolled into Dillon, a pretty little prairie town in southwestern Montana's cattle country. It was still too early in the morning to drop in on his brother, and JP had no room for them to stay, anyway. He had two cats of his own, a sick wife, and enough troubles. So Michael pulled over outside the Native American historical museum, across the road from JP's house. He put Tabor in her carrier, and he and Kyle gathered up their packs, shook the tweaker awake, and thanked him.

They waved good-bye, watching the taillights of the car fade away. Michael shouldered his pack and picked up Tabor's carrier, and he and Kyle staggered along the side of the road, ragged and worn. They decided to sleep out under the stars, on a patch of green near the museum, where Michael had camped out before. They had to climb over a fence, but there was a ladder on both sides.

Once they were over the fence, Michael clipped on Tabor's leash and let her out of her carrier and down on the grass. With Tabor slinking alongside them, they walked to a huge, hollowed-out oak tree. "We can sleep here," Michael said, looking up at the crescent moon. "And in the morning, we'll hitch a lift to Helena."

They dropped their packs and unrolled their sleeping bags next to some dense, trampled-down bushes. Michael put Tabor back in her carrier as Kyle kicked off his shoes and conked out on top of his bedroll as though he'd been dropped out of the sky. He was asleep instantly. Michael lay in his sleeping bag, listening to Tabor snoring in her mobile home beside his head.

Gazing up at the moon, Michael thought about what the tweaker had said: like those sheep in the Bible, Michael had gone astray. He'd been running away his whole life. He knew where this fury and restlessness came from, but not how to deal with it. For the past ten years, he'd thought of himself as essentially being alone, and he'd spent a lot of time feeling lost, constantly longing to be someplace else.

Now, with Tabor at his side, he wanted to leave the past behind and to live again, not drift like a ghost across the country. Tabor reminded him what an amazing feeling it was being with someone you cared about and the way it changed how you felt about everything.

The moon was so bright that it lit the splashy-red Indian paintbrush flowers that crowded around the tree beside him. Michael was wired and couldn't sleep. He sat up in his sleeping bag to light a cigarette, thinking they should pass by JP's in the morning, since he lived across the road. Michael fell in and out of sleep beside the hollowed-out tree. At one point, he heard hooting and looked up to see a huge, great horned owl. In the stillness, he could hear coyotes howling in the distance and small night creatures scurrying in the underbrush.

By the time Michael drifted back to sleep it was already getting light. Soon after Tabor started meowing to wake them. Michael and Kyle got up, gathered their gear, and walked across the road to JP's. They met up with him and his partner, and some of their friends who lived in the same little apartment building. Afterward Michael got JP to drop them off in the pasture where he'd camped once before on previous visits.

They were on the last stretch home to Walter—and a long, relaxing break away from everything.

Chapter 18

Black Magic Woman

In Portland, Ron gazed out the bay window of his living room. It was a beautiful weekend in early June. The sycamores were full of crows, and the magnolia was in bloom. A warm breeze blew in through the open windows and screened porch door, making the gauzy white curtains billow like sails, and scattered petals across the pavement.

Ron normally felt a thrill at the first flush of summer, but now he rarely left the house except to go to work at his guitar store and to shop for food at the corner store. He had become self-absorbed and solitary, often with only the cats for company. His friends—who were throwing barbecues, going to music festivals, open-air movies in Berkeley Park, and weekends away on the coast—kept trying to get him to come out. His friend Evan had actually persuaded Ron to go out that night to Pok Pok, Ron's favorite Thai restaurant, which was a few blocks away on Division Street, Portland's buzzing culinary hub.

After finishing his weekend shopping and cleaning, Ron was hit by what he called the black wave. To lighten his dark mood, he tried to make himself get up to go to the park to get some fresh air and mix with the summer crowds, but he barely made it around the block. He wasted the whole afternoon slouching on the sofa and listening to 92.3 FM, the classic rock station. But Bonnie Tyler wailing away about a heartache, terrorizing him and the cat over the radio, didn't help his mood.

"Is this really music?" he asked Creto, who'd buried himself deep in the folds of the sofa.

He needed to do something to make it to the evening when Evan would arrive.

Just at the right moment, Jim slipped through the screen door with his rusty meow and bits of leaves sticking to his tail. Jim sometimes pulled the porch screen door open with his claws—a trick that he'd taught Mata and Creto—so that they could sneak out of the house whenever they wanted. Ron calculated that between the first and second time Mata had disappeared, she had been gone for a total of fifteen months, and she was only three years old. Ron picked up Jim and stroked him, disentangling the leaves from his tail, as he purred away.

On the couch beside him, Creto was sprawled out grooming himself, balling up one small white paw into a little fist like a boxer, licking it, and then stuffing it into his ears. Usually Ron thought it was the funniest thing, but lately, Creto had started over-grooming himself, stripping the fur off his belly and the back of his legs. He looked like he had mange, but he had a feline anxiety disorder and was suffering from the loss of his sister. The vet prescribed various remedies and skin oils, but nothing worked. Since Mata had disappeared, Creto spent most of his time following Ron around the house and garden, and he waited mournfully on the porch every night for his sister to come home.

After nine months, Ron had not given up on Mata. Her loss still consumed him. He missed and mourned her daily—all the quirky little things she did: the way she draped herself around his shoulders when he sat at his desk; when she sat under the propped-up cat-flap using it as an umbrella when it rained; and how she liked extra-virgin olive oil and drank it out of an espresso cup with her paw. Everywhere he looked held a memory of her. Whenever Steve was out and Ron was home alone, the black wave crashed over him. Some days he hid in his attic sanctuary to cry in peace. He didn't want his friends to see how depressed he'd become, to judge him, or to say things like "It's only a cat" or "Why don't you get another one?"

A few days earlier, Ron had called Rachel, the psychic, again and left her a message explaining that he had a nagging feeling his cat was out there somewhere, and it was driving him mad. When Rachel returned his call a day later, she said that she had had a dream so strong that it had left her with a debilitating twenty-four-hour migraine.

In that dream, she said, "Mata came to me from paradise. She told me that she's quite happy there. She wants me to tell you that she loves you very much, misses you, and not to worry about her. She also said that her life with you was wonderful as short of a time as it was. But there are things that Mata doesn't want me to tell you, like the details of how she passed away or where her corpse is."

Ron listened quietly, but all he could hear were the words *passed away* and *corpse* and his heart thumping in his ears. "Oh, my God," he said, freaked out. "I'm sorry, I've gotta go." Deeply distressed, he immediately rang Suzy. They hadn't spoken since Jack had moved away and vandalized his house and car. Ron relayed what the psychic told him, but Suzy reiterated what she told him months ago, that she and Jack were away for the Labor Day weekend.

Despite Rachel's premonition, Ron couldn't shake off the feeling that Mata was still alive.

As evening fell, Ron became strangely overexcited and jittery. He tried to calm himself down and remembered the story his grandmother had told him, passed down the generations, of how during the Civil War families had left candles in the windows for the return of soldiers who had left to fight. Like the glow of a lighthouse, the candles guided the war-ravaged men through the darkness to the safety of home. Since he could only find one half-melted candle in the house, he went to the corner grocer and bought a couple of dozen red votive candles, and he put them around the house, on windowsills, and the glass coffee table in the living room.

He lit the votive candles, and soon every space and surface was glowing red. As Ron was finishing, Evan came to the front door. Creto, who was now wary and suspicious of everyone and every noise, heard him before he even had walked up the porch and pushed open the screen door, and scrambled to get behind Ron, alerting him.

"My God," said Evan, a slight, small-boned guy with short coppery-brown hair, a pale Irish-mist complexion, and arms inked with girly butterfly tattoos. He stood in the doorway, surveying the living room, stifling a laugh. "It looks like the house from *The Exorcist*. Are you trying to burn it down?"

"Funny," Ron replied, breaking into a half-smile.

"Wouldn't it be more sensible to go across the road and set that miserable bastard's house on fire . . . preferably with him in it?"

Evan was always good for a laugh. Before moving to New York and becoming a photographer, he'd worked for a British tabloid and wrote the captions beneath the half-naked Page Three girls, things like DELICIOUS DEBBIE . . . SHE'S GOT BIG TITS. Ron called him "international man of mystery" and was drawn to him for his quick wit and quirkiness—he'd say things like: "They've chosen the new Bond and he's only got one eyebrow."

"And since when have you become such a mystic?"

"Since my life's been ruined," Ron said, picking up and cuddling Creto. "I just miss her so much."

"Look, I know you miss her," Evan said sympathetically, and slid down on the sofa arm beside Ron. "But this is a little crazy."

"Creto misses her, too. He won't come in at night, and I hear mewling on the porch," Ron said, setting down the cat, who curled into a black ball of fur on the sofa. "Look at him. He's going bald and he's half the cat he was. He creeps around the house and hides in the mattress, where he's dug out a little hole for himself. Whenever the doorbell rings, he disappears into the basement. It's so dank down there, but he pulled an old blanket off the shelf and made himself a nest. He never goes on little adventures or visits the neighbors like he used to. The only thing that makes him happy is mint gelato."

"You feed the cat mint ice cream?"

"Yeah, he loves it," Ron replied, distracted. "Maybe I need to find a cat whisperer."

"For Creto?"

"No, someone who can communicate with animals to help find Mata."

"Have you lost your mind?"

"Yes, I think I have. The not knowing is killing me," he said, and then proceeded to tell Evan about a dream he had the previous night in which he was lost inside a decaying old, cobwebby mansion sealed up like a time capsule, following a cat's shadow up endless stairs. "The higher the floors, the more dilapidated and mysterious it is. Somehow, I end up outside in this wooded area that's apocalyptic. There's mud everywhere, and Creto and I are looking for Mata. In the distance, I keep seeing an emaciated little cat with bleeding paws trying to find her way back home through the woods."

"Burning candles isn't going to bring her back. And you have to prepare yourself that she might be dead."

"*Stop*," Ron snapped, "she's not dead."

Evan, seeing the despair in his eyes, gave Ron a big hug. He loved Mata, too, but he was increasingly worried about Ron's sanity. "I'm sure she's having an adventure out there in the blue yonder," Evan said, humoring him.

Chapter 19

Dillon, Montana: Holy Cow

It was the tenth of June, one of those hazy summer days when the air is still and the sky burning blue. Outside the city limits of Dillon, Michael, Tabor, and Kyle were trying to get to Helena but were following dusty desolate roads that led nowhere. By midday, the only other signs of life in the heat-shimmering emptiness were a jackrabbit scurrying into scrubby brush and a pack of wild turkeys slinking out of the dried yellow grass to peck the ground.

They passed a lone red barn back on a quiet country lane with a rickety sign nailed to the gate: TRESPASSERS WILL BE CRUSHED TO DEATH.

Kyle laughed and said, "That's a bit harsh." He leaned his long, rangy frame against the gate, beads of sweat dripping down his face. "I can't walk anymore. My feet are covered in blisters."

Beyond the sign, the lane was overrun with scraggly brush and frilly, white clusters of giant hogweed. Past the barn was a rambling wreck of a farmhouse surrounded by cottonwood trees.

"C'mon," Michael said, turning. "Just a few more steps until we find some shade trees."

"No, I *can't*," Kyle moaned, slumping down on a patch of soft, cushiony green moss, exhausted from the heat and heaviness of his pack. "I feel like my feet are bleeding into my shoes."

"Don't touch the hogweed. It'll give you a rash like poison ivy."

Michael kept on moving, and finally Kyle got to his feet and followed, lagging behind, sulking and staring at the ground. They were both worn-out and irritable, but even when they argued they'd get over it a little while later. Kyle liked to say their friendship was like a river: you could throw stones in it causing a ripple, even a huge splash, but it would always keep flowing.

The cat was cranky, too, and had been complaining for a couple of miles from her perch on top of Michael's backpack. "She needs lunch," Michael said as they walked past the fields. "When she gets too hot and hungry, she gets into a temper like a tiger."

Kyle froze midstride and his face turned bright red. "Oh, God!" he said.

Michael turned around, exasperated, "What's wrong now? Has your foot fallen off?"

"There's a huge snake crawling out of the grass."

Michael stopped walking and looked back. "What shape is its head?"

"*What?* Triangle. And it's hissing at me."

"Poisonous snakes usually have triangular heads."

"You're kidding, right?"

"No, I'm deadly serious. But if it hasn't attached itself to your leg, you're all right. A few harmless snakes have triangular heads, too. And some of them mimic the poisonous ones."

Michael walked back to see for himself, without getting himself or Tabor too close. The snake was beige with brown blotches. "It's just a prairie rattler," he said. "They're not aggressive, you just startled it. Just stay calm and back away slowly."

Kyle stepped backward, took a wide detour around the snake, and started running as if he were on hot coals.

"That snake looks small to me. It's just a juvenile," Michael said when he caught up to Kyle. "It's the babies that are the deadliest if they bite you because they haven't yet learned to regulate the venom in their bite."

"Why does everything out here wanna kill you?"

"It doesn't. There are actually very few animals that can kill you. It's pretty straightforward: you leave them alone and they'll leave you alone. Rattlesnakes are actually quite beautiful and vital members of the community."

Kyle looked at Michael like he was insane. "I'm happy to never see another snake."

They climbed over a fence and into a hilly meadow where Michael had camped the previous summer on his way to Walter's house. Passing a stone cattle trough, Michael put Tabor down on the ground, then bent over the trough and splashed water on his face. Scooping a few handfuls, he then smoothed down Tabor's coat to cool her off a little. She seemed to like it and calmly stood beside the trough, purring.

Michael led them to his secret place, a shady spot where they collapsed beneath a row of blossoming cottonwood trees whose silvery-white branches trailed down to the ground. He unpacked some of their gear and changed Tabor's leash to the long lead, tethering it to the strap on his pack so she could roam a little but not run off.

A few hundred yards in the distance, a lone cow showed up on the crest of a hill. Then a couple more joined her. Every time Michael glanced up after digging through his bag for the cat's dishes, a new one had appeared.

Kyle got out the radio and a deck of cards to kill some time before they moved on. "How about playing a loser deal, five-

DILLON, MONTANA: HOLY COW   167

card draw or something? Whoever loses deals the next hand. There's no money or anything."

"That's handy 'cause I don't have any," said Michael. He scooped Tabor's Fancy Feast chicken lunch into her bowl and started riffling for his tobacco pouch.

"Or we can play for pennies," Kyle added, taking a handful of copper out of his bag. "Look, I found one with your birth date on it . . . 1916."

But Michael was miles away, thinking back to the warm summer nights when he and Mercer held all-night poker games with a revolving group of regulars at their home in St. Louis. For a while, they shared their three-bedroom apartment with another guy, and sometimes the place was like a flophouse, with a bunch of others crashing and all sorts of drugs floating around. Michael liked to say he and Mercer were partners in grime.

"I'm gonna teach you how to play poker properly," Michael said, rolling himself a cigarette.

"Cool," Kyle said, half listening. He'd begun trying to make peanut butter sandwiches for them from the scrapings of a virtually empty Skippy jar. "Where'd you learn to play?"

"Montana."

"From Walter?"

"Noooo," Michael said, firing his roll-up. "I learned to play when I was sixteen. I was a dealer in a private game in someone's house. It didn't hurt that I could mix cocktails, too. When Mercer and I lived in St. Louis, we started a poker game every Sunday night. We had some famous people come by, one of the Hiltons. He was a friend of our old landlord, and he wasn't a good player, either. We thought we'd make some money, but Hilton was a cheap motherfucker. He'd lose twenty-five dollars and get out of the game. I walked away from that table seven times out of ten a winner."

"Were you hustling everybody?"

"No, I just knew how to play. When I was seventeen, I was dealing blackjack in a casino in Montana. And I knew how to figure out which ones were the weakest players."

Michael started dealing the cards. As he paused to put out his cigarette, he looked back over his shoulder and noticed that even more cows had joined the herd on the hill.

But Tabor was the first to sense that the herd's mood was changing. She looked up from her dish toward the hill, and her eyes widened and her ears flicked back and forth. Her tail swelled out into a brush, and the fur along her back stood up, making her look like a spiky porcupine, and she snarled. She was badly spooked and started growling and spitting like she was possessed.

"Holy shit," Michael said when he looked over his shoulder again. The herd was big now and restless. The leaders in front were stabbing their horns downward and staring in their direction. It was early summer—calving season—when cows can be territorial and protective of their young. Michael knew, having worked on a dairy farm, that if cows were staring intensely in your direction, you could bet they were coming your way. And these were longhorns, not the more placid dairy cows he'd worked with.

Michael scrambled to his feet as the herd started moving down the hill toward them. He stepped on Tabor's leash before she could bolt to the end of it, shrugged on his backpack and, in the next second, the cat went crazy. She tried to tear out of her collar, bit the leash, and threw herself on the ground, pulling, bucking, and kicking angrily like a tiny wild mustang. When Michael tried to pick her up, she latched her claws onto his forearm and tore a huge gash. He could barely keep hold of her.

"We've gotta make a run for it," he shouted to Kyle, clutching the cat in his arms again. "Just pack up as fast as you can."

"What the hell?" Kyle said, freezing momentarily, like a startled woodland creature. Their stuff was spilled out everywhere. He grabbed and packed frantically, wedging everything into his bag, but some items fell out as fast as he crammed them in.

Suddenly the ground shook. Dozens of rangy longhorns were scrambling down the hill through the trees, getting closer. A large, swelling herd was lowing and scraping, surging toward them, kicking up the earth.

Gripping Tabor protectively, Michael urged Kyle to hurry and then ran toward a dense grove of cottonwoods, thinking the cows wouldn't want to risk getting tangled in the trees. Tabor was screaming and clawing, trying to escape his arms and jump up into the branches. Her little heart was racing. Terrified, she bit down on his wrist and then dug her claws into him again, raking both of his hands badly. But he felt no pain. He was too scared about dropping her and losing her under the trampling hooves.

Now about fifty yards away, the cows were rapidly closing in on them. Michael worried that they wouldn't make it to the fence and out of the pasture. Kyle was catching up to them and was almost on his heels when Michael remembered the fat guy who had charged the bear in Yosemite. He yelled back to Kyle: "Run at them and wave your arms and scream at the top of your lungs. Keep doing it until they back off."

Kyle didn't like the idea, but he made a short run at the cows, waving his arms back and forth and shouting halfheartedly. The herd stopped short. Some even retreated long enough for Michael and Tabor to run from the grove to the fence. Then the herd started moving toward Kyle again.

"These frickin' cows won't stop!" Kyle shouted.

"Just keep doing it!" Michael yelled back. "When they back off, move to the edge of the field, and then run like hell."

Kyle continued shouting and screaming until the cows dispersed, little by little.

Michael threw his pack over the fence and then climbed over with Tabor. "Come on, hurry," he called out to Kyle, a blur of flying hair and limbs, now barreling through the grove.

Kyle reached the fence, dropped his pack, and wriggled through a hole in the fence. He didn't have time to struggle to climb over it. He got scratched up by the thorny blackberry brambles and nettles, but reached back to pull his pack through, too. As he stumbled into the road, he staggered beneath the weight of his heavy pack and fell over.

Some of the larger cows were still agitated and had followed them all the way to the fence. They were now angrily pushing against it, determined to get to them for invading their territory. Michael stood back from the fence, Tabor clinging to his chest like a burr. He wiped his bleeding hands on his olive-green T-shirt and beige canvas trousers, which were already smudged with beer, dirt, and grass stains.

Slumping over to catch his breath, Kyle was flushed and shaking. A city kid, he'd rarely left Portland.

"Here, hold Tabor for a sec," Michael said, pushing the cat into Kyle's arms. "I don't wanna mess up her fur." He took out his water bottle and washed the blood and dirt off his hands. Then he went to a nearby pine tree and scraped goopy, honey-colored liquid from its bark and smeared it all over his arm and hands.

"Whaddaya doing?" Kyle asked.

"You'll never be cut out for country life," Michael said, grinning. "It's pine sap to stanch the bleeding and disinfect the wounds. It's what injured trees produce to protect themselves from infection and insect invasions. You can also make moonshine out of it."

Looking at the slash that ran the length of Michael's arm from his wrist all the way up to his elbow, Kyle said, "That looks really nasty."

"Man, oh, man, does it hurt!"

"Those cows were so close I could've touched them."

"Yeah, that was a close call," Michael said, taking Tabor back.

"Poor Tabor," Kyle said. She was panting hard and drooling, still trembling in Michael's arms. "I didn't know cows could be that angry. What was that, Groundscore?"

"That was a stampede if I ever saw one. Lesson learned. If you see cow pies, head to another field." The cows could've easily killed them. In that moment Michael knew he would've laid down his life for Tabor in a heartbeat.

As they walked along the road to look for another field to camp in safely overnight, the cows kept pace with them on the other side of the fence.

. . . . .

The morning after the stampede, Michael, Kyle, and Tabor got a ride into downtown Helena. They arrived just as the sun was cresting the ridge of the Big Belt Mountains, lighting the empty streets' vintage storefronts in glimmers of pale-gold light. Last Chance Gulch, the main street and heart of town, was unchanged after decades, including the Parrot Confectionery with its century-old soda fountain, Dave's Pawn shop sparkling with antique gems and pistols, and the Fire Tower Coffee House with its glowing art deco Rock-Ola jukebox in the window.

Seeing all his old haunts, Michael was kind of excited to be back in his adopted hometown with his two best friends. Every building, every corner, and every little pathway along the four-block boulevard held memories, both good and bad. They passed the Montana Flea Market, where he had bought used paperbacks and which still had the same old sign from the '80s: LIFE'S TOO SHORT TO DRINK BAD WINE.

As they walked by Rock's Western Bar, Michael lifted Tabor to the window so she could look inside. "This is where I used to live," he said to her. "I used to go for a late-night beer and a game of pool after a long day's work and stay there until they chucked me out."

He felt a sense of pride about his work in Helena. "I used to deliver milk here. I was about your age," he told Kyle as they walked through the wide boulevard between Victorian gas lamps and turn-of-the-century rose-stone buildings, many built by gold and ranching money. "Wouldn't you have liked to know me back then," he said to the cat on his shoulder.

Tabor looked around curiously, peering at everything. Michael showed her and Kyle the federal courthouse, where Ted Kaczynski, the Unabomber, was tried after the FBI nabbed him in his hideout in a cabin out in the Montana woods.

Kyle wasn't familiar with that history, so Michael explained: "He was an American terrorist. He killed and crippled a load of people in the nineties. But he was smart. He wrote about how technology was dehumanizing people. And now you can see the old bastard was right."

When they reached the next block, Michael said, "Every spring I planted marigolds and dusty millers that spelled out 'Montana' outside the statehouse, which is not too far from here. I made enough money doing that to go camping pretty much all summer."

"You were a gardener?"

"Yeah . . . I had a business card that read MICHAEL KING, THE ROYAL GARDENER: ROYAL WORK FOR A MERE PITTANCE."

"Cool. Guess I always think of you as a city guy."

"I've always had a thing for plants and nature. When I was

seven years old, I used to pull up the tiger lilies that grew along the railway tracks and then replant them in our backyard."

Michael paused and pointed at the gargoyles and winged lizards perched on top of the imposing gray-stone building on the next corner. "See that? That's a magic salamander that can't be destroyed by fire. The two dragons beside it protect it. The town has burned to the ground many times. So the city included those symbols to ward off fires. The salamander, in the occult, is thought to be an alchemical creature that can live in fire. And see the statue of the man on the building? That's the Titan Atlas, the Greek god who carried the world on his back."

Leaving downtown, they wandered along Euclid Avenue past low wood-frame houses in neat little rows that all looked the same. They turned onto a side street and walked a few blocks over to Walter's house. They were in the foothills of the Rocky Mountains, below Helena's historic Mansion District, a five-mile stretch of graceful Victorian mansions along a hillside, which overlooked downtown Helena. When they reached a modest yellow-and-white clapboard cottage, Walter's place, at the corner of a peaceful cul-de-sac, Michael started around to the back door, and Kyle followed. Behind a square sliver of yard, a fleet of old cars and a rusting pickup blocked the patchy grass and weedy dirt alleyway. As Michael crossed the backyard, he noticed that the sunflowers he had planted last summer in a border on one side of the chain-link fence had grown into giants. Their lovely, lionlike heads were turned skyward.

"Walter," he shouted, letting himself in the screen door and holding it for Kyle. Country music drifted from the stereo.

Tall and stooping, Walter stepped from the living room into the kitchen. Now in his seventies, he had a shock of white hair, silver-rimmed eyeglasses, and a permanent frown on his face. Retired and living alone, he had the heavy look of a kindhearted man worn down by life. When he saw Michael with the cat clinging on to his shoulder like a caterpillar, he couldn't believe his eyes.

"Is that a cat?" he asked, looking at Michael as though he'd grown two heads. "You walked across America with a cat on your back? That's crazy. Just plain crazy."

"I found her on the street. She was hurt and starving."

Walter looked him up and down—the dirt, blood, grass stains on his clothes and his crusty, scarred, scratched-up arms that looked as if he'd been clawed by a grizzly. "You look like shit," he said, and walked out of the room.

"Thanks," Michael said, gazing after him.

Setting Tabor down on the kitchen floor, Michael looked at Kyle and sighed. "I'm sorry, Walter's in one of his moods. And don't call me Groundscore in front of Walter. He *hates* it. To him it just means being homeless, drunken, and sleeping under a tree." Though Walter could be grumpy he had a sharp sense of humor. Once, when Michael posted a picture of himself on Facebook, panhandling, with his cardboard sign: COULD USE A LITTLE HELP TODAY, Walter commented, MICHAEL YOU NEED MORE THAN A LITTLE HELP. YOU NEED A LOT OF HELP!

Like Michael, Walter had a soft spot for animals and had once filled his home with stray cats, injured birds, and other wounded creatures. He still put out leftover food for raccoons. After returning from the Vietnam War in 1967, animals became his refuge from the stresses and horrors of war. Animals had also helped him stay sober for thirty-eight years. When he first met Michael at AA, he told him, "Anyone who's on the down-and-out heals himself with animals."

Kyle sat down at the kitchen table with a tired sigh and looked around. The kitchen had a down-home coziness, pine cupboards bursting with mismatched dishes, and a line of dusty copper mugs hanging above the windows, which overlooked the backyard. The double-door fridge was covered in a mosaic of sun-faded *Vote for Obama* and *Ready for Hillary* stickers, a magnet of an American flag, with a *God Bless America* caption, and a frayed postcard of a yawning otter floating on his back. Above the kitchen table, pictures of Michael and his twin brother, JP, when they were seventeen years old, hung on the wall, along with photos of Elliot, a fifteen-year-old Korean American orphan whom Walter had adopted after Michael left home.

Michael walked over to the fridge and got out a can of Mountain Dew for Kyle. Then he followed Walter into the living room. The cozy room had a wood-burning stove, handcrafted wooden furniture, and worn scatter rugs. Tabor trotted in casually behind him. And then she froze in her tracks at the sight of another cat on the sofa.

Walter had a large smoky-gray blue-eyed Himalayan named Gus, who, seeing a strange cat in his house, hissed and swished his powder-puff tail. With his flat face and frowning mouth, the fluffy tom looked like a hairy little old man. Tabor scrabbled up Michael's leg onto his shoulder, where she stared down at Gus from the safety of her perch. Gus leaped off the sofa and ran down the stairs to Walter's bedroom, his usual hiding place.

Walter sat in a distressed, mustard-yellow recliner, with his back turned to Michael, where he had been enjoying his morning cup of Nescafé and the soothing, sorrowful tones of Johnny Cash before they had arrived.

"Are you mad at me?" Michael asked, cradling Tabor in his arms. "Have I done something wrong?"

Walter hesitated and huffed, "Well, for a start, you've upset Gus. I don't hear from you for ages, and then you show up with another cat."

"Sorry. I've been traveling and trying to look after the cat."

"You could've picked up the phone and called me. What, have you lost the use of your hands?"

"I know. I know. You're right . . . and I'm sorry—"

"I don't wanna another cat," Walter cut him short. "I'm in my retirement now."

"But I'm not trying to dump her on you." Over the years, Michael had rescued countless strays and taken them home to Walter's. As a teen, he had brought home barn kittens in his pockets and named them Sassy and Kassy. It was Walter who taught Michael how to raise cats, and Sassy and Kassy had grown into huge, happy adults.

"When Gus dies, I'll bury him in the yard next to Sassy and Kassy, and that'll be my last cat."

Gus, whom Walter sometimes called "my old buddy," was now a skittish thirteen-year-old. Michael had found him, too, one summer twelve years ago. Walter had also adopted and fed a feral, outdoor cat, a massive tom he named Michael who, once arriving in Walter's backyard, never left. He would come by the back steps outside the kitchen door for his twice-daily takeouts, though he preferred to sleep under the porch or a bush.

"I swear, we're just visiting."

"I don't want that cat upsetting Gus," Walter went on. "He hates change and gets easily upset by just about everything."

"But Tabor's really laid-back, and she gets along with other cats."

"I don't care," Walter said in a voice as dry as dust. "When you have an animal, I don't care whether it's a dog, cat, parrot, or bear; it's a real commitment."

"I know," Michael said. "And I'm trying."

Kyle appeared in the doorway. "It's true," he said, trying to stick up for his friend. "Michael takes good care of her. You should've seen Tabor when he found her."

Walter eased up. "I know Michael has a soft spot in his heart for cats. We had cats and kittens running around the house everywhere. Michael was in seventh heaven. He'd stand out here in the backyard and toss 'em on the roof of the garage, and they'd turn around and jump down on him. It was a circus out there.

"Anyhow, I got Gus in the house. He's an old man now, and I don't want to take any chances. We better take that cat to the vet first thing. There's no telling what mites, ticks, and diseases she might've picked up on your travels."

"She's fine," Michael protested. "Tabor doesn't have any diseases."

"I don't want Gus catching any diseases," Walter shot back, as barbed as a scorpion. "He's old and he's fragile."

"But Tabor's perfectly healthy."

"You're making a mountain out of a molehill," he said firmly. "She's gotta go to the vet."

"Okay," Michael agreed, before wandering back into the kitchen with Kyle. There was no arguing with Walter.

Chapter 20

Portland: A Summer Storm and Full Moon

It was nighttime, and storm clouds were gathering over the rooftops of Northwest Portland. A flash of lightning streaked across the sky. Beneath a garish Tiffany ceiling lamp in a neon-lit parlor, a small, bent old lady with coiffed white hair sat on a plastic-lined armchair as if it were a throne. This was Madeleine, a psychic who had a reputation for finding lost animals, at least according to her ad in the back of *Cat Fancy* magazine. Blue light filtered through her storefront window from the giant neon hand that advertised her tarot reading and other otherworldly services. The parlor walls were lined with gilt-framed paintings of saints, and every surface was covered with crystals, Celtic runes, and the clutter of mysticism and spirituality.

Ron perched on a couch across from Madeleine, a small card table between them. Evan had accompanied him but gone outside for a moment. Ron told Madeleine about Mata and that on the last morning he'd seen her, she'd sat on the kitchen counter and watched him scramble eggs, then gone outside to sit on the porch to catch some sun.

"Some days I just can't stop crying," he said, glancing out the big window, seeing the rain start to pelt down and people rushing home to their lives. "The hardest part is dealing with the lack of closure. I can't move on."

Madeleine pointed at the window to the shadowy trees outside. "You see how the moon is barely visible? People and animals can be like that, too, hidden behind others."

"Hidden?" Ron looked confused. "What are you saying?"

"I'm saying sometimes the clues are all around us, in dreams or in our instincts, for example."

Evan came back inside and sat beside Ron. He'd gone outside because he needed to laugh after noticing the psychic's troweled-on makeup, which looked as if it had been flung on with a spoon, and at the ridiculousness of it all. When Ron had asked him to come along on this visit, he'd said, "You need a therapist, not a psychic. The spirit world is a big fat lie."

Madeleine stared intently at Ron. "I can see this unresolved grief is hurting your soul."

"Yeah, it is," he said, staring at a painting of the Sacred Heart Christ with his chest bursting with flames. He felt it, too, that burning of a broken heart. "The pain just won't go away."

"You have to let yourself heal," she said in low, calming voice. She paused and, with her eyes fixed on Ron, asked, "What is your psychic feeling about your lost cat?"

"That's what he's paying you for," Evan muttered under his breath.

Ron shot him an annoyed glance. "I don't know. I'm hoping that some little old lady found her and Mata's bringing joy to someone else's life, but I know there are bad people out there who do terrible things to animals. Ever since I spoke to Rachel, the psychic who told me that Mata was dead, I can't think of anything else."

"A psychic told you your cat was dead?" she said, frowning.

"The way she described heaven was straight out of Ezekiel and Revelation and exactly as I imagined it: a tropical paradise."

"So she said your dead cat has gone to a tropical island?"

"Yup, to this tropical paradise where people and animals alike are happy. It even says in the Bible, 'God loves his animals and you'll be with your animals in heaven.'" Ron stopped and took a deep breath. "I just need to know if Mata's still alive."

Madeleine clasped her hands over her chest. "I know deep in my bones that your cat's not dead." She laid a weathered deck of tarot cards on the little card table between them. "I want you to shuffle the deck and choose the first card that presents itself to you."

Ron shuffled the deck and chose a card. When Madeleine turned it over, Ron saw that it was the Hanged Man, and the color drained from his face. "Oh, God, does that mean she's been strangled?"

"This card is telling you you're at a crossroads. You have to let go, and the angels will help you. Everything you release will either be washed away from you or returned to you, healed.

"Now, at this point in a session, people usually give me pictures of their missing pet, and I look into their pets' eyes to connect with them and try to find out where they are."

Ron pulled a dog-eared snapshot from his wallet and handed it to her. "Here's a picture of Mata."

Madeleine leaned across the table, sparkling like a gaudy chandelier in her multicolored jewels. "With a summer storm and a full moon, there's a lot of electricity in the air, so it should be easier to reach your cat."

She lit the white and black candles, drew a pentagon on the

dark felt cloth table in front of them, and put Mata's photo in the circle. "Okay, I'll tell you what I see," she began. "I can feel that your cat's anxious. She knows that you and her brother have been missing her."

Closing her eyes, she traced her finger across the cat's photograph. "I can see a cat walking through the desert. She's not alone. It looks like there's someone with her who's trying to keep her out of harm's way. She's a long, long way from home, but she's trying to find her way back to you."

Chapter 21

Helena, Montana:
Mysteries of a Feline Heart

On the morning of June 13, two days after their arrival in Helena, Walter drove them to the vet in his old white Subaru sedan. Kyle rode shotgun, and Michael sat slumped in the backseat with Tabor, who was pretty chill as usual, curled up on his lap, her slender forepaws stretched out, happily watching the view of sky and pines roll past.

But Michael was worried. The moment he had awakened that morning, after tossing and turning all night, he'd had a terrible intuition that he was going to lose Tabor.

As they parked outside the vet, Michael caught his reflection in the side mirror. The lines around his mouth had deepened, and the bags beneath his eyes had gone black. He was starting to look like Bela Lugosi, he thought.

The Helena Veterinary Service was housed in a white-and-blue ski chalet–type building with a giant paw-print logo out front. Michael didn't say anything about his fear to Walter or Kyle, but when they entered the vet's office, Tabor was on edge now, too. Kyle waited in the reception area while Michael and Walter took her in to be examined.

The consultation room smelled of disinfectant. When Michael put Tabor down on the stainless-steel table, her little body tensed and she tried to jump off. Michael caught her midair, but she managed to slip out of his hands and bolt to the corner of the room, where she tried to squeeze herself into a shallow open drawer of a medicine cabinet.

The vet, a soft-spoken man with thinning, gray-flecked blond hair, chubby cheeks, and nerdy glasses, carefully pulled her out of the drawer. "It's okay, sweetheart," he said, patting her reassuringly. "It's okay."

Dr. Bruce Armstrong had been Walter's vet for more than fifteen years. Before settling in Montana to set up his own practice, he had worked all over the world helping animals, from a wildlife refuge in California to relief work in Saudi Arabia. He also had a small horse ranch outside of Helena, with his wife, where they grew hay and alfalfa.

Dr. Armstrong asked about Tabor's history, and Michael told him about finding her under a table on the street in the rain, living on the beach, and escaping a cattle stampede. The vet smiled as he continued to pet Mata on the table.

"Sounds like she's had quite an adventure." Addressing the cat, his voice dropped to a whisper. "Let's take a look at you, young lady, and make sure you're doing okay."

He felt Tabor's joints and put a small stethoscope to her heart. "She's in great shape. You've obviously taken very good care of her," he said, and pried her mouth open to look at her teeth. "I'd say she's between two and four years old." Then he placed her on the scale. His brow furrowed. "She's twelve pounds, a little overweight for her frame."

Michael laughed. "Yup, she's a little chunky," he said, stroking her head. "That's because she's lazy and wants to be carried everywhere. But I figured a little extra weight couldn't hurt her, since we live outside."

"We should get her vaccines all caught up," Walter said.

Dr. Armstrong nodded and whisked her off the table to be vaccinated in the back room. Slung over the vet's shoulder, Tabor shot Michael a look of betrayal.

They were in the back room for what seemed like eternity to Michael. He sensed something was wrong.

When Dr. Armstrong reemerged with Tabor in his arms, he had an odd expression on his face. "She's now up to date with her shots," he said, putting her back on the exam table between them. "But there's another issue."

"Is she okay?" Michael asked, immediately alarmed.

"She has a microchip."

"Heck, I knew it," Walter said, grinning.

Michael stood there, thunderstruck. "A *chip*?"

"Yes, she has an owner," Dr. Armstrong said. "She was reported missing in Portland in September 2012."

Michael felt his heart shatter. His eyes welled up, and he excused himself and walked out of the exam room, through the reception and out the front door. He was heartbroken and angry at the same time. He needed to smoke a cigarette and pull himself together.

When Kyle saw Michael sweeping through the waiting area, he knew something was wrong, too, and thought, *Oh no, Michael's gonna lose Tabor.*

Walter put Tabor back in her carrier and looked at the vet. "Mike's homeless, and it's tough. He's gotten very attached to the cat."

Dr. Armstrong wrote down the telephone numbers associated with the identification chip and gave them to Walter. Then he asked Walter if he could tell the local paper about Michael and Tabor's journey, as it may inspire more people to microchip their pets. Walter thought it might also help Michael to come to terms with losing Tabor to tell their story of traveling together.

Then Walter took Tabor out to rejoin Michael and Kyle and take them home.

Shortly after they left the clinic, the veterinary technician, Maddie Parker, who had scanned Tabor and called the microchip company after finding the chip, called the number for her owner and left a message on Ron Buss's answering machine that the Helena Veterinary clinic wanted to speak to him.

Chapter 22

Astral Weeks

The water was so clear you could actually see fish and turtles swimming beneath the surface. Mata was propped up beside Ron on the wooden seat of a little rowboat, watching the water rippling. Suddenly she grew anxious. She flashed her teeth, hissed and screeched, then scrambled down to hide under Ron's legs. Peering over the boat's edge, Ron could see a dark, bulky shadow. As they drifted toward the shore, he saw that it was a crocodile gliding in the reeds and shallows.

Ron screamed, gripping the cat.

Ron jolted awake out of his scary dream. The sun was streaming through his bedroom windows through the half-open blinds. He lay motionless for a while, blinking sleepily at the streaky light coming in and splashing across the walls. Then he got up and made his way to the kitchen to give the cats breakfast. Creto and Jim sat on the counter next to a glass bowl overflowing with oranges, peaches, and grapefruits, meowing impatiently.

After they were fed, Ron made himself a peach-and-orange smoothie and put on the radio, sending the sounds of the '60s into the street. Settling into the breakfast nook, Ron sat in a daze listening to the Easybeats' catchy 1966 mod classic "Friday on My Mind." Then, straining to remember his dream, he called Miguel, out on the coast.

"I always see Mata by the water and in the woods," he said to Miguel, telling him about his nightmare. "I still sense she's alive, either lost or someone has her. Do you think he might've drowned her and then buried her in the woods by the river—"

"Look, you need to stop analyzing dreams," said Miguel curtly. "It means nothing."

"Yeah, you're right," Ron said, to placate his friend. He was exhausting his friends' sympathy. "I have a million things to do this morning. I need to food shop, water the garden . . . and I need to start thinking about what to pack."

Ron had been invited to the memorial for a friend in Texas the next weekend. The previous summer he'd befriended some rock 'n' roll guys in a group called Ministry from Austin, Texas, through his guitar business. A multiplatinum-selling '90s industrial-metal band, many of their members had been well-known for their life of excess, hardcore drinking and drugging, so it wasn't a surprise when their guitar player collapsed onstage and died of a heart attack at the age of forty-seven. Six months later, the surviving band members were throwing a party to celebrate his life.

Ron got off the phone, slipped a Ministry CD into the kitchen stereo, propped open the back door with a cast-iron statue of a Sphinx, and went out into the backyard. Creto and Jim were already splayed out on top of the garage, sunbathing. Gordon, his neighbor Ann's cat, a tough-looking, yellow-eyed black tom, was up there with them—the garage rooftop was like a tomcat sun-worshippers social-club hub. Ron unraveled the garden hose as Ministry's "Jesus Built My Hotrod" blasted out of the kitchen.

While watering the strawberry plants and raspberry bushes, Ron remembered how Mata went mad for the smell of strawberries. She would roll around in the strawberry patch with her legs up in the air, sniffing and rubbing her head against the strawberry flowers and leaves as though they were catnip. Afterward she'd zoom around the house the way she did after a whiff of catnip.

It was already noon by the time Ron came back inside the kitchen, clutching a bunch of inky purple anemones he'd picked. As he arranged the flowers in a vase in the breakfast nook, he noticed the red light blinking on his BlackBerry. He had two missed calls, one from his sister and another from an unfamiliar area code.

It was a call from a vet in Helena, Montana, telling him his cat had been found. Ron burst into tears as he pressed the callback number. He spoke to Dr. Armstrong, who explained that a homeless man who had been visiting his foster dad had brought in the cat for a checkup, and they had scanned her as they do routinely with strays.

"I can't believe Mata's in Helena, Montana," Ron said, smiling, tears running down his face. "This is the craziest thing I've ever heard. What's your address? Can I come get her now?"

"It's not our responsibility to hold the cat if we find out it belongs to somebody," Dr. Armstrong said, "just to inform you. The person who has her now says he wants to bring the cat back. I have his foster dad's number."

Ron dialed the Montana number that the vet gave him, but there was no answer. He would try again a little later.

He was ecstatic and overwhelmed. After visiting Madeleine, the psychic, something had shifted in Ron. He had registered Creto as a therapy cat, as he'd planned months ago after seeing the poster for the "lost alpaca" with the fuzzy Phil Spector Afro, so he could take him around to hospital patients to spread a little happiness.

The previous weekend, Ron had been tinkering with his guitars in the attic, listening to a marathon of Van Morrison, and when "Astral Weeks" came on, he felt shivers down his arms. It was as though the lyrics about venturing into the slipstream and being born again were a portal into a wider truth.

When Mata had disappeared the first time, Ron, in his desperation, asked for God's help and made a promise that if he brought her back, he would become a better person and help others. But he had conveniently forgotten his promises, and she had vanished again. That night, and every night after, he said a little prayer before going to bed asking God to keep Mata safe wherever she was.

Now, it seemed, Ron's prayers for her return were being answered. He looked out the kitchen window, distracted, his eyes drifting toward the pristine blue sky, remembering why he thought Mata's return this time, like the last, was divine intervention. He'd been visiting his old friend Joe in Bakersfield, California. Joe had moved to Seattle and had been shot during a robbery while working as a security guard. He'd slipped into a coma for a long time and, when he came out, claimed God sat with him and held his hand during the entire time. Ron was at Joe's house when he got the call from the microchip company the first time Mata strayed.

After canceling his flight to Texas, Ron posted a picture of Mata, lying on her back, with her eyes half-shut and glinting in the sunlight, on his Facebook page and typed a quick caption: *Missing since Labor Day 2012, my beloved Mata has been found in Helena, Montana.*

His happiness and sense of relief were exhilarating, like kicking open a fire door to escape a burning building. He rushed next door to tell Ann, on his way shouting out to the sunbathing cats on the garage: "Mata's coming home, boys." The three little cat heads popped up and stared down at him sleepily.

Afterward he tumbled down on the back porch steps, calling everyone, Mata's vet, his childhood friend Randy, Miguel, his father, and Evan, telling them what the Montana vet had told him.

"So a homeless guy took her to Montana?" Evan asked.

"Well, the psychic did say Mata was a long way from home on an adventure."

"What could she possibly know? That woman was a hundred years old and almost blinded by mascara."

"Mata's very smart and her inquisitiveness gets her in trouble," Ron carried on. "Sometimes she's followed little old ladies down the street after they petted her. But out of all the homeless people in the world, she found the greatest one she could get."

Chapter 23

The Most Beautiful Girl

Walter looked out the kitchen window at Michael sitting on a stack of logs against the back of the garage in the backyard, chain-smoking. Tabor was playing in the dry grass, batting her paw at the twilight moths, blissfully unaware that her life was about to change again. The vet had given them Tabor's owner's phone number, and Walter had given it to Michael. Now it was up to Michael to call.

Ten months earlier, Michael hadn't wanted a cat, and now he couldn't imagine living without her. For a long time before Tabor came into his life he had felt like he was living for nothing and hardly cared about anything. His life had been ripped apart when he lost Mercer, but this little cat had helped him start putting the pieces back together. Tabor chased away some of the loneliness that shadowed him like a dark cloud. He'd started to feel somewhat normal again. She filled his days with warmth and laughter. Before he found Tabor, he had been consumed by negative thoughts. But she had quieted the bad thoughts long enough to let in a glimmer of hope.

Kyle came outside, pausing to light a half-smoked roll-up.

He shook out the match and flopped down on the back steps across the yard from Michael. "I was checking my Facebook on Walter's computer and someone posted a video of a stumbling drunk raccoon that broke into a warehouse full of booze. Everyone's been saying it's probably Michael in a raccoon suit."

Michael glanced over with a faint smile but didn't say anything.

Kyle could see he wasn't in the mood for jokes. "It's a bummer about Tabor," he said sympathetically.

"It did cross my mind. You know what? I had this sixth sense when we walked into that vet. The first thing I'm thinking, *If that cat has a fucking chip, I'll be pissed*. And she had a chip."

"Maybe you should just keep her."

"I can't. It's not right. She deserves to go home." Michael knew he could easily hit the road and disappear, like he always did. He could pretend the trip to the vet never happened. *He lost her. I found her*. But Michael also knew he'd be desperate if Tabor suddenly disappeared. The last thing he wanted was to cause somebody else that kind of pain.

They both watched Tabor leaping after the moths and fireflies. "She's so sweet and mellow," Michael said wistfully. "My first thought every morning is why is this cat tugging at my beard and licking my eyelids?"

"Remember whenever we walked down Hawthorne the way she used to jump back and forth from your pack to Stinson's?"

"Yeah, that was awesome. Sometimes I felt like a ship in the ocean walking around with a full-grown cat swaying on my pack. I'm stumbling around and people are looking at me, and I wanted to say, *No, I'm not drunk. The cat's just moving around*."

Walter had been watching them through the screen door and, after a few minutes, came out to join them.

"I know this is tough," Walter said, crossing the small yard to put a hand on Michael's shoulder. "Sad times, but not all sad . . . The cat's going home. I'm happy to make the call if you like."

Michael nodded. He pulled the piece of paper out of his pocket and handed it back to Walter. "But I want to take her back myself. Have one last trip with her."

The fading light turned the backyard violet. The faint sounds of Charlie Rich's "The Most Beautiful Girl" drifted from the '60s coffin-box stereo console inside the house. Michael thought it sounded like the saddest song in the world.

∗ ∗ ∗ ∗

Later that night, Walter made himself a tonic and lime and put Dean Martin on the stereo. The old grandfather clock ticked.

Michael sat slumped on the couch, thinking how lucky he was to have Walter. He admired his resilience and his ability to be alone—he'd have his tonic and put on his music, and all was well with the world.

Then Walter reclined in his ragged, old yellow easy chair, which had been scratched to the bone by all his cats. Tabor came into the room and, springing onto the coffee table, leaped into Michael's lap. Gus lounged on his usual spot on the back of Walter's armchair, sharpening his nails and keeping a watchful eye on the intruder in his house.

Walter picked up the phone and dialed the Portland number. "Hello, is that Ron Buss?" he said. "I think we got your cat here."

"Oh, my God, I'm so glad you called," Ron shouted at the other end. "I got a message from the vet in Montana, who told me you'd brought her in. I'm so grateful, thank you. I can come get her now if it's convenient."

Walter looked across the room at Michael and Tabor. She was nuzzling her face against his beard, and he tenderly stroked her while staring straight ahead in a daze.

"I knew it! I knew she was still alive. I could feel it," Ron carried on excitedly.

"Mike, my son, found him on the street, and they've been traveling together across the West Coast. We took him to my vet for his shots and, well, it was a big surprise that he had a home. But, heck, I was happy."

Michael forced a little smile. It was amusing the way Walter kept referring to Tabor as him.

"Mike feels terrible about taking the cat," Walter went on, "and wants to bring him back home."

"You honestly don't have to go through all the trouble," Ron said, sounding a little wary. The microchip came with insurance that would cover Ron's airfare. "I can fly there tomorrow and pick her up myself."

"It's no trouble at all," Walter cut in. "Mike's heading back that way anyway. He sometimes lives in Portland, where he found the cat. He'd like to take one last trip with the cat. They've spent the last ten months together. Leaving him so abruptly would be too hard for both of them."

Walter sensed Ron's reluctance and attempted to put him at ease by telling him Michael's story. "Mike's a good man. He's got a big heart. Rest assured, he'll bring her back to you. I can vouch for that."

Ron had been silent on the other end of the line as Walter spoke. Then, he said, "Um, sure. I'm just over the moon and so unbelievably happy and grateful she's okay. If Mike wants to bring her back, that's fine."

After Walter had hung up, Michael got up from the couch and went into his bedroom. Tabor stood, too, stretching and yawning, gave him a little mew, and trotted after him. He turned on the computer and posted a Facebook message for his Portland friends: *Just took Tabor to vet. She has a chip in her and the owners are going to take her back. Sad, sad day for Groundscore.* He immediately got a lot of commiserations but couldn't even read them. He went to bed, Tabor tucked in next to him.

·   ·   ·   ·

The next morning scattered clouds drifted overhead, warning of rain. Michael, flushed from sleep and dazed, woke completely disoriented. Hearing Dean Martin crooning like a rooster, he thought he was in some old-timey Italian restaurant. It took a moment for him to remember that he was at Walter's, and Walter was an early riser. Seeing his eyes open, Tabor, who was lying on the pillow beside his head, jumped on his chest and started meowing and tugging at his beard.

Michael got up and felt like the walking dead. He stumbled to the kitchen with Tabor snapping at his heels, tangling herself around his legs. Meowing in her whiny, raspy voice, she demanded to be fed. Michael said good morning to Walter, who was standing at the window with his mug of coffee. He dished out Tabor's breakfast and then he joined Walter at the kitchen window, where they looked out onto the backyard. A ragged blue jay with disheveled feathers had been coming into the yard and perching on the bird feeder. Walter liked to keep an eye out for him and the other wildlife that paraded through his back garden.

Taking a sip of coffee, Walter read the sky. "Looks like a thunderstorm's sweeping in," he said, and turned his head to meet Michael's gaze. "You don't want to be caught in the storm with a cat."

Early summer in Montana was the tail end of the rainy season. Weather changes could be sudden and dramatic. Michael knew they should stay, at least until the rain stopped, and he found comfort in the thought that he would keep Tabor a little longer.

Michael nodded and turned back to make breakfast, huckleberry and buttermilk pancakes for Walter and Kyle. The three of them sat in the kitchen drinking black coffee and listening to the thunderstorm breaking outside and to Johnny Cash's prison blues streaming in from the living room stereo.

Since they would be staying at least a day or two longer, before taking the cat back to Portland, Michael spent the morning scrubbing the house and fixing little things. Walter usually saved all kinds of housekeeping jobs for Michael to do, which turned out to be just about everything. Walter never lifted a broom or ran a vacuum, although he watered and mowed the lawn and fed the birds, rabbits, squirrels, and deer that came to dine on the daily feast of bread, nuts, and seeds that he left out for them.

After Michael had finished, Walter took Michael and Kyle shopping and insisted on buying both of them new backpacks and sleeping bags. Walter was fond of saying, "We're supposed to take care of the downtrodden and protect them." While in Vietnam, he and some of his fellow soldiers stumbled across an orphanage and leper colony and marched straight in and starting helping patients.

By the afternoon, when the clouds cleared and the sun broke through, Michael wanted to show Kyle around Helena and take an overnight trip camping in the Helena National Forest, on the outskirts of the city. They had planned to visit for a couple of weeks, but now getting Tabor back home had become his priority.

Before they went into Helena, Michael gave Ron a call to reassure him. "I'm really sorry I took the cat," he said, after introducing himself. "The last thing in the world I wanted was a cat, but I knew I had to help her. I know you don't know me, but I really want to backpack and have one last adventure before I bring her back to you. I'm going to have a cell phone, and I'll try to call you every day to let you know where we are. It's just really important that we have this one last trip together. You have to trust me."

"Oh, absolutely, I do," Ron replied, and he did. He sensed Michael's sincerity and could just feel it in his voice.

After hanging up, Michael posted another Facebook update: *We talked to Tabor's owner, really nice guy. Leaving Montana by Tuesday, I will be giving Tabor (Madda) when I'm there. Don't be sad, it's time for celebration, Tabor's going home.*

A short drive from Walter's, the Helena National Forest surrounds the east, west, and south sides of the city. After driving along the curving mountain roads that wound through densely wooded hills about fifteen miles outside Helena, Michael pulled over on a high bluff on the edge of the road where they could go on a hike.

Surrounded by the big, blue western sky and the Big Belt Mountains, they walked across a swath of farmland, crossing over a barbwire fence, to climb to the top of a large hill. Tabor clambered up the steep, flower-choked slope on her lead, as sure-footed as a little mountain goat, pausing to sniff mouse burrows and paw the wispy heads of dandelions.

Usually when they were walking together, Michael would point out different types of birds, trees, and flowers to Kyle, but he was subdued and distracted. Halfway up the hill, Michael picked up Tabor and turned around to go back to the car, while Kyle continued the rest of the hike.

Twenty minutes later, when Kyle walked back across the field, Michael was sitting on the hood of the car, Tabor nestled beside him, wistfully looking at the peaceful piney valley below. Michael was marveling at how he and Tabor seemed to sense each other's moods and feelings. He would do anything for this sweet little cat, and he wondered how he was going to cope once

she was gone. She filled nearly all his waking hours with an un-
conditional love that he hadn't known he needed.

Tabor had been half-asleep in the sun but suddenly sprang to
her feet, her ears and whiskers flickering, on the hood when she
heard Kyle crunching gravel as he approached the car.

Kyle was out of breath from the hike and said, "I found
these three piles of stones on the hill. I took a picture," showing
Michael his phone. "They were sort of arranged in a row . . .
knee-high piles of stones that looked like shrines."

"They probably are," Michael said, and went silent for a
moment. "This is where I hit a deer about twenty-five years ago.
I was heading home after finishing someone's garden. And this
buck came running out of nowhere, and I hit him. He was a
mess and screaming like a baby, lying across the road with one
of his legs broken. I had to slit his throat with my pocket knife."

Kyle looked a little shocked. "Couldn't you take him to a vet?"

"He was in very bad condition," he explained, clearly disturbed by the memory. "You can't imagine how upset I was to
take someone's life like that. I went on a bender for three days."

Afterward Michael hauled their things out of the car. He had
packed some food, water, and beer. He hadn't had a drink since
being at Walter's. He led them to a place where he had camped
before, along the banks of a stream, nestled in the middle of a
canyon.

They found a spot near the creek, cocooned by spruce, aspen,
and lodgepole pines, and unrolled their sleeping bags. Michael
always felt at home among the trees—and sleeping under the
sheltering pines and star-filled skies of the Montana woods was
like nowhere else. And the sharp, luxuriant scents of spruce and
sage were intoxicating. It stirred up good memories of when he
was working as a gardener and had sometimes made enough
money to spend much of the summer camping.

Just before dusk, as the sun faded into the trees, they got out the radio and deck of cards. When it got too dark, Michael made a fire and they continued playing by the firelight. Tabor was dreamily immersed watching fireflies, swiping at them without leaving Michael's lap. Afterward Michael grilled up some burgers, potatoes, beans, and greens and whipped up a little feast. But he didn't enjoy any of it. For him, it felt like the Last Supper. For a long while, with Tabor between them, Kyle and Michael sat silently huddled around the campfire, watching it burn down.

Michael was inconsolably sad. Kyle didn't quite know what to say to take away his pain. He'd grown fond of Tabor, too, and dreaded the thought of parting with her. They banked the fire and took to their sleeping bags, Tabor nestling in with Michael with a rumbling purr.

Waking the next morning, Michael fed Tabor and left her lying on his sleeping bag in a stream of sunlight that filtered through the sky-skimming trees. He wanted to enjoy every moment with Tabor while he could, but he had a keen sense of sadness as he prepared mentally to lose his best friend, his road trip buddy.

As he was riffling through their supplies to brew some coffee and fix them some breakfast, Michael caught sight of something dark and furry dipping in and out of view behind the pines on the other side of the creek.

"Oh, my God," Michael said to himself quietly, "there's a bear down by the creek."

Tabor saw it, too, her eyes large. She sniffed the air, her head shifting side to side, and peered curiously at the dark, fuzzy shape darting through the trees. Michael called it her "ole 'I smell a bear' look." But while Michael was getting anxious, Tabor remained calm and unruffled, watching. Having become a seasoned bear wrangler, she seemed to know this bear was not trouble.

The bear saw Michael and shot up a tree. His fur, shimmering in the light, was as black and shiny as onyx. He was mesmerizing, but much smaller and cuter than the brown bear that they encountered at Yosemite—not really an adult or a cub, but somewhere in between.

"We'll have to leave," Michael said to Kyle, who was tying his shoelaces. "If there's a juvenile bear prowling the neighborhood, I'm sure he's got a mother, too." While there was a kind of unexpected thrill in running into a bear in the woods, he decided he ought to get Kyle and Tabor back to Walter's.

Chapter 24

The Cat Was a Rainbow
in a Dark World

On Saturday afternoon, when Michael, Kyle, and Tabor got back to Walter's after camping, an elegant older gentleman sporting a silver walrus mustache was sitting at the kitchen table with Walter.

Walter was telling him the story of how he and Michael had met at AA in the fall of 1981. As the three of them came through the back door, Michael and Kyle caught the tail end of their conversation: "Michael was traveling through Helena at the time, and that started the journey."

Then, looking up at Michael, he said, "This gentleman's here to see you from the newspaper." He got up, excusing himself by saying, "And I've got a hungry cat." Gus was squalling grumpily in the living room doorway, and Walter got his food from the cupboard and filled his little porcelain cat dish on the counter.

The mustachioed staff reporter was Al Knauber, from Helena's *Independent Record*. He stood up and shook hands with Michael. He had heard the story about Michael and the traveling cat from the Helena vet and wanted to talk to Michael before he and Tabor left town.

Kyle went outside to the garden for a smoke. Tabor leaped onto the kitchen table and collapsed on her side, purring, blissed-out and beat from her adventure.

"She's worn-out. My friend Kyle and I took her camping up in the mountains," Michael said, and then told the story of finding her. "I see cats all the time. I didn't pick her up because I wanted a cat. She was wet, scared, thin."

He looked at Tabor spilled across the table, her beautiful, fluffy chrysanthemum head drooping over the edge, her slanted eyes, half-closed, watching him sleepily, and choked up.

"I really needed the companionship," he said, his eyes welling up. "I'm homeless. Depression is a big thing out there. The cat was a rainbow in a dark world."

Michael paused as Gus walked out and then back into the kitchen. "She's going to go back home where she belongs," he said after a moment. "It's going to be a sad day. There's going to be six or seven men crying the day I give her away. I've grown attached to her. My pack will be twenty pounds lighter, but a big hole, a big hole."

After their talk, Michael walked Al Knauber out to the front door to say good-bye. Tabor lifted her head drowsily and meowed, her eyes following Michael as he left the room. Soon afterward he checked his Facebook and saw that the cat's owner Ron had sent him a message: *Check out Mata's baby photos, Mike, on my photo album* MATA PLEASE COME HOME. *Time to roll out the welcome carpet and celebrate.*

Michael wrote back, *Hi Ron, the local paper came to my dad's today, they wanted a scoop. The story will be in Monday's paper, the Helena Independent Record.*

Ron replied back, *Thanks Mike, They already called me and I talked to them this morning. Looking forward to reading it.*

Before he even had a chance to have a good look at Tabor and her four littermates' kitten pictures, the doorbell rang. It was the photographer from the *Independent Record*. Tall, lean, and clean-shaven with short, curly blond hair and sparkly blue eyes, Dylan Brown was usually the only Saturday photographer working for the town newspaper and had to dash from story to story. Walter let him in, and Tabor trotted in from the kitchen to join Michael in the living room.

As Brown hurriedly snapped a few shots of Michael with Tabor, he was immediately struck by the deep affection between the man and the cat.

Tabor loved the fuss, prancing and posing in the glow of the flash.

"I love this cat," Michael said, beaming at her with his broken-toothed smile. "I don't even think I should be in the pictures. Everyone wants to see the cat. Not a dirty old bum like me." As if on cue, Tabor jumped on the TV stand right in front of Brown and stared directly into the camera, her eucalyptus-green eyes warm and soulful.

Two days later, on Monday, June 17, 2013, that was the shot that appeared in the *Helena Independent Record*, beneath the headline THE CAT WAS A RAINBOW IN A DARK WORLD.

. . . .

On that Monday morning, Michael sat at the kitchen table and flipped through the paper to find the article about himself and Tabor. He showed it to Walter, who was hunched over the counter making coffee.

"Tabor looks so beautiful," he said, and as he continued reading, he was a little stunned when he found out the cat had jumped in the back of a car and Ron got her back six months later. "Oooh, this makes me mad," he added. "She's done this before."

Just as he said this, Tabor shot into the kitchen, scurrying across the tiles, kicking around a plastic water-bottle top between her paws. Kyle followed after her, lugging his backpack.

"I'm glad they used that picture of her," Michael said, showing it to Kyle.

Peering over his shoulder, Kyle laughed. "They blurred you out in the background."

"That's exactly what I was hoping for."

"Mornin'," Walter said to Kyle, and set out a pot of coffee and a stack of waffles on the table in front of them.

They ate and sipped their coffee in silence. Tabor ran around their feet until she tired herself out. She sprang up onto the table and slumped onto her side. Walter got up and started making sandwiches for them for the road. He had also offered to take them to the nearest highway.

Michael had had a vivid dream. "I dreamed about these two elk," he began telling Kyle. "It was the same dream I had when I stayed at Walter's the winter before I got Tabor. It had snowed that night. I look out the window and I see two big female elk lying in the snow pack against the house. I see them getting down in the bedding, and then I went to sleep. Next morning, leaning out of bed, I look outside again and see these elk shake off the snowflakes. As they walk out of the front yard, they start fading into rainbows and then turn into two Native American women dressed in buckskins."

"Were you drunk?" Kyle asked, grinning.

"You know I can't drink in Walter's house."

"Whaddaya think it meant?"

"I have no idea." Without a word, Michael got up, cleared

away the breakfast plates, and started loading their belongings into Walter's Subaru. He was itching to get going.

Just as Walter was wrapping up the sandwiches in brown waxed paper, the phone rang. Walter answered it and called out the back door to Michael, "It's Kathleen . . . your mother."

Michael came in and dutifully took the receiver. He could not remember the last time his mother had called him and wondered how she knew he was there. "Hi, Mom," he said into the receiver.

"Michael!" she shouted in her crisp English accent. "You're in the paper."

The story had been syndicated across the country.

"My neighbor saw you and the cat in the paper this morning," she said. "So you're returning the cat?"

"Um, yeah . . . today," he said, stumbling on his words. "I'm taking Tabor back to Portland . . . back to her owner."

"That's very nice of you, Michael."

It was the first positive thing she'd said to him in a long while. It felt good, though at the same time, he didn't need her approval. He had Kyle, Stinson, and an extended family of drifters across the American West. He had Walter, and, for the time being, he had a cat that he loved. They all gave him the warm, nurturing sense of family that he had never felt from his own family.

"Thanks," he said. "Well, we were just getting ready to leave."

"Okay, love. Have a safe trip back."

Hanging up, he turned to Kyle and Walter. "She saw the story in her local paper."

Walter grabbed his cup of coffee and the paper and went to his armchair in the living room to read the article. Gus trailed along.

Kyle looked at Michael quizzically and said, "I didn't know you were on speaking terms."

"I call her once in a while to check that she's okay," Michael said, looking away as he did when he didn't want to talk about something. "She's the only mother I've got. I have to forgive her. She's seventy-eight and all alone. I wasted a lot of time and energy hating her. Whatever she did to me, it doesn't matter anymore."

Walter came back in the kitchen and said, "Everybody has a story. It's what you do with your life after you've recognized the fact you've had a tough time," he went on. "There's no place for bitterness. I hated my dad. He was a loving man who came from Montana. He was the oldest of five, and his dad used to whip him. He brought into his marriage and family what he'd learned. When I stopped to look back many years later, I saw that he was nineteen years old when I was born and had five kids while he was still in his twenties. He was putting a roof over my head, food in my stomach, clothes on my back, sending me to Catholic school. Here I am bad-mouthing him when he'd done the best he could.

"When I sobered up and looked at what this man had accomplished, I was ashamed of myself. Michael's mother had a tough childhood, too. She had five kids, and Michael's father had to support them all on a policeman's wage. Of course she'd get frustrated like any normal person would. That's why I say you need to put all this stuff back into perspective: people are going to do what they need to survive."

Kyle shared his own story. "My mom had nine other children from seven different fathers," he said. "Never met her or even know what she looked like. I heard she passed away in 2007. One of my half brothers, who I accidentally met at a friend's house, told me that she was with some guy who shot her and then shot himself."

"I'm sorry about that," Michael said. "That's too bad."

"She was never part of my life, and, from what I hear, that's a good thing," Kyle said, leaning back in a mellow slouch in the chair. "So do you have a picture of your mother?"

Leaving Walter and Kyle at the kitchen table, Michael disappeared into his bedroom and brought out a yellowing photo album.

"That's my mother on their wedding day in London," Michael said, pointing to a black-and-white picture from the '50s of a smiling young couple outside an ancient, soot-covered graystone church. She wore a high-necked, cinch-waisted lace gown, with her hair swept up in a wave. Beside her was a rakish, boyishly handsome man in an army uniform, with thick and disheveled black hair and the same pale, gleaming eyes as Michael's.

Michael closed the album and took it back into his bedroom.

When Michael put the wedding album back under his bed, he flicked on the computer to have a quick look at his Facebook. He shared the *Independent Record* article about himself and Tabor so all his friends would be prepared for losing the cat before they got back to Portland.

While posting, he noticed a message from Ron from the night before: *Mata's definitely a rambler. Did my first newspaper interview readable online as of midnight. Go to Helena.air.com, it'll be front page news.*

He saw that Ron had posted a video, too, that morning and titled it "Mata Hairi 007." When he played the link he realized Tabor was on the news on KGW Channel 8, the local Portland television station. The picture of Tabor and Michael from the Helena *Independent Record* flashed across screen, with a ticker strip sliding at the bottom, announcing: THE RETURN OF MATA HAIRI.

A glossy-maned, fortysomething newswoman came on and said: "After an adventure all over the Northwest, a cat named

Mata Hairi is headed home. It doesn't get more Portland than this," she added, looking like she was trying to suppress a laugh. "Mata Hairi the cat was picked up by a wanderer in Portland who put a leash on her and took her all over the West Coast."

"She ended up in Montana," her male co-anchor cut in with a coat hanger smile, "and in a few days is headed home to Southeast Portland. Here our news anchor Erica spent the afternoon talking to the owner."

A willowy, blue-eyed, blond reporter, standing in downtown Portland, came on: "Mata Hairi, you guys, has a knack for getting lost and then getting found. A wanderer who goes by the name of Groundscore Mike says he found her near 38th and Hawthorne in Portland last September. He took her camping to Ventura, California, all the way to Yosemite, before ending up in Montana, where he took her to a vet and they scanned her for a microchip. The vet called the cat's owner in Portland."

A picture of Ron Buss with a beard (when he still had hair) sitting on a sofa and holding Mata and her black-and-white littermate flashed on screen. Then Ron himself appeared, saying: "She traveled thirty-five hundred miles with him. She went to Yosemite National Park with him . . . and, um, went camping all over the United States. I'm hoping she doesn't like him better than me when they get back," he added with a nervous laugh.

Erica, the pretty blond reporter, came back on: "Now, the cat is expected to be back this Wednesday or Thursday. By the way, this isn't Mata Hairi's first road trip. Two years ago, the cat ended up in Vancouver, Washington, after she went missing for six months."

Back at the television studio, the two newscasters were cracking jokes about the hitchhiking cat. "Somehow, you can't quite believe that story," said the glossy-maned newswoman.

Her grinning male co-anchor signed off with a raised eyebrow: "Well, catching mice will seem boring after that adventure."

"Catching mice ain't going to be the same again, that's for damn sure," Michael said aloud, and then posted those exact words to Ron, adding, *We still have to hitch-hike back to Portland!!!!*

Michael went back into the kitchen and told Walter and Kyle that he and Tabor were on television. His head was spinning a bit at the fact that they were all over the news in the Northwest.

* * * *

It was a perfect summer day, sapphire-blue sky, shimmering bright sunshine, when Walter dropped them off on the edge of town near the on-ramp to I-90. He hugged Michael and patted Kyle on the back warmly.

"Behave yourself," he said to Michael, and turning to Tabor, gently ruffled her fur. "Take care of him and make sure he gets home safe."

"I will," Michael said, grinning at Walter still referring to Tabor as a tomcat. He promised to call when they got to Portland.

As Walter drove away, the three of them waited by the side of the road. Kyle messed around with his skateboard, Michael chain-smoked furiously, and Tabor hunkered down on Michael's backpack, purring. Michael thought of how much he was going to miss her and all her funny little quirks: the way she licked his face to wake him; tugged at his beard when he tried to sleep in; and sometimes scooped her food with her paw. Thinking these things while she purred there beside him only made the prospect of losing her even more painful.

Less than ten minutes passed before they got a ride to Missoula. And there as soon as they flashed their sign, NEED RIDE TO PORTLAND, they got another one. A small light-blue compact car stopped for them, driven by two smiling Native American women with a little tawny-brown puppy that looked like a baby version of Madison's dog, Bobby, riding between them.

"Been there long?" the driver asked, rolling down her window.

"Wow, is that a cat?" said the woman in the passenger seat before they could answer.

They were heading north to Spokane, Washington, and offered to drive them all the way. As soon as Michael and Kyle hopped in the car, the driver, glancing back smiling, said, "We never see hitchhikers anymore."

Michael smiled back at her, thinking, *You don't see them because they're always getting rides.* Although they looked clean and less rumpled than usual after staying at Walter's, he was sure that Tabor was responsible for getting them the ride.

Sitting in the backseat, Michael looked at the back of the women's heads and leaned toward Kyle, wide-eyed, to whisper, "Remember the dream I told you about the two elk? Déjà vu or what?"

It took a minute to register, but then Kyle said quietly, "Wow. That's so weird."

The women were very chatty and friendly, asked about the cat, and offered to buy them something to eat, but Michael thanked them and told them they had already eaten.

With Tabor nuzzled on his lap, Michael stared out the window at the widening views of seamless sky and clouds swirling above the plains, slivers of light flitting through the pines, the white-tailed deer and elk grazing in the distance. He tried to enjoy this last adventure, since it was an extra-special trip, a sort of victory lap, but he just felt sad.

The woman in the passenger seat turned back and asked, "What're you gonna do once you take the cat back home?"

"Dunno," Michael said, hanging his head, unable to explain

the heartsickness that he felt. "It's gonna be hard because I've spent the last ten months with her in my lap. I don't want to stay in Portland crying about the cat. I'm thinking of disappearing in the woods in Prineville, Oregon, with some of my friends."

An hour into the ride, Kyle saw that Michael was anxious and wanted to get out of the car. Under normal circumstances, a long ride like this was like gold, but this one would have only cut down the time he had left with Tabor, and he wanted to prolong the journey home.

Finally Michael asked the women to be let out early in St. Regis, a tiny backwater hidden in the mountains on the edge of the western Montana wilderness—hours away from anything. He could see the flash of fear in the women's eyes after he asked them to stop in a remote wooded area before they'd even gotten to Idaho. They must've thought they'd picked up a pair of lunatics.

"Here?" the driver asked as she got off the highway to let them out. There was nothing in sight from the exit but dense fir forest.

"Yup, this is great," Michael said, grinning and swinging open the door. "Thank you." He sprang out of the car, pulled their stuff out, and scooped up Tabor.

The moment the women drove away, leaving them on a desolate country road near the exit ramp of the I-90, Kyle asked, "Whaddaya think it means when your dream becomes real?"

Michael didn't respond as he clipped on Tabor's leash and set her down to stretch her legs. She squatted on the side of the road to pee. After scratching the dirt around a bit, she leaped back up on Michael's pack.

Walking down the rural road, surrounded by gigantic pines, they saw a big yellow sign looming ahead, with a black image of a cow, warning: ENTERING OPEN RANGE. EXPECT COWS ON THE

ROAD. There was another yellow wildlife crossing sign with an image of a deer kicking a person.

Kyle looked around a little warily.

The sky was darkening, and swirls of purple clouds floated over the mountains. Summer thunderstorms in Montana were dramatic, but also dangerous, sometimes sparking forest fires. It started to drizzle, then turned into a downpour.

Tabor grumbled on Michael's shoulder—she hated getting wet, so he zipped her inside his hoodie with her head sticking out. Then, gripping her tightly, Michael ran across the wet, squishy grass, with Kyle following, to take cover under a freeway overpass. There they set up a small camp.

Michael gathered whatever twigs and branches he could find nearby and lit a small fire. Then he unrolled the new sleeping bags Walter had bought them, and they ate the packed sandwiches he had made them. Tabor immediately snuggled into Michael's bag.

It poured all day and all night—not a heavy, drenching Portland rain—but there was nowhere to go. So they stayed under the overpass beneath the roar of traffic, talking and listening to the distant rumbles of thunder breaking over the mountains. They also drank until the booze ran dry, having packed a family-size bottle of vodka for the road.

Michael was grateful for every minute he had with Tabor, who spent most of the time cozily cocooned, shifting between Michael and Kyle's sleeping bags.

"I've hardly told this to anyone," Michael began. "The night before Mercer died, I'm in the back bedroom, and the living room is over here on this side. I walk toward the kitchen, take a quick left, and it's where Mercer is in his hospice room. I'm sitting there tinkering with something, and I hear the floorboards creak and feel like someone has stepped into the room. When I look up, there's nothing there. All of a sudden, these three shadows float by. I nearly faint. The first guy had on glasses and a brimmed hat. The second was an old lady with curly hair. Then behind the old lady was a taller gentleman in a jacket. And I thought, *They're coming to say good-bye.* Mercer died the next day."

"That's pretty heavy."

"I told one of Mercer's sisters about it after the funeral, and she goes, 'Oh, that's Uncle So-and-So, that's Mom, and that's Dad.'"

"Whoa . . . you can't make that up."

"Yeah, that's why I don't like talking about this stuff. It's so crazy." Michael went quiet for a minute. "It hurts even for me to talk about—" He broke off shakily. Even mentioning Mercer's name felt like a betrayal of sorts.

Almost ten years after Mercer's death, and now faced with losing Tabor, Michael felt there was no way to get rid of the loss and emptiness. Under the freeway, he was plagued by night-mares. In one, it was shortly after Mercer's burial, and Michael was alone at their home in St. Louis, getting ready to leave for good. He wanted to talk to someone, so he called his mother and through sobs told her Mercer was gone.

As cars and trucks rumbled overhead, Michael snapped awake, shaken. The corner of his sleeping bag was damp with tears. Daylight was already fading, and he realized he must have slept away most of the morning and afternoon.

. . . . .

That second day under the overpass, Michael couldn't stop thinking about all the sad things that happened to him. He wished he could disappear. He stared in a daze at the falling rain, the wet road reflected with streaky car lights, smoking his roll-up while stroking Tabor with his other hand. Tabor looked into his eyes, picking up on the gloom settling in Michael. She got up from her nest in the sleeping bag, stretched her legs, and then snuggled closer.

As she moved onto his lap, mussing up her fur, he thought about their days under the tree in Ventura, the drowsy afternoons and dreamy sunsets. What stayed with him most was Tabor playing alone in the surf and her sweetness and he could hardly stand it. He knew no one else could understand his broken heart and the hollowness he felt. This cuddly little cat, with her sparkly personality, vivacity, and wholehearted friendship, had been like a furry salve, a great comfort—whisking away his anxiety and glum thoughts. Nothing would be the same without her warm and constant presence.

While Michael didn't hesitate for a second to return Tabor to her owner, deep down, he struggled between his conscience of doing the right thing and his profound love for her. He reflected again on what Walter had told him when he was a teenager and brought home sick and starving barn kittens: "In nourishing others we find ourselves."

But after a while, Michael wanted a drink to blot out his thoughts and emotions. When Tabor drifted back to sleep, he scooped her up and carefully tucked her into her mobile home. He looked over at Kyle, who was listening to the radio and playing a game of dice on his own.

He stood up and slipped on his hoodie. "I need to get some beer. . . . Be back in a bit," he said, and slunk away into the pouring rain. Kyle knew that he couldn't reason with Michael in one of his black moods.

Michael followed the road from the underpass, hoping to find a beer store, until he spotted a giant neon buffalo sign for a bar flickering red and white, advertising "poker, keno, and Miller Light."

Hours later, when he came back to their camp, Michael was completely wasted, and he had spent all their money—the entire eighty dollars.

· · · · ·

The following morning, they got up with the sun. The sky was a glorious blue and the air dense with the fresh, woodsy scents of pine and sage. As soon as they had packed up and moved from the underpass toward the on-ramp, they put out their PORTLAND, OREGON sign and managed to snag a ride. A young guy with tousled hair and a friendly face in a dusty compact car with Washington license plates stopped.

"You're in luck, I'm going to Seattle," he said as he jumped out and helped load their stuff.

He told Michael he had picked them up because he loved cats and took them all the way to downtown Seattle.

Four hundred miles later, when Michael finished telling him the whole story about Tabor, the guy said, "We'll just end your trip here, and I'll get you bus tickets to Portland so it's easier for you." He pulled over on the next junction, took out his phone and his credit card, and bought them tickets on the Greyhound. But when they got to the station, they found he'd paid for only one ticket.

Shrugging, Kyle told Michael, "Get on the bus, I'll figure it out." He waved to them and set off to find his own way back.

Deeply tired, Michael boarded the bus and settled into his seat, Tabor in her carrier on his lap. He was sick at heart but ready to finish their journey.

Chapter 25

The Long and Winding Road

Portland was in full bloom when Michael and Tabor returned on June 20. The green lushness, the heady scents of pine and roses, the fruit hanging on trees along the sidewalks, and the warm sultry nights could make even drifters feel like they were living the good life.

Arriving in the early evening at the Greyhound bus station downtown, Michael walked solemnly across the city, with Tabor slunk on his pack, his shoulders slumped, his eyes ringed with shadows. That feeling of hollow sadness that he had felt under the overpass stayed with him.

In the end, it took three days, four hitches, a gallon of vodka, a few six-packs, and a bus ride to get back to Portland.

He wandered through the orange glow of early-evening light, which took the edge away from everything. Downtown Portland was overrun with transients and junkies, kids on the run, and kids on the game. Great swaths of the city had turned into a sprawl of cardboard boxes, tents and shopping carts heaped with all their possessions. Homeless people moved in slow motion across Burnside Bridge.

Michael walked down Hawthorne, Tabor riding on his pack, passing the strip of art deco storefronts and eclectic cafés, book and record shops. In a doorway outside Crossroads Music store, a girl and a guy dressed in vintage threads, with an acoustic guitar and tambourine, were singing an indie-folk duet, aptly about traveling around the world. A few doors down, a handsome lone busker with long dark dreads and sharp cheekbones played an electric violin, churning out a moody, bluegrassy tune.

They were heading back to their old squat by the loading bay. It was a bittersweet return. He loved Portland, and the only reason he'd left was the harsh winters. But now it felt tainted and oppressive. As he made his way through the flow of summer tourists and friendly locals, he saw that most passersby still smiled at the cat. He spotted his name still in graffiti on the fire hydrant outside the supermarket where he, Kyle, and Stinson usually panhandled.

"Well, Tabor, we're here," he said, when they got to the bay. "Back in our first home."

The cat's eyes widened with wonder when she saw where they were. She flew off his shoulder, sniffing the air, prowling the bushes, and rubbing her cheek against everything to leave her scent, like she was reclaiming her lost kingdom. As Tabor sharpened her claws on the maple tree marking her territory, Michael thought back to the nights he was kept awake because she couldn't sleep, distracted by the streetlights and police sirens, and the way they had played hide-and-seek together, when she would vanish behind that tree or a bush, but with her tail poking out, thinking she was well hidden. He wondered whether cats recalled memories in the same way.

He gave her a tin of her favorite Fancy Feast chicken in gravy and then settled in the doorway to smoke. She grabbed a mouthful of food and dropped it by his feet to have company while she ate, then she licked her dish clean and finished the stray bite. She promptly fell asleep on his backpack with her tongue sticking out, which always made Michael smile.

The cat allowed him to touch another world and see beauty in the smallest things.

After her nap, they walked all the way down Hawthorne, even though it was dark. They found some friends, told them what happened, and camped out together in the park. Kyle had texted that he was on his way, and Ron had messaged Michael that he was going to give a homecoming party when they got back. Michael wanted to wait to give Tabor away when Kyle returned, and he wanted to go together with his friends.

·   ·   ·   ·

When he woke up the next morning, Michael called Ron to say they were in Portland and would come by at 3 p.m. Then, with Tabor riding on his shoulder, he returned to the UPS bay to wait for Kyle. He sat there the whole morning, smoking and feeling sorry for himself. Tabor seemed to sense his sadness and kept jumping back and forth from his lap to the backpack sitting beside him.

Kyle showed up by midmorning and found Michael slumped in the doorway staring down at the cat half snoozing in his lap. She had a paw across her eyes to keep out the sun. The light streamed around Michael like sun falling across a ruin.

"That didn't take long," Michael said. He was red eyed and rumpled.

"Yeah, it wasn't too bad. I called my dad and he got me a bus ticket back," Kyle said as he plunked down beside him. "You got a snipe?"

Michael pulled out a couple of cigarette butts from his pocket, lit them, and handed one to Kyle.

Michael took a long, pensive drag. "Damn the luck," he said, watching the drifting seam of blue smoke. "If I loved this cat any more, I'd blow up and die. Kyle, if you ever like a cat this much, I'm going to beat you up."

"I'll try to remember that."

They sat in silence until Tabor woke up. She stretched out her front legs, blinking sleepily, with her wide, lazy yawn, and pulled herself out of his lap. Then she looked up at Michael expectantly, as if to ask, "Where next?"

Michael set her on the ground and stood up, flinging on his pack. "Okay, Tabor," he said, scooping her up and swinging her into his arms. "Time to go."

Tabor melted into his chest with a loud purr, rumbling like a mini tugboat, ready as ever for a new adventure. Michael could barely feel the ground beneath his feet, knowing that this was their last fling and their time together would be over in hours.

The two men walked down Hawthorne to Colonel Summers Park and community gardens, to the old redbrick, military pavilion, where Stinson, Madison, Whip Kid, Jane, and their friends were waiting for them. Tabor seemed especially happy to see Stinson. She jumped on his shoulder and started pawing at his Medusa-like tangle of hair.

"I heard you guys got stuck in the desert in Idaho," he said to Kyle as he untangled a paw out of his hair and pulled Tabor into his arms.

"Yeah," Kyle said, "we were sitting on the side of the road for, like, twelve days and no one gave us a ride."

"*Seriously?*" Stinson let out a wild laugh. "I had hard luck for stretches before, like in Utah because of the police efforts to keep me out and, um, the quality of the traffic. But I'd commit suicide if I had to hitchhike for twelve days."

Michael flung himself down on the grass beside Madison

and Bobby, Whip Kid and Jane. They couldn't believe Michael was giving Tabor back. All of them wanted Michael to keep her.

Tabor was part of the gang, their small-community cat. This sunny little tabby had such a big spirit. She was the brightest ray of light in their lives.

But when it was time, they all grabbed their packs to make an entourage for Michael, who carried Tabor in his arms. They wanted to support Michael, but they were also expecting a party, with some free food and booze. Yet the entire way to Ron's house, the homeless kids kept trying to persuade Michael to keep the cat.

"Let's turn around now," Stinson said, flanking him on one side, Kyle on the other. Madison, Whip Kid, Jane, another friend, and three dogs followed behind. "I mean, you've had her for almost a year. She's basically yours."

"I could've been the jack-off that said, 'No, I'm keeping the cat' and hitchhike out to the East Coast," Michael said, staring straight ahead. "But she's not my cat."

Whip Kid came alongside them. "But, Groundscore, we were on Hawthorne for three months with the cat," he protested. "We carried her around for all that time, and he never saw it. He doesn't deserve that cat."

Kyle tried to reason with them; he saw that they were only upsetting Michael. "I'm not sure Michael could keep the cat even if he wanted to now that the whole world knows about it," he said. "The story is all over the papers, and on the television."

"You can't own a cat, anyway," Michael said. "I'm just the caretaker, making sure she has a safe passage home."

Sensing his unease and the tension around her, Tabor kept looking up at his face, trying to figure out what was wrong. As they neared Berkeley Park, a few blocks away from Ron's house, Tabor suddenly dug her claws into Michael's shirt. For a moment he was back with her in the snow, his hoodie zipped tightly around her as they trekked out of Oregon. He felt a lump in his throat, but he kept walking.

"You can always rescue another cat," Whip Kid said, trying to lighten the mood.

"It wouldn't be the same," Kyle said. "It's like, 'Oh, I'll get another girlfriend. This one died.' It doesn't work that way."

On the corner by the Bagdad Theatre, a grand old Jazz Age picture palace, they hung a right and walked a few blocks down SE 37th Avenue, where pretty, flower-filled cafés spilled onto the pavement with courtesy dog water bowls outside. Farther along, brightly painted vintage bungalows had shutters, planters, window boxes with geraniums, and velvety green front lawns.

Tabor scrunched herself into a little ball against Michael's chest as they got closer to her home. The rest of the homeless parade shuffled behind them. They stopped in front of a white two-story house with gold-painted pillars, half-hidden behind a lovely old juniper tree.

A normal house for a magical cat, Michael thought.

Ron spotted the ragtag little band from the window and thought, *Oh no, he's brought everyone he knows*. He had been expecting only Michael—and he'd expected him an hour later. Nonetheless, Ron ran down the porch steps and greeted them with happy tears. "Mata!" he shouted.

Before Michael could even introduce himself, Ron had slipped his hands behind Tabor's shoulders and pulled her into his arms.

"Oh, Mata, Mata, my sweet potata, I wish I may, I wish I oughta," he sang to her, cradling her in the crook of his arm. "It's a song I wrote for her." He looked up at Michael. "Cats love being sung to."

Michael thought, *She looks seasick*.

For a minute, everyone stood around as Ron fawned over the cat, who for once seemed overwhelmed by the attention.

In the patch of garden alongside the house, another cat appeared, a sleek, long-legged tuxedo with a crooked mustache and silvery-green, leaf-shaped eyes like Tabor's. Behind him was a big, buff chocolate-faced Siamese with two different-colored eyes. But when Creto and Jim caught sight of the dogs in front of the house, they got spooked and took off to the neighbor's back garden.

"The black-and-white cat's mine," Ron explained. "He's Mata's brother."

All of a sudden Tabor, who'd been writhing in Ron's arms, hissed at him and scrambled away to crawl up Michael's leg onto his shoulder. Ron looked a little sad, but his lodger, Steve, came out of the house to see Mata, ruffling her fur as she lay in Michael's arms.

Ron introduced Steve, who smiled at everyone and then left on his own business.

· · · ·

"Come inside," Ron said, motioning his visitors into his pristine house. Michael's friends made a beeline for the porch, their dogs scrambling behind them.

Still carrying Tabor, Michael reluctantly followed. He felt kind of embarrassed. What could he say? "I'm sorry, Ron, here's your cat. Sorry I took her to California and Montana." As he walked by the porch swing sheltered by a trellis of jasmine, he imagined Tabor lounging there with Ron and the other cats on warm summer nights, watching the world go by.

Ron welcomed them all with a gracious and easy charm. "I bought pizza and soda so we could have a little shindig for Mata."

The squadron of homeless people and their three dogs swept

into the creamy-white living room and arranged themselves on Ron's snug couches. Stinson settled between the stone fireplace and the glass coffee table, sitting cross-legged on the polished honey-wood floors. The two bigger dogs, a brown mongrel and a gray brindle pit bull cross, circled around him.

The scent of freshly cut freesias wafted from a vase on the mantelpiece. Wind chimes rattled above the opened window. The living room was full of cat art. Silver sculptures of lions and leopards sat beneath a glossy green asparagus fern whose fronds spilled off a bookshelf. Prints of nineteenth-century Parisian Le Chat Noir lithographs lined the wall, along with a silver-framed photo of Mata. Plumper and more kittenish, she had the same glow in her eyes.

Michael sat on the sofa by the bay window. "There you go," he said to Tabor as he put her down on the floor. She looked confused and hid under his legs.

Buzzing around excitedly, Ron was all smiles. He headed to the kitchen to get his guests some Cokes but got distracted, worried that his cat didn't recognize him anymore. He quickly rang his friend Stefanie, the former neighbor who'd found Mata and her litter under her porch and had their tabby brother Hank.

"Come quick, the party's started earlier," he said quietly down the phone. "I feel like I'm on drugs. Mata hates me. And all the homeless people in Portland, and their dogs, are in my living room."

When Ron returned, he had forgotten the Cokes. "So tell me some of your stories," he said. "Where has Mata been this whole time?"

"I'm in a daze right now . . . can't even think," Kyle said, slumped on the arm of a corner armchair by the stone fireplace. Whip Kid was sitting in the chair with Bobby in his lap, and Madison had propped herself on the other arm of the chair.

Michael couldn't answer. He was staring down at the cat and fighting hard to hold back tears.

Stinson could tell that his friend was hurting, so he jumped in for him, saying, "Well, we were heading down Hawthorne for a sleeping spot late one night, and we saw her under the picnic table of a café. She was kinda freaked out when we found her. I grabbed her, thinking she was a stray, and thought my friend who lost a cat might want her. She hung out with us and then we put her picture on Craigslist. It was the most used lost-pet section."

"And that was the only one I hadn't checked," Ron said. "Isn't that strange?"

At that moment, Tabor peeped her head out behind Michael's legs, anxiously glancing around the room, and jumped on a low-slung, midcentury sideboard in the alcove hall opposite the front door. She sat there, a little agitated, staring down at the two dogs that were still milling around Stinson.

Michael walked over to her and stood by the sideboard, stroking her, trying to calm her.

"The first week or two we were hanging out with Tabor, or, um, Mata," Kyle said, "we were squatting in a parking lot at night on Hawthorne, and for the first few days she'd go off at night and come back."

"Yeah," Ron laughed, "she'd wander a three-block radius around here just making friends and influencing people."

Jane chimed in, "When I met Groundscore a couple of weeks after he found her, she acted like she'd been his cat forever. And she became a bit of a celebrity around Hawthorne. Everyone loved her."

"Oh, Maaata, sweet girl, Honey Bunny," Ron cooed at her.

"Michael took good care of her," Kyle added. "When we got to Montana, Michael's dad, or, um, foster dad, took us to the vet to get the cat checked out. And he said that she was in perfect health, a pristine cat. Apart from her teeth, which were a little dirty."

Turning around to look at his cat, who hadn't moved from the sideboard, Ron could see that Michael was getting more upset. For a mad split second, he thought that if Mata was unhappy and preferred to be with Michael, he would give her to him. But then he thought about how much Creto missed her and how much they both loved her, and decided that she just needed a little time to remember where she was and settle back in.

"And there's Groundscore with Mata," he said anxiously, trying to draw Michael into the conversation. "I thought it was funny how you told me she'd grab your beard and then kiss you on the mouth."

"She did that to Stinson, to Kyle, too," Michael said, without taking his eyes off Tabor.

Stinson laughed. "Sometimes I'd wake up with her paws in my hand."

"Anybody else have any stories?" Ron asked. "I heard you went camping in Yosemite. How was that?"

"It was pretty cool," said Stinson, who was still on the floor tussling with the two dogs. "Madison and Bobby were there," he added, pointing toward them in the corner chair. Madison smiled at Ron and waved. "We saw a bear. Michael started yelling, 'There's a bear.' And I was like, 'There's no bear.' And Tabor and Bobby were freaking out. In the end, it was okay, the bear didn't eat us."

"We got run out of a squat in Montana by a herd of angry cows, too," Kyle said.

Ron looked across the room at Michael as he stood quietly beside Tabor, stroking her. "I can't thank you enough," he said to Michael. "I'll always be grateful to you for treating Mata so well."

"She was good to me, too," he said, without looking up. "I carried her for thirty-six hundred miles on my back. All over Oregon, California, Idaho, Montana. And she's probably only walked about half a mile. She was like the Queen of Sheba."

"The Queen of Sheba—I love it." Ron smiled. "This is so great." He was proud of his mad, beautiful cat.

"I read that she'd run off before and ended up in a trunk of a car," Stinson said.

"She was kidnapped by a neighbor," Ron said, and told them the story. "What's mystifyingly weird is that you brought her back today on June twenty-first. The first time Mata went missing, it was December twentieth, 2011, and the animal shelter in Vancouver called on June twenty-first to say she'd been found. Poor Mata ended up living alone in the woods for six months."

"So how did she survive in the woods for that long?" Kyle asked.

"I guess she must've hunted and lived on mice."

They must've been arthritic mice, Michael thought to himself. He had never seen Tabor hunt, apart from harassing seabirds and the deer mouse that she'd caught in the long grasses and let go. He couldn't imagine her surviving alone in the wilderness for more than a day.

"What's really incredible is that she survived all the coyotes, hawks, and God knows what else," Ron rambled on. "There was this black tomcat who lived across the street called Raoul, who was friends with my cats. His owner moved away and took him back to her hometown by Yellowstone Park. He got out and was eaten by a coyote. She found his head."

This gave Michael the chills, and he flashed back to the night those coyotes circled him and Tabor under the trees in Ventura. *She's definitely better off here*, he thought.

Jane, who'd been sitting quietly at the end of sofa and looking out the window, saw that three news vans had pulled up outside the house. She suddenly rose to her feet and said, "We gotta go."

The others got up, too, and quickly shuffled toward the back door, the three dogs in tow, legging it down the road.

"I just don't wanna deal with those people," Michael explained to Ron, who suddenly realized that was why he had arrived an hour early.

Tabor jumped down from the sideboard and sat in the living room doorway. She looked directly into Michael's eyes as if she sensed he was leaving her.

At that moment, all his conflicted feelings hit him. It was like freeing a bird after nursing her back to health and seeing her fly—sad but certain that it was the right thing.

Michael picked her up one last time, burying his face in her silky fur. He couldn't stop the tears as he kissed her good-bye. "You be good, Tabor," he murmured into her fur. "Love you."

"Hey, you can come visit her anytime you want," Ron said, touched. "That's no problem at all."

"Yes, I'd like to," he said, glancing up at Ron. "I'm gonna split town soon, but I'd like to see her again before I leave."

When he handed her to Ron, she hissed at her owner. When Michael had left and Creto shyly peeped his head into the room, she hissed at him, too, and dived under the sofa. Only her eyes showing, Tabor watched Michael slip out the back door.

Soon after Michael and his friends had gone, Mata fled from under the sofa into the quiet of Ron's bedroom off the little hallway between the dining room and kitchen. Ron closed the blinds so it was nice and dark and she could have a little peace and calm to settle in. He had put down food and cat milk there for her. He had made her favorite treat—ground-up raw chicken with egg yolks and vitamins that he used to feed her and Creto as kittens—but she refused it.

When he set out a litter box, she immediately went and sat in it, looked up at him sadly, then sank deeper in the litter and buried her head in her paws. She was showing withdrawal behavior—she was distressed that Michael was gone.

Creto swung his head around the bedroom doorway, sniffing around cautiously. Jim trotted in after him and, muscling his way past Creto, padded toward Mata, suspicious and challenging. Mata stood up, spat and snarled, and Jim wailed. They had a brief yowling standoff.

"Jiii-immm, stop it! Don't be such a brute." Ron snatched him up before he could get his claws out and pushed him out of the bedroom, shutting the door.

Then he flicked through his LP records. His cats loved music. A cat's taste in music was a mysterious thing, but all the household kitties, past and present, seemed to favor melodic '60s stuff, particularly the Beatles. Miles Davis's *Kind of Blue*, which Ron used to leave on repeat for Mata and Creto whenever he left them alone as kittens, was another favorite.

Ron put a Beatles 45, "And I Love Her," on the turntable and said, "This is for you, Honey Bunny." When she heard the crackly sound of the needle on the vinyl and the soft strum of guitars, she looked up at him as though it jogged her memory.

Creto hopped on the bed, watching quietly with his huge searching eyes, purring. She stared back at him from the litter box, a glint of recognition in her eyes.

Ron sat on the bed with Creto.

After a little while, Mata jumped on the bed, and before long she and the tuxedo tom were sniffing each other and touching noses. Then she looked at Ron and suddenly seemed to realize she was home. She rolled over on her back and purred away.

She was finally home. Ron wanted to let everyone know the happy news. He pulled his phone out of his shorts' pocket and snapped a picture of Mata sprawled out on the bed, posting it on Facebook:

Missing: 12/20/11. Found: 6/21/12

Missing: 9/1/12. Found: 6/13/13

Thank God for pet chips.

He watched the two cats snuggled together on the bed, thinking this was the best summer of his life. Then he posted an old picture of Mata and Creto, both staring up into the camera, from beneath a scarlet rosebush in his garden, and jotted out another quick post:

Mata Hairi, Creto Von Bruiser and I thank everyone for all your prayers and kind thoughts for her safe return. The three of us are a team once again.

Chapter 26

Portland Again:
Sweet Emotion

Nine months after Tabor became Mata again, Michael came back to Portland, this time on Amtrak. It was March 2014, and he had spent the winter with Walter in Montana. He returned to share a house with Kyle and his two roommates. He took a spare room in their tumbledown bungalow with worn furniture and a wild garden full of weeds and occupied by a family of raccoons. But the place was peaceful, and it was a chance to live another life.

The first thing Michael had done when he arrived, though, was to head straight to the corner house on SE 37th Avenue where Tabor lived. Halfway down the street, he saw her on the picnic table lazily stretched out in a ray of sun, grasping at the sky with her paw, her white tiger-striped fur glistening in the morning light.

She looked in his direction and watched him intently, and he could see her ears twitching back and forth.

"Ta-bor . . . Ta-bor," he shouted, and then he whistled the

Tabor whistle once he was at the corner. She jumped off the table and ran toward him, meowing.

Before he could put down his backpack, she had sprung up on his shoulder the way she used to with a kittenish *prrrrp* sound. Hot tears streamed down his face as she nudged and licked his cheeks and dug her soft muzzle under his chin, all the while purring. He wept from joy that she hadn't forgotten him.

He cuddled her like an infant. As he looked down at her, bathed in sunlight, her silvery-green-gold eyes gleaming like jewels, he thought she was the most beautiful thing alive.

After he had returned Tabor to Ron the year before, Michael had got blackout drunk for the better part of two weeks. For many teary and sleepless nights, he sat out in their old UPS squat, imagining her shooting out of the bushes, tail up in the air, trilling.

He had made it through that dark time, and although he still missed her, she had enriched his life, and changed him—he was calmer, more at peace with himself and the world.

Michael sat at the picnic table on the front lawn. Tabor shot straight onto his lap, mewling softly and kneading his stomach. He noticed that she still wore the red-and-orange-checked dog collar that he'd bought her, but her heart-shaped ID tag had been replaced with a new copper one. She was back to being Mata Hairi again.

Her littermate, Creto, stared out from the blaze of fire-orange wildflowers in the corner garden. A kitten shadowed him, a yellow-eyed calico beauty in a patchwork coat of orange, brown, and black. She was a tiny parcel of eyes, limbs, and fur as wispy as a dandelion. With a high-pitched squeak, the baby cat leapt on the bench beside Michael and played with his bag strap. Tabor licked the kitten's head and put a protective paw on her neck as she edged her way into Michael's lap, too.

Michael assumed Ron had gotten another cat. He couldn't believe he'd gotten a third cat after he'd lost Tabor twice, and though he was happy to see Tabor, he was surprised Ron still let her roam outside.

A voice behind him said, "Her name's Puzzle."

He looked up at the porch where Steve was standing, and recognized him from their fleeting meeting outside Ron's house on the day he'd returned Tabor. He was clearly keeping an eye on the cats and might've thought he'd come back to get the cat.

"I was just saying hello to Tabor," Michael said wearily, half-expecting Ron's young lover, or whoever he was, to pull out the cutlery and start throwing it at him.

Steve smiled and said, "She's the new addition to the house. Somebody moved away and left her in an empty house, so I rescued her as a sister for Jim."

Shifting on the bench uneasily, Michael smiled and set Tabor down on the picnic table in her spot of sun. He got up to start walking back up the road but turned to look back. Tabor was following him with the calico kitten trailing behind her. But Steve chased after them in his bare feet and scooped them both in his arms.

Just seeing Tabor happy in her old life was enough.

Chapter 27

Seven Steps to Heaven

The following fall, just after seven in the morning on October 15, 2015, Michael stood in front of a dozen homeless kids who were sprawled out on the green in front of the old military pavilion of Colonel Summers Park. Many of his old street pals had moved on. Stinson was off the street and living with his girlfriend and had a job working in an Asian food factory. Whip Kid and Jane were also happily settled in new jobs and their own apartment. But there were plenty of kids still out there, living rough, who, like him, were troubled and lost, and he couldn't turn his back on them.

It had been two years, three months, and three weeks since he had returned Tabor to Ron. Now, when talking about the cat, he would smile and tear up, but he would always collect himself and say, with some perspective, "We all miss things in our lives."

But today, he felt good as he welcomed the motley crew to what they called their 707 meeting. "Good morning," Michael said, scanning the faces of the street kids.

Two years ago, after the long drinking binge that had followed giving up Tabor, Michael had found himself standing outside a liquor store on Hawthorne, waiting for it to open at

7 a.m. A group of drunks and addicts were waiting with him with a sense of grim camaraderie. When the doors opened, they shuffled in, bought what they could afford, and prepared to get smashed.

But that day, Michael suggested that they do something slightly different. He proposed that, after getting their booze, they walk to the nearby Sewallcrest Park and talk. Everybody could still drink, but it might also be helpful if they shared what was going on with them. That was how the 707 meetings got their name: They were held just after the liquor stores opened at 7 a.m., and it took seven minutes to walk from the liquor store to the bleachers in the park. Michael hosted them once a week whenever he was in town. It gave him a point to his life, a purpose.

Most of the skinny, scruffy street kids in their early to midtwenties who hung out in the park looked high and mellow, smoking whatever, cradling cans of beer or swilling malt liquor from a paper bag. Many of them came from unstable, uncaring families and migrated up and down the West Coast with the change of seasons. Some of them thought of themselves as outcasts, but all were still desperate to belong, and they found a sense of family and community among themselves. Tumbling from doorway to doorway, they moved and grazed in packs, divvying up whatever food, drink, and cigarettes they had and guarded one another's scant possessions.

Michael knew most of them pretty well and usually started off these meetings by checking in with each person. "Shane, how ya doing?" he asked a gangly kid with long, messy brown bangs. "Have you talked to your mom?"

When Shane admitted he hadn't spoken to his mother in a while, Michael handed him the pay-as-you-go phone that Walter had given him years ago; it was now battered and the screen was cracked, but it still worked. Shane had borrowed it in the past to cajole money out of his mother, but Michael wanted him to talk to her without asking for anything.

"C'mon," Michael urged him, handing him the phone, "just talk to her."

Shane wandered off with the phone. Others in the group talked about their problems. He shared some of his feelings, too, although he didn't mention Tabor.

Over the last couple of years, he'd occasionally visited her at Ron's house. He would stand on the sidewalk, shout out her name, do the "Tabor whistle" and throw down his pack. She'd run down the porch steps and jump on the pack, kneading it.

But at his last visit that spring, after a nine-month stretch of not seeing her, he realized something had shifted. She was sauntering across the grass of the front yard when he arrived, and she trotted up to him. He had expected the usual warm welcome, but she was standoffish and just stared at him. Then she scrambled up the porch steps, pulled open the screen door with her claws, and scuttled back inside the house.

Michael could almost hear her thinking: "No way you're taking me back to Idaho on another four-thousand-mile road trip." At that moment, he felt sad that she no longer needed him, but happy that she was safe and content at home.

At the park, Michael encouraged a heroin addict to go to the methadone clinic. He told a crystal meth user to stick to weed and booze. Michael understood that there was no magic fix to their problems. Part of the reason people listened to him was because he wasn't much better off than they were: he still drank and lived on the street. But people showed up because it was clear that Michael cared.

Later that afternoon, a car from a local mission pulled up to the pavilion, as it did every day, to distribute free food. The volunteers—many of whom had been out on the street them-selves—handed out cups of coffee, sandwiches, potato chips, apples, and bananas to the homeless people around the park.

After sitting down to a communal lunch with his buddies, Michael said it was time to go. There was a crispness in the air, the weather was getting colder. He was leaving that afternoon for warmer climes. He had less than ten dollars in his pocket. It would only get him on a local bus or train—but it was enough to get moving again.

AFTERWORD

On June 20, 2013, I was researching an article when the headline *Homeless Man Travels 3,600 Miles to Take Cat Back Home* caught my eye. After reading the story of the stray cat and homeless drifter traveling across America, I knew I had to find this man. His story was filled with love, loss, adventure, mystery, and tenderness.

First I called Michael King's foster father, Walter Ebert, in Helena, Montana. I told Walter that I wanted to write a book and help change Michael's life.

He just laughed and said, "Good luck. I've tried to get him off the street for years but finally gave up. Money is like water in Michael's hands. He's got a good heart, but he's a big drinker." At that moment, Michael was hitchhiking his way back to Portland to take the cat home to the original owner, but Walter said that if he heard from him, he'd pass on my message.

Afterward I contacted Ron Buss in Portland. And that same day, while hitchhiking to take the cat back home, Michael phoned and poured out his heart to me, a total stranger, about giving up Tabor, how it was the hardest thing he ever had to do. When I met him in Portland three weeks later, he looked crushed, and his sea-blue eyes misted at the very first mention of Tabor.

I have followed Michael's and Mata's lives ever since and have interviewed Michael, his street friends, and Ron for this book. In May 2014, Michael invited me to meet Walter in Montana. Kyle was also visiting at the time; he and Michael were planning a camping trip around Montana, since their previous trip with Tabor had been cut short.

While sitting in the kitchen with the three of them, I asked Michael if he was still drinking. He went quiet for a while and then said, "Yeah, but mostly beer. It takes the edge off of sleeping in cold doorways. I didn't want to lose her, so I had to keep it together quite a bit."

Seeing Michael upset, Walter recounted his own long struggles as a drinker. "It's not easy quitting," he said. "When you get sick and tired of being sick and tired, maybe you'll do something about it. I had bottles by the half-gallon out in the garage, one out on the tree stump, and one on my kitchen windowsill, so when I went out to mow the lawn, I knew exactly where my drinks were. Until I looked at myself in the mirror one hot summer day, and I called this friend of mine and said, 'That's it, I've had enough.' I checked myself into the state hospital and I drank half the bottle on the way there. When we got out of the car, I hid it under a tree in the parking lot. About five minutes later I decided I needed a drink and came out of the hospital waiting room to find it. Somebody snatched it, and I was mad as hell.

"Everybody that sobers up has that moment. All the talking in the world isn't gonna do any good. Like my friend Father Joe Martin, who was an alcoholic, said: 'There are those of us that won't get sober in this lifetime.'"

· · · ·

In the summer of 2015, I went back to Portland again to see Michael, Ron, and Mata. I met Michael in Colonel Summers

Park. These days Michael has a renewed sense of purpose and sees it as his mission to watch out for the street kids and young runaways along Hawthorne.

He still drinks and struggles with depression. He had recently returned from Montana, where he had spent five months nursing Walter, who was very ill, and looking after Walter's cat, Gus, as well as another rescue. "Walter took in a young black-and-white called Winnie who'd been attacked by a dog," Michael explained. "I talked to Walter the other day about how I've got to stop doing this. He wants me to retire in Helena, but I don't know what to do there. If anything, I'd house up in Portland."

While looking after Walter, he was stone sober, but slipped back into street life when he came back to Portland. "I'm tired, almost done with this life," he said, recounting how, last October, he tried to stop drinking. "I went out to the woods in Sisters, Oregon, and DT'd for two days. I was sick as a dog, and I just looked back over the last five years and went cold turkey. I don't want to be that guy constantly blacking out in alleys, not knowing where I am. Maybe I'll retrain as a nurse. I looked after Mercer, and my father just before he died."

But it would be another eighteen months before Michael would go to rehab. One day, the realization that many of his friends were either dead or in jail hit him hard. He finally "got sick and tired of being sick and tired," as Walter had put it, and realized he needed to deal with his addiction.

Michael also knew his days on the streets were numbered. Turning fifty was a game changer, he said. "I can't be a beach bum anymore. The sun bothers me." Though he often thinks back to his days on the beach with Tabor in Ventura as some of his happiest. And meeting Linda Tabor, the kind pensioner who regularly brought him and Tabor food, was the start of a grand friendship. They still write each other letters, via Walter's address, and Michael sees her whenever he goes to California.

Michael, Kyle, and their friends still miss Tabor and the spring and summer they had her brought them closer together. Her spirit and energy was everywhere, and Stinson, Kyle, or one of the other kids would mention her being someplace, a park, a doorway, or doing something amusing.

Kyle claimed that Michael never really got over the heartbreak of losing the cat. "When he went to say good-bye to Tabor on his own the morning after we took her back, Ron gave him a little money as a thank-you, but he didn't keep any of it. When he came back to the squat, he was pretty depressed and throwing crumpled twenty-dollar bills at people with tears in his eyes."

Michael shrugged his shoulders and laughed. "Guess I fell in love with a cat," he said, and for a while, she was his happiness, but looking back on it now, he thinks he was meant to pick up the cat to bring her back to Ron.

When I suggested adopting another cat, he said, "I'm done with cats." But soon afterward, Michael would rescue a black-and-white kitten he named Wendy. He took Wendy on the road for a few days and found a home for her in San Francisco. He would eventually find a tiny, tawny puppy, whom he called Abbey Road and kept.

Kyle is back to being homeless after the shared house he lived in with friends fell apart. When I asked him what he planned to do next, he shrugged sullenly. "There's nothing romantic about waking up in cold doorways and feeling useless," he said once his friends dispersed, but he hoped to go back to school if he could figure out what he wanted to do. "I don't want to only make it to forty and die. But making that transition back into society makes me nervous."

When I visited Ron, he whisked me inside to see the cats. He opened the door to his bedroom to show me one of Mata's favorite spots. "Norwegian Wood" was drifting out of the room, and on the dresser in a pool of sunlight, Mata was cuddled up to the calico kitten, Puzzle, now a full-grown stunner.

Mata leaped off the dresser and ran to me, clawing her way up my leg, as if she were greeting an old friend. Ron said, "Mata's turned into a couch cat and rarely goes out like she used to."

Outside in his back garden, Ron shouted out to Creto, who was sunbathing on the roof of the next-door neighbor's shed. Nearby, stirring up the dirt beneath a rosebush was Jim, the buff chocolate-faced Siamese.

Since it was a breezy, sunny June day, Ron thought it would be lovely to take the cats to the seaside. On the drive up to Sauvie Island, just north of town along the Columbia River, both cats sat calmly like seasoned travelers. Mata hopped onto my lap and stayed there. She clearly loved road trips, her little head swiveling from the road ahead to the passenger window to get a good look at the scenery whizzing past.

Ron took us to a quiet part of the beach edging the woods, where dogs weren't allowed, and we sprawled out on a blanket. Mata nestled between us; Creto hid in the shade of a bush just behind us.

As we sat there, over a picnic of veggie sandwiches and root beers, watching the setting sun and stragglers along the shore, a raggedy black kitten suddenly appeared out of the thicket, crying. Seeing the other cats and the food, she approached us meekly and meowed.

She was a pitiful sight, with big, sad eyes that swallowed her heart-shaped face, and pointy ears and paws too big for her bony body. This tiny, starving creature had clearly been left to fend for herself in the woods. She looked weary, but her desperation and hunger made her bold. When I called out to her, she immediately padded over. She wolfed down two tins of Sheba, one after another, and meowed for more. Mata and Creto couldn't take their eyes off her. Mata seemed to feel sorry for her.

"We have to help her," I said to Ron as we watched the kitten polishing off her last tin of Sheba without pausing before guzzling a cup of water.

"Oh, absolutely," he replied. "Poor thing, she wouldn't survive here much longer with all the coyotes, ospreys, and owls."

For about an hour, Ron left me with the cats while he went up and down the beach, asking if anyone knew anything about the little stray. When he returned, he said, "I asked everyone I saw . . . about fifty people, and only one person said he saw an elderly man with a black kitten but saw him leave without her. Guess she's going with us. . . . How shall we do this?"

"We don't want to spook her," I said, opening a can of tuna and placing it in Mata's carrier. The kitten willingly walked in. When Ron shut the door behind her, she looked over her bony shoulder and carried on eating.

After finishing, she head-butted our hands through the bars of the cage and brushed her whiskers against them, purring loudly the entire time. As I spoke to her softly, she thrust out a skinny paw and touched my face. The little pads on her paws were worn and burned, probably from days of walking on the hot sand.

Ron hoisted the carrier, and we walked back to the car. I stumbled behind them in the sand, holding the other cats' leads, trying to keep up as they pulled me in different directions. Creto was happily trotting ahead toward home, but Mata wasn't quite ready to leave the beach. I had to carry her, squirming and screaming, back to the car.

As Ron put the carrier with the kitten on the backseat, Creto jumped in beside it. Ron looked at me and said, "You know, we almost didn't come here. I was thinking about going to Rooster Rock, but at last minute I thought you should see this place. It was fate. But Mata rescued her as much as we did."

He named her Sauvie and took her home. The next morning, he took her to his vet, who said she was about four months old, severely dehydrated, and probably hadn't eaten for ten to fifteen days. Ron believed that he was meant to find her.

That following weekend Ron put "found kitten" posters in Sauvie Island's general store and on the trees along the beach, but no one responded, so Sauvie became a permanent member of Ron's feline family.

As Ron said, "It's the perfect ending to a pretty amazing story."

AUTHOR'S NOTE

Rescue—Don't Buy

I hope *Strays* will inspire you to help any animal in distress that crosses your path.

How we treat the voiceless and vulnerable is a reflection of our decency as a society—and while our treatment of *some* animals has improved over the last few decades, we still have a long way to go. In America, there are an estimated 70 million homeless and abandoned animals—and, according to Cats Protection, nearly 10 million stray cats and 1.5 million ferals alone in the UK. Many suffer and die in the streets from starvation and exposure, and some are poisoned, shot, and tortured. Those few that manage to survive rely on the goodwill of compassionate people.

Being homeless is a death sentence for animals. Every year nearly 6.5 million lost, abandoned, and abused cats and dogs enter shelters across the United States.* The lucky ones get adopted and a few reunited with their families, but many don't make it out

*American Society for the Prevention of Cruelty to Animals. http://www.aspca.org/animal-homelessness/shelter-intake-and-surrender/pet-statistics

alive. Of the cats and dogs being taken into shelters, a staggering 70 percent are killed, and horrifically, sometimes in front of each other—many public shelters find it easier to euthanize healthy, adoptable animals rather than save them and at the annual cost of about $2 billion to taxpayers.* In my research, I discovered that motherless kittens are systematically killed because most shelters don't want to waste resources to care for them. Every single one of these animals is precious, and all they need is someone to give them a chance to be saved. No animal, domestic or wild, should have to suffer and be denied "their little share of the earth's happiness," as the great animal-rights author Matthew Scully put it so eloquently in his dazzling and deeply moving book *Dominion: The Power of Man, the Suffering of Animals, and the Call to Mercy.* The successful shelters, such as Best Friends Animal Society, North Shore Animal League, and NKLA (No-Kill Los Angeles), have long embraced no-kill policies.

If you're thinking of adding a furry family member to your home, *adopt*, don't shop. Save a cat or dog from a sad and uncertain future—*NEVER* buy from breeders or pet stores, which contribute to the pet overpopulation and appalling suffering at kitten and puppy mills. What many people don't realize is that when they buy a cat or dog from a pet store or on the Internet, that animal most likely came from a kitten or puppy mill—"factory farms" for cats and dogs—where mothers are forced to produce litter after litter until they drop dead, and kittens and puppies are usually sick, weak, riddled with infections, and living in filthy, cramped, and grim conditions. This cruel, inhumane multimillion-dollar trade is a worldwide problem, and the only way to end it is for people to always neuter and stop buying

---

*Roughly 71 percent of cats and 57 percent of dogs that enter shelters are killed, according to AmericanHumane.org.

animals altogether. Meanwhile, according to the Humane Society of the United States, only about 30 percent of pets in homes come from shelters or rescues.* In light of the continuing crisis, there's no such thing as a responsible breeder—just varying degrees of parasitic greed and awfulness. Even if you have your heart set on a particular breed, such as Maine coon or Siamese, for example, turn to the shelters/sanctuaries/rescue societies. They have every type of pedigree desperately waiting for homes, too. Every time someone buys a companion animal from a pet store or breeder, they are condemning another one to death at a pound that could've otherwise been rescued.

If these numbers of unwanted and discarded animals languishing in cages or being destroyed are upsetting, I suggest doing something positive. We can all make a difference in the lives of homeless animals: supporting your local charity or humane society by donating money, bedding, food, and toys or by fostering and volunteering; helping that poor hungry stray on your doorstep; and feeding, neutering, and caring for feral colonies in your community, whose very existence relies on our compassion (AlleyCat.org is a brilliant and helpful resource).

It's always the countless small deeds and kindnesses of individuals that have consistently made an impact on the world.

---

*Humane Society of the United States. http://www.humanesociety.org/assets /facts-pet-stores-puppy-mills.pdf

ACKNOWLEDGMENTS

I would like to thank Michael King and Ron Buss for their gracious help, extraordinary stories, dark wit and humor, and patience for enduring seemingly endless interviews. Without their generosity and kindness, I could not have finished this book. Walter Ebert, Kyle Brecheen, Josh Stinson, Linda Tabor, Kathleen King, Xavier Armand, Rockwell Mills, Dr. Bruce Armstrong, Maddie Parker, Al Knauber, and Dylan Brown for all their invaluable contributions. Mata Hairi, Creto, and Sauvie for their own incredible adventure stories and feline charms.

I owe so much to my amazing agent, Bonnie Nadell, who believed in *Strays* and instantly found it a home at Atria Books, and for all her wisdom and guidance along the way. I am particularly grateful to Joshua Davis for originally commissioning *Strays* for *Epic* magazine, his keenness for Michael, Mata, and Ron's story, editing suggestions, and for introducing me to his agent Bonnie. Stephen Elliott and Harry Spritzer for additional editing and research, respectively, on the original *Epic* story. And Scott Carney for putting me in touch with Joshua Davis.

I am indebted to my brilliant editor Leslie Meredith, who loved this story from the start and greatly improved it with

249

her light touch, careful pruning, and exacting standards. She constantly pushed me to try harder and dig deeper. Her love and understanding of cats, too, was an unexpected and much-appreciated gift.

I am hugely grateful to my new editor Jhanteigh Kupihea for jumping in at the end, her thoughtful touches and insights, as well as indulging me and fulfilling my wish for a cover that best conveyed the story. I would like to thank Patricia Callahan for her sharp, sensitive copyediting and suggestions that improved every page, and production editor Mark LaFlaur. I must also thank art director Albert Tang and interior designer Kyoko Watanabe for their perfectionism as well as Leslie and Jhanteigh's lovely assistants, Natasha Rodriguez, Melanie Iglesias-Perez, and Loan Le, and the rest of the talented team at Atria/Simon & Schuster for the skill and enthusiasm they brought to the book and for bringing *Strays* into the world.

Tiziano Niero, for his unwavering love, encouragement, and insightful and sometimes hilariously mean critiques, and filming the stunning book trailer for *Strays*. Kevin Grady, my dear old pal and twice-Emmy-nominated creative director, for the gorgeous cover and sheer genius. Endless love and gratitude to my wonderful friends for their relentless support and humor: Stewart Brotherton, Chris Brock, Chrissy Iley, Julia Snell, David Garner, Sibéal Nic Ginnéa, Ludovica Niero, Steven Ludwin, Marion McKeone, Harriet Green, Sharon Walker, Caroline Carpenter, Marc Walker, Dawn Chapman, Jill Starley-Grainger, Jennifer Johnson, Sharon Parham, Trevor Bowen, Stephanie Theobald, Babette Kulik—and especially Victoria Clarke and Jasmin Naim, whom I probably drove mad with countless un-solicited readings of my manuscript.

Special thanks to Jeffrey Moussaieff Masson for writing the foreword for *Strays*, as well as for being a fearless and eloquent voice for society's most vulnerable and powerless. His impassioned, thoughtful books about the complex emotional lives of animals have provided so much joy and inspiration and serve as a reminder that cats, dogs, cows, pigs, and other fellow creatures in their vulnerability can teach us humility, decency, boundless love—the things that really matter in this world.

I am humbled and grateful to have crossed paths with Andrew Tyler, Celia Hammond, Francis Battista, and Michael Mountain, who have devoted their lives to rescuing animals and fighting for their rights to be treated with respect, empathy, and dignity, and not being denied their lives for our whims and consumption. Their deep compassion and perseverance for the cause continues to inspire me.

Finally, for Bobby Seale, my spirited six-year-old, orange-eyed marmalade goddess of a cat who loved life and people so much. She was murdered in London on September 23, 2009, by teenage thugs who set their pit bull on her for fun. Bobby's brutal death shook me to the core and made me fight even harder for abused, abandoned, and suffering animals.

And for all my other lost cats, Tallulah, Edie Sedgwick, Coco, Dylan, Halo, Reverend Baloo, Pixie, Tad, Mowgli, White Baloo, and especially Honey, my ginger Maine coon stunner and cancer survivor who had more character than anyone I'd ever met. They've taught me the meaning of morality, brought so much happiness, and left their paw prints on my heart.

I am so grateful for my current little wildcats, Lola, Jimmy Ciambella, Shadow, Stevie Tigerface Wright, and little Murzik Meerkat, who in their own subtle ways left their mark on *Strays*. I have so much love and reverence for them all. In the words of my favorite writer, Charles Bukowski, "I think the world should be full of cats and full of rain, that's all, just cats and rain, rain and cats."

ABOUT THE AUTHOR

Britt Collins is a British journalist and writes for the *Guardian*, the *Sunday Times*, the *Independent*, *Harper's Bazaar*, *Condé Nast Traveller* (UK) and Billionaire.com. Her volunteer work tending animals at sanctuaries around the world, from big cats and baboons in Namibia to wild horses in Nevada, has inspired features for the *Guardian* and the *Sunday Times*. While writing for the British tabloid the *Sunday People*, she has raised hundreds of thousands of dollars for many international charities through her investigative animal-cruelty stories; as an activist, she has helped shut down controversial breeders of laboratory animals. She lives with her cats in London.